TV Chefs

TV Chefs

The Dish on the Stars
of Your Favorite Cooking Shows

KAREN LURIE

RENAISSANCE BOOKS
Los Angeles

Library of Congress Cataloging-in-Publication Data
Lurie, Karen.
    TV chefs / Karen Lurie.
        p. cm.
    Includes bibliographical references and index.
    ISBN 1-58063-073-1 (pbk. : alk. paper)
        1. Cooks—United States—Interviews. 2. Cooks—United States—
Directories. I. Title.
TX649.A1L87 1999
641.5'092'273—dc21   99-21725
                                                              CIP

10 9 8 7 6 5 4 3 2 1

Design by Tanya Maiboroda

Cover photos courtesy of: (front, left to right) Rom Eckerle, AP Photo/Jim Cooper, AP Photo/Douglas C. Pizac, Dickinson; (back, left to right) Bill Lyle, TBS, Inc./Chris Cuffaro © 1997, George Selland, Jason Bell.

Distributed by St. Martin's Press
Manufactured in the United States of America
First Edition

For my sous-chef

Contents

Appendices

Acknowledgments

The author would like to thank the following for their assistance:

IN THE FOOD WORLD:

Curtis Aikens, Stephanie Banyas (*re* Bobby Flay), Ginny Bast (*re* Martin Yan), Mario Batali, Mark Beckloff, Fern Berman (Fern Berman Communications, Inc.), Sissy Biggers, Bob Blumer, Susan Cahn (*re* Mario Batali), Julia Child, Amy Coleman, Marti Dalton (*re* Emeril Lagasse), Clarissa Dickson Wright, Nathalie Dupree, Susan Feniger, Bobby Flay, Norma Galehouse (*re* Jacques Pépin), Paul Gilmartin, Annabelle Gurwitch, Mollie Katzen, Graham Kerr, Kris Kruid, Emeril Lagasse, Michael Lomonaco, Claud Mann, Mindi Martinez (*re* Susan Feniger), Carolyn McCool (*re* Burt Wolf), Mary Sue Milliken, Jenny Morrison (*re* Caprial Pence), Sara Moulton, Molly O'Neill, Jennifer Paterson, Caprial Pence, Jacques Pépin, Torri Randall (*re* Mollie Katzen), David Rosengarten, Nick Stellino, Jacques Torres, Ming Tsai, Martha Wright (Border Grill), and Martin Yan.

IN THE TV WORLD:

Kimberlee Carlson (TBS), Geoffrey Drummond (A La Carte Productions), Corinne Field (Optomen Television), Lesia Figueira (Food Network), John Jenkins (Food Network), Bill Kossman (Food Network), Jim Lautz, Gina Mackenzie (TBS), Charles Pinsky (Frappé, Inc.), Marjorie Poore (Marjorie Poore Productions), Melissa Quezada (West 175 Enterprises), and Jonathan Rosenthal.

IN THE BOOK WORLD:

James Robert Parish (Renaissance Books) and Allan Taylor (Freelance Services).

IN THE WEB WORLD:

Stephanie Masumura.

IN THE REAL WORLD:

Robert Schnakenberg.

Key to Chapters

Each chapter includes a profile of a chef or chef team. The chapter begins with a box of "at a glance" factoids, which include birthdays, hometowns, parents' and siblings' names, favorite junk food, favorite food smells and sounds, items that can always be found in the subjects' pantries and refrigerators, and "Fantasy Last Meal," which is what the chef would want to eat if the world ended tomorrow.

After the profile is a "Tvography" of that chef or chef team's TV shows and specials, with the years of broadcast and networks. If the show is still being produced, the entry looks like this:

Cooking with Kumquats (PBS, 1996–)

If the show is no longer produced, but reruns are still being aired, the entry looks like this:

Cooking with Pomegranates (Food Network, 1996– *)

If the show is no longer produced, but reruns are still being aired, but only occasionally, the entry looks like this:

Cooking with Bananas (PBS, 1996– occasional)

Serious researchers should be forewarned that, unlike networks such as NBC, which show almost the same programming all over the United States, PBS stations are more independent and can air almost wherever they want. This means that any individual public television station may still be rerunning older shows. The TVography is an educated estimation based upon whether at least one station was airing a particular TV series at the time this book was written (1998).

After each TVography is a list of books written by the chef. This list is followed by the addresses of any Web sites associated with each chef.

Okay, dear reader—dig in!

Prologue

CHAPTER 1

Introduction:
The Edible Complex

In the broadest of terms, during the 1970s in the United States, people seemed consumed with looking good, even though, in retrospect, we looked pretty bad. Still, it was the decade of the fashion designer, and names like Halston and Ralph Lauren were as common on the labels of our back pockets as they were in magazines. The 1980s were about procuring money, so the negotiators, lawyers, and Hollywood agents such as Mike Ovitz became household names. In the 1990s, when the word "home," either making one or working out of one, came back into focus, the food industry has become hot. Even at fine restaurants in the 1970s, chefs were opening canned mushrooms to use in their recipes. But today, for example, even Friendly's fast food restaurants offer a portobello mushroom sandwich.

In today's era of heightened awareness of fine food, are Americans turning on TV cooking shows to learn specific cooking techniques? Or are they watching these programs to find out about cultures they may not be familiar with through the demonstration of food customs and cuisines? Although some viewers are motivated by one or the other of these reasons, many are not concerned with either one. Typically, people cook only one or two recipes from any of the cookbooks they buy. So, besides the charm of the hosts, why watch a television cooking show if you don't cook that often?

Some maintain that for baby boomers, food has replaced "sex, drugs, and rock and roll." The boomers, who spent all that money in the 1980s in restaurants, had kids and settled down in the 1990s. The generation that likes to think it invented everything is inventing a food revolution epitomized by the consumption of all possible cuisines, including TV food. This "revolution" can also be seen as the vehicle for a backlash against feminism. When citing a reason for the popularity of food and cooking shows on television, more than a few viewers mention a longing for something missed while growing up in a family where the mother entered the workforce instead of staying home and cooking.

Maybe viewing TV cooking programs has a kind of sex appeal. They take you from the tuna fish and pasta you eat almost daily, to an exotic world of truffle oil and uni. You can watch people do all kinds of strange things with foodstuffs, and the presentation of the finished recipe is something you would rarely bother with at home.

Some publicists believe cooking shows are similar to music videos in capturing an audience. After all, music videos started out with the purpose of selling records. If you want to make an impact on people so they remember your record the next time they are in the record store, you make a memorable music video. For TV chefs, those who want their cookbooks to stand out among the throngs of books on shelves in the cookery section of bookstores do cooking shows, so next time you're browsing, you'll say, "Oh yes, I've seen that guy on TV. I'll buy his book."

Then, there's the nostalgia factor: the weird comfort you get from feeling as if somebody's in your house, even if only on TV, making something delicious that must smell good. This process arouses sense memory and reminds you of family and tradition and the hearth, but with a bonus: you don't suffer any family dysfunction.

Maybe tuning in to TV cooking programs is more like watching sports on TV. After all, like sports, cooking is something you know a little about, and maybe even have done yourself, so you can relate to it. However, the thrill comes in watching it done by someone better than you, whether it's a gravity-defying slam dunk, or a smooth, artful deboning of a salmon. However, unlike when the home team loses or someone gets injured on the playing field, a television cooking show is never upsetting or stressful. Yes, there are knives, but they're only chopping vegetables.

Or maybe it's the same sense of satisfaction you get from watching a play, something with a concrete beginning, middle, and end. The characters, or ingredients, are introduced first, then the plot is the challenge of following the recipe. The suspense rises with every chop, the climax arrives as the food comes out of the oven or refrigerator, and the resolution hits when it's brought over to the table and tasted. No cliffhangers or unfinished business with a TV cooking show. Like a sitcom, where the hero's problems are solved in twenty-two minutes, the Perfect Plate (referred to as "the hero" or the "stunt food" in the TV food biz), emerges, piping hot, or properly chilled, paired with the perfect wine, and you get an empathetic sense of accomplishment.

"I think what our viewers are doing," says Marjorie Poore, producer of *Home Cooking with Amy Coleman* (PBS), "is accumulating information that they may not necessarily put to use because they may not have the time, or the energy, or the right kitchen. It's almost a 'collecting' mentality—they're collecting information and they want to know these things. It's more like an informational quest that we're solving for them. Plus, it's fun to watch the food come together; it's almost like magic. You take all these ingredients, a little flour, a little sugar, and all of a sudden there's this gorgeous, delicious cake. And it could even be vicarious pleasure of eating it, too. People are accumulating the information, getting vicarious pleasure, and they're fascinated to watch it come together, almost by magic."

Some have compared cooking shows to the launching of a yacht—you know you're never going to do it yourself, but it's fun to pretend. Maybe the fantasy is the lure. You get a vicarious experience in not just creating, but also eating, without your hands getting dirty or your tummy getting bigger. And who wouldn't eat more vegetables if a sous-chef was chopping them for you?

"They are empowering," says Geoffrey Drummond, producer of *Baking with Julia* (PBS). "Whether you cook or just dine out, it's easy to grasp—much more so than rebuilding an old house or playing a better game of golf. Most of us spent our early childhood in the kitchen with Mom, so it's a comfortable place to return to. And it's rewarding, whether you've just passively increased your knowledge and can apply it the next time you read the menu at a restaurant, or whether you've truly taken the interactive path and used what you learned in your own kitchen. More and more people are watching because they want to learn about cooking not even so much to cook, but because dining and restaurants have become more of a popular activity. So you can go in and know what a compote is, know what goes into a vinaigrette."

The key to a successful TV food show is that it all looks so possible. Unlike traveling to Bali or installing a toilet, you have a pretty good shot of some day actually experiencing what you see on the screen, even if you're only ordering it in. Food is the great equalizer, the common denominator of all people. After all, everyone has to eat.

Overview:
Television's Food Court
Through the Years

Cooking shows are no longer only for people who cook; the shows have entered the pop-culture Zeitgeist. If there's any doubt of that, consider *Mr. Nice Guy* (1997), Jackie Chan's first feature film shot entirely in English. In this action comedy, Chan portrays an affable TV chef in Melbourne, Australia. In the story line his instructional cooking video gets mixed up with one featuring footage of a local drug lord making illegal deals, and Chan, the hero, ends up taking on two opposing Australian crime gangs before all matters are resolved. The beginnings of the food genre were far less striking.

The first cooking shows on television in the United States go back as far as the beginning of commercial TV and with a good American enterprising reason: Food companies were sponsors of the first shows. Sometimes, performers did commercials during their shows; other times, home economics experts (wearing white lab coats) would come in and talk about the four basic food groups. Unlike the first educational television stations, commercial stations had built-in kitchens because advertisers promoted food products and stations produced the commercials. Food companies weren't just sponsors, they also influenced what went out on "their" airwaves.

One of the first American TV cooking shows, *In the Kelvinator Kitchen* (NBC), was also one of TV's first consumer-oriented shows. It was hosted by Alma Kitchell, at the dawn of commercial television in 1947.

Kitchell was a radio singer, and back in 1939, during RCA's first experimental TV broadcasts, she sang the part of Ruth in the first televised opera, Gilbert and Sullivan's comic operetta *The Pirates of Penzance*. Kitchell hosted *In the Kelvinator Kitchen* until 1949, when she retired from public life. She lived to be 103, and died in 1996.

In 1946, Borden's "Elsie the Cow" announced "Elsie presents James Beard in *I Love to Eat!*" (NBC). Beard (1903–1985) demonstrated cooking techniques and stumbled over his lines, but showed skill with utensils. *I Love to Eat* began as a fifteen-minute spot on the network, expanded to thirty minutes, and then was canceled the following spring by its new sponsor, Birdseye. Beard integrated Birdseye commercials into his commentary and used their products in creating his dishes. Although he had theater experience, Beard never seemed comfortable in front of the TV camera. However, he didn't stay off the tube. The Canadian-produced *James Beard: Better Living and Better Cooking* show ran on America's syndicated airwaves from 1964 to 1966. This was more like a "happy homemaker" show.

The first TV cooking teacher to use authentic French technique was Dione (pronounced Dee-o-nee) Lucas, who was born in 1909 in England, studied at the Cordon Bleu in France, and died in 1971 at the age of sixty-two. Lucas opened the Cordon Bleu restaurant and school in New York City in 1942. *Dione Lucas' Cooking Show* ran in prime time on CBS from 1948 to 1949, and in its early weeks was called *To the Queen's Taste*. The half-hour program also ran locally in New York from 1948 to 1953. "She was a marvelous technician," recalls cooking maven Julia Child.

Creative Cookery, hosted by chef François Pope and his sons Francis and Robert, was broadcast in 1953 to 1954 from Chicago. NBC ran an hour-long version on Saturday mornings, and ABC ran a fifty-five-minute version on weekdays. NBC's *Home* show (1954–57) was hosted by Arlene Francis, and was an extension of the *Today* show. The program had a magazine format, complete with "departments." Poppy Cannon, who wrote the *Can Opener Cookbook* (1952), occasionally appeared, usually demonstrating how to cook with canned ingredients such as Campbell's soup. (Years later, in the 1970s, Cannon jumped to her death from her twenty-third floor New York City apartment.)

Hi Mom! ran on weekday mornings on NBC in the 1950s, and was hosted by Shari Lewis (with puppets Lambchop and Charlie the Horse). This show's premise was to offer advice to young mothers and entertain very young children. The program included a cooking segment with Josie

McCarthy, who made full menus of "nice meal(s) for a man to come home to." We're talking beef stew and hot vegetable salad here.

One day in 1962 a six-foot-two-inch woman with an unusual voice was featured on a fledgling educational television book review program to promote her latest cookbook. To fill air time, she whipped up an omelet with ingredients she brought with her. People loved her, and soon Julia Child began her renowned half-hour PBS-TV show, *The French Chef* (1962–73). Child attributes her success to timing. People were able to travel more easily in the 1960s, and therefore were exposed more frequently to different cultures. Also, President and Mrs. Kennedy hired a French chef for the White House, raising people's consciousness about finer foods. But in many ways, Child represented the early 1960s' awakening of both food and women in the United States.

American TV cooking shows in the late 1960s and early 1970s were epitomized by the groovy cocktail party that was the *Galloping Gourmet* (1968–71), hosted by the British-born Graham Kerr in front of a live audience. The liberating libertine opened each half-hour syndicated episode with the mantra "You're the greatest there is."

In the button-down 1980s, the gourmet was Frugal. The anti-Kerr, minister Jeff Smith brought cooking shows to a new height. After hosting a local TV program in Tacoma, Washington (1973–77), he went national in 1983 with the half-hour series *The Frugal Gourmet* (PBS), based in Chicago. He made so many shows that some credit his popularity to pure volume—people got used to him, like the morning paper, and associated him with cooking on television. His producer, Geoffrey Drummond, sums it up this way: "Jeff Smith was incredibly successful because he was extremely likable on TV. People really felt that a friendly neighbor was dropping by. He had that ability to create a warm, friendly, and very personalized relationship with the audience." Also in the 1980s, people were looking for a new drug-free way to show off all their disposable income, so the restaurant culture expanded in popularity, as did celebrity chefs like Wolfgang Puck. Soon, with surveillance TV cameras focused in restaurant kitchens, you could go out to eat and watch a virtual cooking show in progress.

In the 1990s, the people who spent the 1980s dining out wanted to stay in and cook at home, or at least dine in. They remodeled their kitchens instead of their living rooms, and the right type of pots, pans, and knives became the new status symbols. "Domesticity," a word that would have made people shudder in any decade other than the 1950s, again became big business. The personification of this trend is Martha Stewart, who seems to have polarized a nation.

Stewart, the "Dominatrix of Domesticity," went from a straight-A student in Nutley, New Jersey, to a Barnard College (New York City) graduate and model (doing commercials for Breck, Clairol, Lifebuoy soap, and Tarryton cigarettes), to stock broker, to farm house restorer and caterer, to virtual empress of a media empire. This empire includes books, magazines, and television. Once described as a unique combination of the beauty of the orchid and the efficiency of a computer, Stewart has throngs of fans who want to be her. There is also a cottage industry employing people who poke fun at Stewart, such as 1994's parody magazine *Is Martha Stuart Living?* in which readers learn how to make water from scratch. And then there was Jerry Oppenheimer's 1997 *Just Desserts: The Unauthorized Biography* filled with stories alleging that Martha Stewart, the 1990s perfectionist herself is not so perfect.

As the 1990s wind down, Stewart isn't the only one on TV talking about gardening, cleaning, cooking, decorating, and party-planning. There's Katie Brown, sometimes called "the Gen-X Martha Stewart," who hosts a Lifetime cable show, *Next Door with Katie Brown* (1997), which features remedial homemaking. Brown was once an actress in a Saturn car commercial, a caterer, and an antique store manager before heeding the call of television host. There's also B. Smith, whom the media has dubbed "the black Martha Stewart." Smith charted new territory in 1976 when she became the first African-American woman to appear on the cover of *Mademoiselle*. Now she owns restaurants, writes books, and hosts a TV show, *B. Smith with Style* (syndicated, 1998).

Fragmentation is also a key to popular culture in the 1990s. Everything from radio formats to cable channels have become quite specific. By the time the twentieth century ends, there will be, seemingly, a separate cable channel for every possible hobby (coming soon: the skeet shooting channel!). Already there is an entire network devoted to food (that's *food*, not necessarily *cooking*). The New York–based Food Network started broadcasting on November 23, 1993, with the aim to win over viewers who love to eat. The cable network doesn't really compete with traditional public television shows, which are more specially targeted to gourmet hobbyists. The formats and the audiences are different. This new network is building an enthusiastic and cooking-aware audience, raising people's consciousness about the availability of food programming, much like CNN did for news coverage.

Back when the sitcom *Happy Days* debuted on ABC-TV in 1974, the Fonzie character, played by Henry Winkler, was peripheral at best. He had very few lines, and didn't even wear his trademark leather jacket. But people liked him, and the momentum grew: the Fonz started spending more and more time on camera. Throw in a few catchphrases ("Ay!") and you soon had the most popular character on the half-hour show. At one point the series' creators even considered changing the name of the program to *Fonzie's Happy Days*. The Food Network probably won't switch its name to Emeril's Food Network, but it certainly saw what it had in Emeril Lagasse. He is an outgoing, effervescent, yet down-to-earth chef who appeals to a wide range of viewers because of his zesty approach, and not just by standing next to an outdoor grill in the summertime. This winner of a 1997 CableACE award is getting major national press and attracting viewers, exposing them to the Food Network, and giving them the chance to sample other chefs. A "blue collar" gourmet with T-shirt-friendly catchphrases ("Bam!" and "Let's kick it up a notch!"), he has created a franchise that can establish further the network's identity.

Currently, the Food Network reaches 33 million homes, while PBS, which has many food-oriented shows, is available in 98 percent of American households. American Program Services, which distributes programs to public television stations around the country, handled twenty-eight different cooking shows in 1993. In 1998, that number was up to forty-three. Says TV producer Geoffrey Drummond: "The 'food-as-entertainment' gestalt has a nice glow right now."

The Chefs

Curtis Aikens: The Produce Guy

Born: January 22, 1959.

Hometown: Conyers, Georgia.

Parents: Father, Eddie, mechanic; mother, Laura, homemaker.

Siblings: Older brothers, Eddie Jr. and Jeffery; older sister, Laura Regina; younger sisters, Sophie and Portia.

Schools: Attended Southern University (Baton Rouge, Louisiana), and then University of Georgia (Athens, Georgia).

Favorite Junk Food: "Potato chips. When I'm in a different region [of the country] I try out the potato chips. That's the thing that keeps my belly round. I can kick sugar, but give me that salty, fatty, greasy stuff and I'm down. I'm a chipaholic."

Always in the Pantry: Salt and pepper, beans, pasta, dried fruit, and grits.

Always in the Fridge: Wine, champagne, tofu, eggs, and water. "I like cold water."

Favorite Food Smell: "Herb de provence. It reminds me of sausage cooking as a kid. When I do that combo (sage, thyme, and lavender), I can get a very similar flavor to sausage."

Favorite Food Sound: "The 'chhhhh' sound you get when you get the pan nice and hot. Also, grits. There's a sound that they make that is so country, kind of a 'blop blop' when the grits are really getting right."

Fantasy Last Meal: "Collard greens, black-eyed peas, cornbread, green onions, sliced tomatoes, my mother's fried chicken, might have to throw in some barbecued ribs, sweet potato pie, banana pudding—my last meal would be a whole day."

Curtis Aikens (*Pick of the Day*, Food Network) was born to love produce. Growing up in rural Georgia, he spent summers with his granddad Curtis. "He was a hell of a farmer. This cat grew everything, black-eyed peas, okra, tomatoes, cabbage, lettuce . . . in the summertime he grew these huge-ass collard greens that were just the bomb." His grandfather would grow it and his grandmother would cook it. Aikens' father raised a pig and a cow every year which he had slaughtered so his family of eight would have meat on the dinner table.

Aikens laughs. "Of course nowadays, I don't eat meat, but there was a lot of dedication in [what my father did]." Of his siblings, he says "None of us are crack addicts or in jail, we're all contributing. So Dad and Mom did a damn good job."

The same cannot be said of the school system in which Aikens came of age. He didn't learn to read until he was twenty-six. He didn't develop a basic foundation for reading in high school, then was admitted to college on a football scholarship. He survived a year and a half of higher education by giving his answers verbally, and maintained a B average without being able to read or write. How?

"You get more flies with honey. I got over because I was a nice guy, and people wanted to help the nice guy. I tell these kids [today] if you really want to be something or make something, don't try to tear the door down. Ask someone for the key, because nine times out of ten the person wants to give you the key anyway. I knew that as a kid. I schmoozed my way through. I'm not proud of that now. But it was what got me through."

Aikens got close to success many times, but then ran away from it. "I don't think I could ever walk you through what life was like for me growing up, not knowing how to read and hiding it every day. That was my challenge every day, to make sure no one found out that this boy couldn't read. I spent a night on the side of the freeway once because I couldn't read the word 'Arkansas' to get back to the damn highway. I remember spending five hours trying to get around San Antonio because I couldn't read the street signs."

When Aikens was running his own produce company, Peaches, in 1985 (which he started in 1981 and operated until 1986), he saw a TV commercial for ABC's PLUS (Project Learning U.S.), and decided enough was enough. He called the literacy hotline number and announced he wanted to learn to read, which he did, with the help of tutors. Now he donates half of the royalties from his books to reading programs. In 1992 he came full circle, taping a public service announcement for PLUS.

"I don't want anyone else to go through it, but people still are, every day, and it's time we in America stopped pretending it's not happening and put some money back into public schools. We owe it to society. How much money does one man need? I'm not saying you have to give away your fortune, but I'm willing to give something back, and I'd like to see other people willing to do that, and not only willing, but do it. For me, television was not to become rich, it was to show people that if I could learn to read at age twenty-six, get a goal for myself and achieve that goal, anyone else could do it, especially non-reading adults. So my message to the nonreaders is: 'Don't be ashamed, don't be embarrassed, get help.' The Food Network knows that if I can't promote that on my show then I won't do the show, because that's what I'm all about. Food, for me, has been a way out."

Certainly, it always has been just that. His first real job was in a grocery store, at the Conyers, Georgia A&P Market. He worked in the grocery department, but spent all his free time in the produce department. "The first time I tasted fresh pineapple, it was a whole new world, baby, that really brought it home." Aikens had access to fresh items from different parts of the world, and that fueled his produce fire. He moved to California in the early 1980s, and soon was cooking with 100 different herbs, and tasting things he'd never seen before, such as passion fruit, guava, mango, and papaya. "Yeah, it turned me on."

After running his produce company in the San Francisco Bay area, Aikens moved to New York to head the produce departments at Dorn's Wholesale Market and Balducci's. Then, in 1988, he relocated to Georgia where he established Aikens' Family Produce, which catered to film and TV shoots in his home state. He supplied produce for the TV series *In the Heat of the Night* and the feature film *Glory* and soon started sharing his produce knowledge on local television shows. After a guest appearance on ABC-TV's daytime show *Home,* to promote his 1993 book *Guide to the Harvest,* he began regular appearances on that program.

Aikens has since appeared on *The Oprah Winfrey Show,* CNN, *Good Morning America,* and *Entertainment Tonight. NBC Nightly News* did a feature story on his struggle with illiteracy and his devotion to helping American adults who are unable to read. ABC's *World News Tonight* also featured Aikens, covering his participation in the First Annual Literacy Festival in Cairo, Georgia. He's a speaker at festivals and conferences, and has been a guest at the White House, visiting First Lady Hillary Clinton, former President George Bush, and former First Lady Barbara Bush. As a food consultant, Aikens has worked with the United States Open Tennis Tournament, the New York City Plaza Hotel, the United Nations Cafeteria, McDonalds, Pizza Hut, Pillsbury, and Balducci's. He's nationally recognized as a health food expert, cook, and consumer food advocate.

Aikens likes to refer to himself as "the produce guy." So, is he a vegetarian? "I don't use a label. I don't eat meat, but I think there's a negative connotation to the word 'vegetarian,' so I don't use it. What I try to do in my show is give people options with produce. I'm not anti-meat; someday I might go back to eating meat, and I don't want people to trip out if I do." Some of Aikens' greatest food memories are of Sundays when he was a youngster, when chicken was prepared four or five different ways, including fried, roasted, and barbecued. Notice that he also listed some meat in the description of his "Fantasy Last Meal."

Aikens began with the Food Network early in the network's history in the mid-1990s, hosting shows like *Meals Without Meat, Food in a Flash,* and now *Pick of the Day.* Each series is driven by his personality: "You can't put someone up there who can't relate to the camera; if someone can't relate to the camera, no one's gonna watch the show."

Aikens is currently the only African-American culinary expert to have a regular network TV show. "I think that's a shame. Racism still exists and no one wants to admit it right now. There are no other black chefs on television and of all the minority cats out there cooking, I'm not the best. I'm good at what I do and I present information well, but I could name so many great black chefs, and they don't get a shot on television. Am I happy about it? No. Can I change it? When I start my own network."

So, is Curtis a role model? "[Basketball player] Charles Barkley said [on his sneaker commercial] 'I ain't no role model.' I feel like anytime you put on a sneaker and say 'buy this sneaker' you're a role model. And anytime I stand in front of the camera I'm a role model, for my kids, nieces, nephews, every little kid out there who says, 'There's a black man on television and if he can be on television cooking, so can I.' Or poor white kids in the country can say, 'Curtis is from Georgia, if he can grow up and go off and become a TV chef, so can I.' Anybody is a role model. Once we become over eighteen, we're a role model, whether we're a good one or a bad one."

Chef!

Curtis Aikens wonders why he's the only African-American regularly cooking on television. British stand-up comedian Lenny Henry had the same question about celebrity chefs. In 1990, after reading a newspaper article about superstar chefs in England, he noticed that none of them were black.

As a result, Henry created and stars in the British sitcom *Chef!* which premiered in 1993 as one of the few British TV series ever to cast a black lead actor, and can be seen now on American PBS stations. Henry rose to fame costarring with Tracey Ullman in BBC-TV's *Three of a Kind* and his own *Lenny Henry Show*.

In *Chef!* Henry plays Gareth Blackstock, the chef de cuisine at the fictional Le Chateau Anglais. Blackstock is intelligent, ambitious, dysfunctional, conceited, and high-strung, and manages to be likable even while being obnoxious. To a wine steward: "This doesn't have a bouquet, it has a smell. A bouquet has flowery and fruity scents, it promises delights to come. This smells like the interior of a Datsun minivan. It doesn't promise—it threatens." And to a cook: "Let me put things in perspective for you: on the evolutionary scale of cooking, I am Einstein, and you are a mud-dwelling, uni-cellular speck of jelly with a predilection for consuming its own excrement."

Besides witty dialogue, the show features some yummy food-preparation scenes, which brought in the foodies and broadened Henry's comedy audience. By some accounts, the program accurately portrays life in the kitchen of a five-star restaurant.

Aikens says his children, Curtis Jr. and Cole Bennet, are the "best thing I've done in my life." Their mom, Teresa, and Aikens are divorced, but live in the same neighborhood in Novato, California. "We have houses four doors apart, so when I'm home they're with me or when they want to walk down to her house, they walk down to her house. It's taken us a long time to get to that point, but I'm proud of it. I didn't have kids to be away from them; I don't want to live in Georgia when my kids live in California. I don't understand how these guys can father these kids and just take off like that. Watching [my children] in the bathtub, or eating breakfast, or at their little karate show... I have more fun watching them than thinking about my own stuff."

When he does think about his own stuff, it's usually about cooking. "I love watching cooking shows. It's like dining out at other restaurants to see what's hot in someone else's joint." When asked whether the popularity of cooking shows is just a recent fad, Curtis states that, "I think it's been popular for a long time, but the powers that be, the guys in those big offices weren't watching those shows, so I don't think they had any idea how popular food shows were. I think when a lot of women started climbing that corporate ladder, it became 'okay' to have cooking programs. I don't want to sound sexist because there are a lot of guys who love cooking shows. I think when women and other minorities started really getting involved in programming and developing programs, we started doing things down on the street, street-level. Everybody loves to eat, or everyone HAS to eat. It's one thing we have in common all over this world, that no matter what kind of diet you're on, whether you're big or small, you have to take in some sustenance at some point in the day."

Unlike many of his peers, Aikens didn't learn his techniques from an official institution. "I'm from the 'ghetto school of cooking,' and the 'ghetto school of cooking' is just as good, just different. My mama taught me to cook, and I added to that when I traveled around the country. That's what world cuisine is all about, everybody bringing something different. If we all cooked the same way, wouldn't it be boring as hell?"

Still, there are some who protest that those who teach the culinary arts on television should have an official degree to substantiate their knowledge. "Sometimes people get upset with those of us who didn't go to culinary school, that we're making the money we are and have the profiles we have, but didn't get certified by this [cooking school] entity. One of my biggest peeves with this [TV chef] industry is the label 'master chef.' It was invented by some guy who wanted to keep some other guy down. I'm not a classically trained chef, but I know the five mother sauces. You could put my recipes against any of these so called 'master chefs' and you break it down to the important thing, taste, and my stuff is right there with any of them. So if this guy went to school and became a 'master chef,' or he spent twenty years refining how to make a soufflé or a cake . . . I say, 'So let's cook, baby!'"

Being a master chef might not be necessary, but life experience is. "You can't be a star at fifteen or twenty in this business. It's like the blues. When you get those layers of hard life or living, that's when you become a great blues act. I think that's what happens with chefs. Ask any chef about how they cooked at twenty and now at forty, and how much richer their recipes and food and techniques are now."

According to Aikens, food has the power to break down barriers. "When you sit down one-on-one with someone, there are no problems. It's that group mentality that's the problem. We need to take that one-on-one mentality and put it in a group situation, and I feel like the way to do that is over the table. Sit down and break bread with someone and you can talk about anything. Can you imagine bringing the United Nations together and everybody brings a dish? We all sit down and eat like the other guy does, and then we start throwing topics on the table. That's what I think food is all about. You break bread, you can break any problem. That's my vision of what this culinary world could actually be, especially on television."

TV Series

The Home Show (ABC, 1993–94)
Food in a Flash (Food Network, 1993–94)
Meals Without Meat (Food Network, 1994–96)
From My Garden (Food Network, 1995)
Pick of the Day (Food Network, 1996–)

Books

Curtis Aikens' Guide to the Harvest by Curtis G. Aikens (revised edition) (Peachtree Publishers, 1993)
Curtis Cooks with Heart & Soul: Quick, Healthy Cooking from the Host of TV's from My Garden by Curtis G. Aikens (Hearst Books, 1995)

Web Site

www.foodtv.com

Mario Batali: Chow Batali-a

Born: September 19, 1960.

Hometown: Federal Way, Washington (suburb of Seattle).

Parents: Father, Armandino, retired Boeing Aircraft engineer; mother, Marilyn, retired nurse.

Siblings: Two younger sisters, Dana and Gina.

School: Rutgers University (New Jersey).

Favorite Junk Food: "I don't eat junk food per se. I love chips and salsa, but I don't think anyone in America doesn't. I grew up eating a lot of [fast food] so at this point it's no longer interesting to me. I would just as soon eat a Vietnamese fast food, which, to a Vietnamese person may seem as boring as [American fast food] does to me."

Always in the Pantry: "Great extra virgin olive oil, great balsamic vinegar, Parmesan cheese, garlic, that's a given, and champagne."

Always in the Fridge: "There's always some fruit that's not going to make it. We buy fruit a lot and it just sits around. Also, lots of bottles of water, jam or jelly, at least two kinds of mustard, at least two kinds of hot sauce, and my baby's food."

Favorite Food Smell: "The starch in the air when pasta's cooking. That's an amazing smell. When I was growing up we'd have pasta in the winter, and I would remember all of the windows in the house, for some reason, would just steam up. You walk in the house and smell that starchy spaghetti smell, and it drives you nuts."

Favorite Food Sound: "The sizzle—it's crisp."

Fantasy Last Meal: "I don't have a dish like that in my mind. I would like to be on the Amalfi coast [of Italy] and eat whatever happened to be there."

Mario Batali, host of Food Network's *Molto Mario* and *Mediterranean Mario*, grew up just outside of Seattle, Washington, in a family whose livelihood was based in food production. They made their own pasta and sausages, cured their own olives, and produced their own wine. "We spent the whole year, every year, foraging for mushrooms, blackberries, making pies, making sausage, making whatever we made." His first Italian cooking teacher was his grandmother, starting from when he was old enough to stir.

But like many little boys, he wanted to be a football player. Or a pirate. His family moved to Spain when Mario was fourteen. "I went to high school in Madrid and I decided I wanted to be a banker because I loved Spain so much, and I wanted to go back and live in Spain." So Batali went to Rutgers University in New Brunswick, New Jersey, and earned a degree in Spanish Theater of the Golden Age as well as one in finance. Then he decided he really didn't want to work in finance, and turned to cooking.

He enrolled in the Cordon Bleu School of Cooking in London, but didn't stay long. "I hated it. I dropped out. It wasn't a professional cooking school, it was a housewife school. Not that housewives are bad, but I was looking for an intense professional program, and it was like sixty-one women and three American guys who also got duped, and it moved very slowly, we did like one menu a day. It's a great school, I'm not debasing it, but it wasn't what I was looking for." Batali decided to pursue on-the-job training in restaurants all over France. In 1984, he returned to America, to the West Coast, winning a job at a catering hall that served thousands of people. This experience made him realize that he wanted something more intimate, so he worked as a chef at the Four Seasons Hotel in San Francisco for three years. He remained with the hospitality chain and moved to Santa Barbara, California, to work at the famed Biltmore. "Then they wanted me to move to Hawaii. I realized I didn't want to continue with the Four Seasons, because it was just too slick and too fancy. That's when I retired and went to work in Italy for three and a half years."

Batali worked as a chef at Trattoria La Volta in Bologna, Italy, a restaurant serving rustic mountain cuisine. It was here that Batali mastered the Italian cooking that he began learning in his childhood home. He was getting back to his roots, and that of the traditional Italian table. He learned the fine points of food presentation in the classic Italian style, and visited the wineries, cheese makers, prosciutto curers, and vinegar makers. This experience was the big turning point in Batali's career. "[That's where I gained] the most technique, the most understanding of real, simple, Italian food, and the language and travel. Most Americans consider most Italian food to be spaghetti and meatballs, which are great dishes when they're done properly, but they're Italo-American dishes. The real Italian food is much simpler. It's much more based on the seasons, and it's lighter. There's a lot less stuff in it."

In 1992, Batali moved back to the United States, this time to New York City's Greenwich Village, where he helped recharge and update a friend's seventy-year-old family-owned restaurant, Rocco. Then, in 1993, Batali opened his own trattoria on Cornelia Street called Po. *The Zagat Guide to New York City Restaurants* describes Po as "delicious, original Northern Italian–Mediterranean food." Each day a fresh supply of vegetables and cheese arrives from Coach Farm, a dairy goat farm that includes a vegetable garden and is only two and one-half hours from New York City in Pine Plains, New York. The farm is the family business of Susan Cahn, who became Batali's wife in 1994. They have two children, Benno, born in 1996, and Leo, born in 1998, at about the same time as Batali's second Greenwich Village restaurant, Babbo, came to be.

In 1994 and 1995, Batali won the James Beard Award for Table Design at the Beard House Holiday Auction held in New York City. The James Beard Foundation also cited Batali as a Rising Star of America Cuisine and chose him to be among just six chefs to demonstrate his talents at the James Beard Awards.

Batali, whose laid-back style on the air includes a ponytail of long strawberry blond hair, shorts, and clogs, came to television via the Food Network, starting with a week as the guest host on *Chef du Jour*. He later returned to do the game show, *Ready...Set...Cook!* where he competed against his friend and fellow Food Network chef, Bobby Flay. Soon Batali had his own programs, where he could showcase his own recipes on camera. In the first series, *Molto Mario*, which began in 1996, he explains the differences in Italian regional cooking. In the second series, *Mediterranean Mario*, which began in 1998, he included Mediterranean-style cooking, from countries such as France, Greece, Spain, Italy, and Morocco. "Basically what I hope people see is that across borders, a lot more things are shared than just trade and commerce. There's similar ideas going on in the food in all the Mediterranean, and they're based on Grandma's cooking, not necessarily the best French chefs and high technique. That's what I think people like about the shows. They'll see something that they recognized that their grandmothers made and that will knock them, and they'll say, 'Jeez, I haven't thought about that dish since 1975, or when I was twelve, when I had it the last time, and you know, I forgot about it.' I get letters all the time, 'Oh, I forgot about this dish. It brought me to tears to see you make it.' It's really gratifying, but I don't do it to do that. I'm looking at it more like a road map. The mission is to make accessible and understandable dishes that people may or may not have recognized."

More TV cooking programs feature Italian food than any other style of cuisine. Why? "It's the most accessible. In America, it's enjoyed by the most people, even in the places that are the furthest from any cosmopolitan action, like farm country, they like Italian food. If they're going to have any ethnic, it's going to be Italian or Chinese in little towns. A lot of Italian immigrants came here from the 1870s to the 1930s. They got here and wanted to make their own dishes but they couldn't find the ingredients, so these crafty old grandmas and moms started substituting American ingredients—cream cheese for marscapone, cheddar [cheese] for Parmesano [cheese]. The dishes lost anything they had to do with Italy other than that it was some great cook's attempt to use the local ingredients, which is what Italian cooking is all about. So these Italian dishes are handed down from generation to generation, pretty soon they're not Italian; they have nothing to do with Italian food. You go to Italy, and it's, 'Where's the Turkey Tettrazini? Where's the Shrimp Scampi?'"

Batali believes that with the popularity of cooking shows on television, people aren't just watching, but are actually cooking. "Cooking is the leisure of the next millennium. People enjoy it, and it gives them a chance to understand things from a very earth- or dirt-based level. To see things like wheat be ground into flour and then take that flour and add just eggs, and come up with a beautiful pasta dish from scratch, it removes a lot of the problems with understanding the complex system that our lives have become a part of. Simple cookery is also an expression of art. People love to be able to express themselves once they're comfortable with their techniques and that's a very satisfying thing; you have your friends over, make dinner with them, and eat it with them.

"But for me it also represents a lot of the tradition that I believe a lot of the yuppies in America lost. As they moved away from their families to the city and went to work every day, they saw that rich, satisfying traditional stuff is missing from their day. That's one of the reasons that on the weekends, they really dig [cooking]. It's a good form of leisure."

Foodfellas

Film director Martin Scorcese professed his love for cooking shows in the February 1997 issue of *Details* magazine. "I loved to watch my mother cook. Ever since I was a boy, I've loved to watch cooking shows. I liked the way things were made. It's like little paintings in a way. These shows are soothing, like music. It's fantastic. Now I watch Television Food Network [sic]."

Scorcese, whose late mother Catherine wrote the cookbook, *Italianamerican—The Scorcese Family Cookbook* (Random House, 1996), and appeared in *GoodFellas* (1990), also claimed mozzarella as his favorite cheese and compared making a movie to making a meal. "A lot of the inspiration that you need in cooking—the creativity, the improvisation—is very similar. In a movie, every shot is like making a good meal. But since you do maybe ten shots a day, that's like preparing and cooking ten good meals a day. And you have a lot of pots simmering."

TV Series

Molto Mario (Food Network, 1996– *)
Mediterranean Mario (Food Network, 1998– *)

Book

Mario Batali's Simple Italian Food: Rustic Cooking from Two Villages by
  Mario Batali (Clarkson Potter, 1998)

Web Site

www.foodtv.com

Sissy Biggers: Kitchen Sync

Born: July 3, "the year the electric can opener was invented."

Hometown: Southport, Connecticut.

Parents: Father, William Cargill, marketing executive; mother, Terry Cargill Russell, real estate broker.

Siblings: Older brother, Bill; younger brother, Sam; younger sisters, Molly and Sarah; half sister, Alexandra.

Schools: Barnard College (New York City), Columbia University (New York City).

Favorite Junk Food: "It's not a huge indulgence of mine, but I have been known to enjoy a McDonalds quarter pounder with a bloody Mary on Concourse B at Chicago's O'Hare. I do love a fresh pan of Rice Krispie treats."

Always in the Pantry: "Canned whole clams, olive paste, smoked oysters, canned pomodoro, and corn flakes."

Always in the Fridge: "Pepper jack cheese in a block; broccoli rabe; frozen soaked, black beans; any barbecue sauce on special at the supermarket; and Paul Newman's Caesar salad dressing."

Favorite Food Smell: "Truffle oil!"

Favorite Food Sound: "The gurgle of an expensive Italian espresso machine."

Fantasy Last Meal: "I get 'agita' just thinking about it. I can tell you this much, if I knew it was my last meal the last thing I'd want to do is tuck into a big dinner. If it were a swift glancing blow, let it be outside a five-star French restaurant where I've just enjoyed a rabbit confit and foie gras with a lingonberry glaze."

Sissy Biggers grew up in Connecticut, near the Long Island Sound, about fifty miles from New York City. Her parents divorced when she was twelve. Her father was a marketing executive and expatriate who lived the last twenty-two years of his life in Marbella, Spain, on the Costa del Sol. Her mother has been remarried for almost twenty years, is a retired real estate broker, and still resides in Connecticut. Young Sissy dreamed of growing up to be either soap opera's Susan Lucci or the news world's Jane Pauley. Television was destined to be in her future in some way. She also had a burgeoning interest in food programming on television.

"I used to watch cooking shows casually. In particular I remember Julia Child and the comfortable atmosphere. I used to make her crepes with orange rind. I got so good at it, my mom got me a crepe pan. I remember the *Galloping Gourmet* for his entertainment edge. But what I really watched was variety shows in the afternoon. Bill Boggs on Channel 5 in New York City and Merv [Griffin] and Mike [Douglas], of course."

When she was sixteen, Biggers made her television debut as Impostor Number One (as in "Number One, what is your name please?") on the CBS network game show *To Tell the Truth*. She pretended to be Abby Lee Greene, a baton-twirling magician. She duped panelist Peggy Cass and wound up with a prize of Turtlewax. But the TV bug had bit.

While studying at Columbia University in New York City, Biggers earned her AFTRA card as a regular extra on the New York–based soap opera *All My Children*, featuring Susan Lucci. "I got on through Mary Fickett, who played Ruth Martin for years. I was her [kids'] babysitter and she got me in." Biggers never had any lines, but did what was called "under five" or "special business." "I spent a lot of time on a stretcher at 'Pine Valley Hospital.' Underneath the sheet I was busy reading American literature—my major at Barnard College at Columbia University uptown." In fact, if Sissy hadn't gone into television, she now would be teaching American literature. "Great material and a chance to stand up in front of an audience and, ideally, inspire a generation."

It was at the daytime soap that Biggers developed an interest in production. Soon it was off to Los Angeles where she started as a secretary and worked her way up to production coordinator on HBO cable's *Not Necessarily the News*. She then did similar chores on Fridays. ABC-TV's live, late night sketch comedy program, which attempted to rival with *Saturday Night Live*.

In 1984, Biggers moved back to New York to join the NBC network as the Director of Late Night and Specials Programming. She supervised *Saturday Night Live, Late Night with David Letterman,* and the launch of *Late Night with Conan O'Brien*. She managed *Macy's Thanksgiving Day Parade, The Miss America Pageant,* and several comedy and information specials including *Spy Magazine's How to Be Famous* and the Emmy-award winning, *Lucy & Desi: A Home Movie*. In 1985, Sissy married Kelsey Biggers, who works on Wall Street in banking informational services. They have two daughters, Sarah and Lucy.

"In the specials area, the highlight had to be snagging my kids and my husband roles on the 'Fruit Juice Valley Float,' which they shared with Kelsey Grammer at the Macy's Thanksgiving Day Parade. When the float hit Herald Square the director [of the TV special] unabashedly favored my family in the shots virtually overlooking Kelsey and his daughter—which Grammer complained about on Letterman the next night . . . not knowing, of course, that I was Gypsy Rose Lee [running the show] in the video truck!"

Saturday Night Live was also a memorable experience. "[I remember] Matthew Broderick was in a sketch called 'Nude Beach' in which we, the programming department, negotiated how many times the word 'penis' could be uttered. But the memory I relish most is having the catered dinner on the eighth floor of 30 Rock[efeller Plaza] before dress rehearsal and choking back food listening to head writer Jim Downey, Dennis Miller, and Dana Carvey carry on. I was especially fond of Dennis, with whom I would hang out on the 'back deck' behind the control booth as he prepared for his 'Weekend Update' segments. What everyone probably remembers about me was my two pregnancies [and how] I'd get larger and larger as the season went on and nights got later. I was a novelty. Not many were pregnant on that watch."

In 1994, Biggers was ready for the other side of the camera—the side where star Jane Pauley works. Sissy landed the job of on-air personality as host of Lifetime cable's daytime talk show, *Live from Queens*, which was nominated for the 1994 CableACE award for Best Talk Show six months after its debut.

Julia Child Meets American Gladiators

If viewing cooking shows is truly like watching sports, then *Iron Chef* (known in Japan as *Ryori no Tetsujin* or *Cooking Iron Man*) is the Olympics. It's been described as *"Monday Night Football* Meets Julia Child" and "a cross between *Yan Can Cook* and *Mortal Kombat*." Produced by Fuji-TV in Japan, it can be seen in most major American cities that carry Japanese programming. It's *Ready...Set...Cook!* kicked up about a hundred Far Eastern notches.

The Emmy-nominated show, which began airing in October 1993, is a real-time cooking competition that takes place in the Kitchen Stadium and centers around a battle between two cooking wizards, an Iron Chef representing the finest of a specific cuisine and a challenger. The challenger can choose to battle one of four Iron Chefs—Japanese, Chinese, French, or Italian. Champ and challenger are given the same theme ingredient, and have an hour to prepare a multi-course menu using that ingredient, while three or four commentators do "color" (making breathless comments such as "I think he may steam that") and sideline reporters and handheld cameras catch all the action (the chefs are also interviewed before the "confronts"). There are even instant replays and statistics from previous battles. Finally, a group of judges taste and critique the dishes, then cast their votes.

That's what the show has in common with sports. Here's what it has in common with theater. It's hosted by Kaga Takeshi, a Japanese actor decked out in a shoulder-length pageboy, black gloves, a frilly shirt, and a sequined jacket (he's been described as "Liberace on speed"). Each installment begins with Kaga taking a bite out of a yellow pepper and, well, leering at the camera. The Iron Chefs, each clad in a different colored satin robe, rise up on motorized platforms. It also falls to Kaga to choose and introduce the theme ingredient, which can be anything from chestnuts to giant crab to game birds still wearing their feathers to entire headless lambs. Kaga reveals the ingredient by either whipping away a silk covering as it emerges from a pit smoking with dry ice, or lowering it from the ceiling. Kaga utters a Japan-icized version of "A la Cuisine!" the Gong of Fate sounds, and the battle begins.

Most of the sweeping musical score comes from the soundtrack to the movie *Backdraft* (1991).

Educational? No, this is pure competition; pure sport. We're talking "improv cooking." The chefs must use the theme ingredient in a multicourse meal (anywhere from four to eight dishes), so you'll see original, creative courses no one has ever even thought of before (or again)—ice cream with baked beef tongue cookies or sun-dried tomato and mackerel napoleons. However, the improv is a big draw for fans, especially those who happen to be culinary experts.

Iron Chef's cult status is proven by the enthusiasts who are hosting Iron Chef cooking parties, where folks take turns yelling out a hypothetical theme ingredient as everyone makes a list of dishes they'd create with it. And yes, there's even a drinking game. The subtitles stopped appearing in mid-1998, and though a massive letter-writing campaign has begun, some non-Japanese-speaking fans are watching the show anyway; others are considering learning Japanese just to be able to view the program. There are many Internet Web sites, including Stephanie Masumura's extremely informative site at www.ironchefs.com. There's also a Usenet group: alt.tv.iron-chefs.

Kaga Takeshi fans might want to know he played the lead in *Jesus Christ Superstar* in 1976, Tony in *West Side Story* in 1977, and Jean Val Jean in *Les Miserables* in the 1994 Japan production. Kaga was the first Japanese actor to portray Tony and Jesus on the stage.

When Sissy Biggers hosted Lifetime cable's *Live from Queens*, a psychic read her aura and said she saw "food around her." "My food background is from a household where my mother and stepfather climbed on kitchen chairs to get overhead shots of their Thanksgiving pies for little [photo] frames on the kitchen counter. So food was important."

"*Live from Queens* was developed around the drive-time radio concept. The studio was kind of messy and even had fake mikes on the desk. My original partner on the show, Susan Korn—who was then replaced by a rotating roster of women, while I remained constant—was a comic, as were Joy Behar and others. I have a natural edge of irreverence and the idea was to give women information at home in a fun, loose way."

Promoting that show brought her back to NBC and *Late Night with Conan O'Brien*, but this time as a guest. She had a little gift for her successor. "I was talking about having to do all these sex segments on television for women, and I worked the word 'clitoris' into my material, knowing that my NBC successor would squirm in his chair for a second."

"What was weird about the appearance," recalls Biggers, "was that Conan never acknowledged that he knew me from my 'former life' as a programmer. I was distracted during the segment because when he said 'So, this is not your first job in TV' I thought we were getting to my behind-the-scenes role on his very own show, but instead he asked about *To Tell the Truth*. I was new to the interviewing game, but I would never have let that ball drop. The fact that I had worked on the other side of those very cameras was really the story."

As a guest Biggers has also been on *Mike & Maty*, *KTLA* [Los Angeles] *Morning Show*, CNBC's *After Hours with Mike Jerrick*, E!'s *Talk Soup*, and the *Today* show. In 1995, Lifetime cable paired Biggers with Marc Summers for the network's live, information-driven talk show, *Biggers & Summers*. She also hosted Food Network's *Hunger Telethon '95* and, later, *Election Night Party* in 1996. In September 1996 Biggers became a regular at the Food Network by replacing Robin Young as the host of the cooking game show *Ready...Set...Cook!*, based on a similar British program called *Ready...Steady...Cook!* How are these two shows different? "Fern, my English counterpart 'presides' over her show...I would say I 'alight' between the two sides."

Basically, on *Ready...Set...Cook!* each of two contestants teams up with one of two chefs, forming the Tomato Team and the Pepper Team (named such to maintain the cooking motif). Both pairs have to cook something in eighteen minutes, using the imaginative, challenging ingredients selected by the team's non-chef. Each different set of ingredients usually costs less than ten dollars. "The contestants give a list of ingredients to the Food Network's kitchen staff which is then shopped for by the kitchen...after all, that tuna steak better be camera ready!" The chefs also get to use what is in the ultra-stocked TV studio pantry, which includes almost every known herb and spice.

During the course of her hosting job on the half-hour *Ready...Set...Cook!* program, Biggers moves back and forth, chatting with the two sides while they concoct and cook as the minutes tick away. The audience then votes on which dish looks better, and then everyone eats. (If there is meat involved, it might need a little zap in the microwave, in case the eighteen minutes didn't allow it to be cooked through. This is why viewers can't retrieve these shotgun recipes on the Food Network's Internet Web site.) Because the chefs on the show must think quickly, be inventive, and have charisma, many of them have been asked to return as guests on the Food Network's *Chef du Jour*.

You don't necessarily watch *Ready . . . Set . . . Cook!* to learn. It's a perfect example of an entertainment-driven food show targeting an audience who loves to eat, not just those who cook. It's also an example of cooking-as-sport. "I think '*RSC!*' is the ultimate vicarious cooking show. As you watch the chefs mull over the surprise ingredients, the playing field [between teams] is even for a minute or two, and the viewer makes their own plan for the leeks and portobellos . . . but inevitably, minutes later, the chef dazzles the home [TV viewer] cook."

Blessed with what she calls an adventurous palette and a high metabolism, Biggers, although not actually cooking for a living, does so at home. She considers herself a foodie, which she defines as "someone who plans their next meal as they tuck into the meal in front of them." At home, she is likely to whip up linguine with clam sauce and olive paste, or broccoli rabe with garlic and a generous sprinkling of red pepper flakes. "I consider cooking my hobby and when referring to me as an entertainer, it should be prefaced by the word 'avid.'"

Biggers' children are starting to putter enthusiastically in the kitchen, too. "Sarah likes to doctor up Lipton's chicken noodle soup with whatever's in the vegetable drawer. Lucy likes to mix up tuna and sneak in relish." The girls appeared with her on the *Today* show not too long ago where they demonstrated the *Better Homes and Gardens Junior Cookbook*. Biggers is spokesperson for the Better Homes and Gardens book group.

Sissy's experiences both on camera and off camera give her a unique perspective regarding the cooking show phenomenon. "I think watching cooking shows is guilt-free television. You can come home and snap on the set and go about preparing dinner or doing chores and not feel that the idiot box (as we used to call it) is a distraction. You can catch a bit of info here and there and file it away. You can follow along in a vicarious manner without having to jot everything down. I think the challenge for food on television is serving the core audience that is really tuning in for traditional cooking on television and the others who are attracted to the entertainment value which the Food Network is beefing up. It is still a maturing—or to use the food metaphor—a simmering medium which has a long way to go before it's done. It's an exciting form of broadcasting."

TV Series

Live from Queens (Lifetime, 1994–95)
Biggers & Summers (Lifetime, 1995–96)
Ready... Set... Cook! (Food Network, 1996– *)

Web Site

www.foodtv.com

Bob Blumer:
The Dali of the Dishwasher

Born: March 6, 1960.

Hometown: Montreal, Quebec, Canada.

Parents: Father, Jack, contractor/developer; mother, Joan, school teacher.

Siblings: Younger sister Sarah; younger brother Billy.

School: University of Western Ontario (London, Ontario, Canada).

Favorite Junk Food: "Store-bought chocolate bars, like Rolos. I've got a real sweet tooth."

Always in the Pantry: "Dried chipotle peppers, Treasure Joe's Chicken Chile, three or four olive oils, vinegar, garlic, shallots, dried pasta, and fleur de sal."

Always in the Fridge: "Tons of oranges, Parmesan Reggiano, pancetta, fresh herbs, fresh pasta, olives, mustards, and greens."

Favorite Food Smell: "Roasting garlic."

Favorite Food Sound: "The smoke alarm. When I'm doing my chipotle dry rub shrimp on the stovetop, I know the flavor is peaking when the smoke alarm goes off."

Fantasy Last Meal: "My last meal really would be different things from different restaurants from around the country: A bottle of

Burgundy, the Ty Cobb salad from a restaurant in LA, grilled asparagus and Fritto Misto from a restaurant in San Francisco, orange chicken from a Chinese restaurant in Toronto, and one of everything on the dessert menu."

He's not the first guy who ever cooked fish in his dishwasher, but he's probably the best-known. He's the Surreal Gourmet, a.k.a. Bob Blumer.

Blumer grew up in the 1960s in Canada with his mother, father, brother, and sister. Unlike most youngsters of his generation, and especially ironic for one who would grow up to appear on more than 200 TV shows, he rarely watched television. "I really believe that if every TV was turned off, we'd be much more creative."

In college, Blumer and his roommate decided that one would cook and the other would clean; Blumer opted for the cooking. "I realized I had a natural affinity for it and loved to go shopping at farmers' markets and stuff like that. Cooking for dates is where I honed my skills."

Blumer took a graduate business program as an undergraduate at the University of Western Ontario, a serious business school in Canada. "I never had a plan. I'm an entrepreneur at heart, so it seemed like a good idea." He decided he didn't want to be a business person, and fell into rock music management when he met eclectic singer and songwriter Jane Siberry, who has released ten albums of her own and collaborated on projects with Brian Eno, k.d. lang, and filmmaker Wim Wenders. Blumer signed on as her manager, and they entered the music business together.

In 1988, Blumer moved to Hollywood, where he still lives. While involved in the unpredictable music business, he still enjoyed cooking and entertaining. "I was out with a friend one night, moaning about not being able to pay my mortgage, and he said, 'Why don't you write a book?' You know how every five minutes someone has an idea of what you should be doing with your life? This was one of those ideas like a bolt of lightning where you go, 'Yeah!' So I started working on my treatment for the book." Out of what he calls sheer naiveté, he called up his future publisher and told them they should have a meeting with him. They did, and he gave them a ten-page outline with ten illustrations and ten recipes.

It worked. The Surreal Gourmet, named for Blumer's surreal illustrations, became a book. *The Surreal Gourmet: Real Food for Pretend Chefs* was published in 1992, and it has since taken on a life of its own. "I never owned a cookbook before I wrote my cookbook. The first book was surprisingly successful, and brought me places I never thought I'd be."

The *San Diego Times Advocate* said of the first book: "This is the perfect gift for irreverent, kitchen-cautious friends who believe cookbooks are boring, tedious tomes for unhip old farts." Blumer followed up in 1995 with *The Surreal Gourmet Entertains: High-Fun, Low-Stress Dinner Parties for 6 to 12 People*. His recipes are followed by his tips on enhancing the whole experience, including matching wine and the music to cook by.

As a result, the books combine cooking, music, and art, and his career is about finding more unique ways to do just that. He is the co-creator of *MusicalMeals*, a CD-series from SONY Music featuring recipes in the lyric booklet and accompanying music-to-dine-by on the disc (including packages by Emeril Lagasse and the Too Hot Tamales, Mary Sue Milliken and Susan Feniger). He was commissioned by the Salvador Dali Museum (St. Petersburg, Florida) to create eighteen surreal martini glasses which auctioned for $3,100 to benefit the museum's endowment fund. He was also commissioned by the Armand Hammer Museum (Los Angeles, California) to design a food-related homage for the opening of the Rene Magritte exhibition. He's also the official culinary artist for Starbucks coffee ice cream. "From the mail I get, people like that it's being treated more like an art now, instead of just a sustenance thing."

Add to that his own line of magnets, posters, postcards, T-shirts, and calendars, and you have what he calls his "accidental career." "I backed into the best job in the world totally naively. When I wrote my book I thought about quitting while I was ahead, while I was on a total high note, so I'd never have to take any knocks, but I decided to go forward anyway, and it just evolved. It sort of fell in my lap, basically. If something falls in your lap when you're a rock manager, you go with it."

Blumer's first TV appearance was itself surreal. It was a ten-minute interview on a public access book show taped at Beverly Hills High School. "I only got halfway through the Caesar salad I was making when my time was up. [The host] took a lettuce leaf from a bowl and dipped it in the dressing and said, 'Oh, this is very nice.'"

Appearances on *Good Morning America* and the Discovery Channel came next. OTS-TV in Austria produced a fifteen-minute documentary, following him through the creative process of a surreal dinner party. He appeared on VH-1's *RuPaul* with fashion designer Isaac Mizrahi, creating dishes for the "RuPaul Supermodel Diet," and was the on-air personality for the Mrs. Dash spice ad campaign. The Food Network learned of him in 1997 and, as a result, Blumer did a week of *Chef du Jour*. To liven up the proceedings, for his flambé episode he appeared in a fireman outfit and for his breakfast installment he wore a bathrobe. He followed up *Chef du Jour* with two one-hour TV specials on the Food Network: *The Surreal Gourmet: Playing with Food*, focusing on the art of entertaining, and *The Surreal Gourmet: My Favorite Martini*, focusing on, well, martinis. He also did a one-hour holiday food special for VH-1, *Munch with the Surreal Gourmet*, featuring recipes and food-related adventures with rock stars and celebrity guests.

Itchin' to Make Something in the Kitchen?

Those of us who remember *Schoolhouse Rock* on ABC-TV Saturday mornings may also recall a more obscure educational Saturday morning cartoon. He's a yellow blob with stick-like limbs named Timer, and he hankers for a hunk of cheese.

Timer, voiced by Lennie Weinrib, the man who voiced H. R. Pufnstuf on the show of the same name, made his first TV appearance in 1974. It was on an hour-long DePatie-Freleng production combining live-action and animation, originally aired as an ABC Afterschool Special and later re-broadcast as a two-part ABC Weekend special. In the story line, Timer miniaturizes two youngsters and takes them on an amazing journey through the human body.

But those of us who remember him can only hear the Saturday morning cry "Time for Timer!" This is the Timer that was later brought back to life by ABC and DePatie-Freleng in 1977 for a series of ABC Health and Nutrition commercials, short public service spots on ABC's weekend schedule that ran throughout the 1980s.

Timer's new mission was to show kids how to make (relatively) healthy snacks, such as putting cheese on Ritz crackers to create "Wagon Wheels," and making popsicles by pouring orange juice into empty ice cube trays, covering the trays with plastic wrap, poking toothpicks through the plastic, and freezing. Voila! You've got "Sunshine on a Stick." The latter irked parents all over the country, who found they never had ice for their martinis or toothpicks for the olives.

Blumer has since retired from the music industry; "Now it's all about me," he jokes. He's made the transition from promoting someone else to promoting himself. "That was really weird at first. I'd be with a [promotional] handler, and get to a doorway, and say, 'After you,' and they'd say, 'No, after you.' It took me a while to realize that now I'm the so-called 'talent.'"

The Surreal Gourmet likes preparing salmon in a dishwasher because it's virtually foolproof, and "it's usually a safe bet that none of the guests ordered the same thing [earlier] for lunch." But he's the first to point out that he's not responsible for creating the dish. "I've never claimed to have invented salmon in the dishwasher. It's a folkloric kind of dish. I tried it, found out it worked, and I've probably done it at a hundred dinner parties by now. If anything, I've popularized it, or at least practicalized it. Somebody told me Milton Berle did it on a television show before I was born. I've done it around the world. In my next book, *Off the Eaten Path*, I'm going to revisit the concept of cooking on a car manifold, which is another thing that everybody knows about, but not many have tried." He's also developing the concept for a restaurant, with a surreal environment and surreal food.

Blumer describes his cooking philosophy: "More of all the tasty things. I'm very heavy handed with my herbs and spices. Professionals might say too heavy handed..." But he's not worried about the comments of professional chefs. As stated on his Web site, "In my humble opinion, one need not be a professional chef to prepare gratifying food, or for that matter, to write about it. I believe that ignorance in the kitchen sweetens the taste of even the smallest culinary accomplishments. And for the uninitiated, those accomplishments need not remain small forever. With a little blind ambition, the culinary world can become your oyster."

Lack of professional training does have an impact on the foods Blumer cooks. "I'm not a mushroom fan, so [mushrooms are] not in any [of my] books. I avoid cooking things that I'm not a fan of. Because if I'm not a fan of it, then I haven't cooked it a million times, so I don't know it really well; unlike professional chefs, who went to school and learned to cook everything. Everything I learn to cook is through my own personal experience. All of my books have my own personal repertoire. The new book will have everything I learned to cook since the last book four years ago."

In a sense, the Surreal Gourmet has picked up the Galloping Gourmet's spatula, because he's focused on food as entertaining. Blumer has forged a career out of combining food with art, entertaining, fun, knowledge, and music. "The real truth of the matter," he says, laughing, "is that I've always been a jack of all trades and master of none, and having the book and the world of the Surreal Gourmet has allowed me to take all of my ad hoc art and creative skills and joie de vivre and given it all a home, and once there was a home for it, I was able to expand my thinking in each of those different mindsets."

After experiencing the music business, what is Blumer's take on the celebrity of chefs? "Chefs have evolved into professional wrestlers. They've taken on personas even though they're all essentially doing the same thing, which is making a meal, like all professional wrestlers are doing the same thing, which is trying to pin the other guy down for a count of three. The fact that they've developed their own individual personas, and you can sort of pick your favorite Beatle, to mix metaphors, has made it much more interesting."

TV Specials

The Surreal Gourmet: My Favorite Martini (Food Network, 1997–occasional)
The Surreal Gourmet Plays with Food (Food Network, 1997–occasional)
Munch with the Surreal Gourmet (VH-1, 1997)

Books

The Surreal Gourmet: Real Food for Pretend Chefs by Bob Blumer, Nion McEvoy (editor) (Chronicle Books, 1992)
The Surreal Gourmet Entertains: High-Fun, Low-Stress Dinner Parties for 6 to 12 People by Bob Blumer (Chronicle Books, 1995)
Off the Eaten Path by Bob Blumer (Ballantine, 1999)

Web Site

www.surrealgourmet.com

Julia Child:
The Spy Who Came
into the Kitchen

Born: August 15, 1912.

Hometown: Pasadena, California.

Parents: Father, John McWilliams, landowner/businessman; mother, Julia Carolyn "Caro" Weston.

Siblings: Younger brother, John; younger sister, Dorothy.

School: Smith College (Northampton, Massachusetts).

Favorite Junk Food: "I don't eat any snacks. I think that's one reason we're such a fat nation. We should eat three reasonable meals and that's it. I think parents should be very careful not to encourage their children to [snack]. I think if you're looking forward to a good dinner you don't want to spoil it with a chocolate bar."

Always in the Pantry: Butter, sugar, salt, pepper, shallots, onions, and potatoes.

Always in the Fridge: Frozen hamburger, frozen pie dough, milk, cream.

Favorite Food Smell: "When you walk into a good French restaurant, and you smell mussels cooking in white wine with shallots and butter, that's a very nice smell as you come into a restaurant. And the smell of a fresh salad with lemon and oil is very refreshing."

Fantasy Last Meal: Foie gras, oysters, a little caviar, pan roasted duck with onions and chantrelle mushrooms, good French bread with Roquefort and Brie.

Julia Child is responsible for defining the television cooking show in the United States, and for giving educational television a healthy push forward. All of this from a woman who didn't appear on TV until she was nearly fifty years old.

Julia Child (née McWilliams) was born to a well-to-do family. She grew to six-foot-two-inches, was perpetually hungry and a mischievous tomboy who, according to her biography, once sent away for a mail-order gun with her sister and fired blank cartridges at passing passenger trains. Reportedly, Child once broke into a neighbor's home, stole a chandelier, and buried it. She hung out at speakeasies during the Prohibition days of the late 1920s and enjoyed playing basketball at school. "I was thrust into the role of jumping center because I was so tall, and when they changed the rules [of the game], that was the end of my basketball career."

Child next set her mind on being a writer. She enrolled at the all-women's Smith College in 1930, at a time when only 5 percent of the American female population went beyond high school education, and only a third of those actually earned college diplomas. Most women who attended college often left with a husband, something else Child did not do. After graduation, she returned to Pasadena but grew tired of her life of leisure and moved on to a public relations job at W. & J. Sloane, a New York City department store.

When World War II began, Child volunteered for the Office of Strategic Services in Washington, D.C., which was the precursor to the CIA. She intended to become a secret agent. She was sent to Ceylon (now Sri Lanka) and then into China, to be a file clerk. It was there that she met Paul Child, a man several inches shorter and several years older. Paul was an OSS mapmaker who was raised in France and well-traveled. "I didn't really get interested [in cooking] till I was married. My husband had grown up with good food and I realized I better do something."

When they married in 1946 and settled in Washington D.C., Julia set out to learn the culinary craft for both of them. She started with a book that was a standard at the time for homemaking—*The Joy of Cooking* by Irma Rombauer.

Paul was soon transferred to the U.S. Information Service at the American Embassy in Paris and the first meal she ate in Paris changed her life. The menu consisted of Oysters Portugaises on the half shell, a chilled pouilly-fuisse wine, sole meuniere, green salad, creme fraiche, and cafe filtre. Upon eating this meal, Child discovered that delving into the pleasures of fine cuisine was a way to enhance one's sensory perceptions. "It was so delicious. In [the United States] you didn't do much with anything, except broiling, like broiled mackerel. It was just a revelation to go over there and eat a piece of fish in white wine. I just couldn't get over it. We were living in Paris for about five years, and food was a national sport. The nutritionists hadn't gotten to anyone yet."

In 1949, Julia Child was thirty-seven years old, and decided to turn her life in a different direction. She enrolled at the Cordon Bleu cooking school in Paris and began taking classes with Max Bugnard, a follower of the celebrated nineteenth-century chef Auguste Escoffier. She was the only woman among a group of ex-GIs. After six months, Child left the Cordon Bleu to study independently with Bugnard. Eventually she became friends with a French woman named Simone "Simca" Beck. When American women living in Paris began to ask Julia for cooking lessons, Child, Beck, and their mutual friend Louisette Bertholle started an informal cooking school out of Child's kitchen. They called it L'Ecole des Trois Gourmandes.

Beck and Bertholle had previously published a little book introducing French food to an American audience. They wanted to expand it and Child joined in. The result was *Mastering the Art of French Cooking* (1961), which was innovative because the recipes included pointers on picking out proper cuts of meat and chopping vegetables. These tips hadn't been included with published recipes before. Child wanted the recipes to include ingredients that the average cook could find at local supermarkets. The book was huge, so huge that Houghton Mifflin, which had contracted to publish the comprehensive manuscript that took nearly ten years to be complete, rejected the finished results. Alfred A. Knopf picked up the rights, and published it in the fall of 1961. This publishing event led Craig Claiborne to enthuse in the *New York Times*: "Probably the most comprehensive, laudable, and monumental work on [French cuisine] was published this week...and it will probably remain as the definitive work for nonprofessionals...."

In 1961, French cuisine was considered the pinnacle of sophisticated culture. President and Mrs. Kennedy, for example, hired a French chef

Rene Verdon for the White House. Also, people were traveling more and experiencing different cultures. Lots of people with disposable income were trying to rise above their middle class background, or at least give that impression, and fancy cuisine was one very visible way to do just that. The time was right for Child's cookbook and within three months it had sold 20,000 copies and was in its third printing. Had it appeared in the previous decade, when cooking meant emptying a can of cream of mushroom soup on canned tuna fish, the same world might not have been so receptive.

According to Julia, "[In the fifties we were putting] marshmallows all over everything. We didn't come out of that, really, until we had air travel, and people could finally get abroad, and then the Kennedys in the White House made a great deal of difference, but that of course was in the sixties. But we had lots of Jell-O pudding, things like that. We were isolated right here in this country. Well-to-do people could take an oceanliner, or spend five days getting abroad, five days coming back. It was only the well-to-do who traveled, so we didn't have immediate access to the trends that were going on."

Julia was invited in the early 1960s by WGBH, a television station in Boston, to discuss her new cookbook on the book review/interview program, *I've Been Reading*. She knew she was going to have to fill a half hour of time, so she brought some eggs, a bowl, a whisk, and a hot plate with her. During the show she chatted and whipped up the eggs into an omelet. That program received letters from many viewers saying they wanted to see this woman cook some more. Soon Julia was hosting her own show.

Russell Morash, who later brought Bob Vila (*This Old House*) into our homes, became the producer of Child's program, *The French Chef*, which debuted on educational television on February 11, 1963. This was the show that brought educational television into the domain of most non-academics. Here was a sensualist, an anti-snob who was messy and forgiving. If Julia cooked broccoli, stores would sell out of broccoli.

The French Chef, taped at the WGBH studio in Boston, won a Peabody Award in 1965, and an Emmy in 1966. In fact, Child was the first educational TV personality to win an Emmy. The year 1970 brought the magic of color to her formerly black-and-white series. "It was like night and day. When it was over we went right out and bought our first color television set. It was spectacular, the difference. The strawberries weren't gray!"

Save the Liver!

In December 9, 1978, Julia Child, already a household name, was truly immortalized for the ages. That night's episode of NBC's *Saturday Night Live* featured Dan Aykroyd as the *French Chef*, complete with wig, apron, and high-pitched voice. "You can't do nothin' without a sharp knife!" says the ersatz Julia, running the knife along a chicken's spine, and slicing off her thumb. "Oh, now I've done it—I've cut the dickens out of my finger." She looks around for a "natural coagulant, such as chicken liver" and applies one to her injured hand. Next, she reaches for the phone to call 911, only to discover, "It's a prop phone. That's a shame." She begins to weaken from the loss of blood, which is gushing everywhere, and she utters "Why are you all spinning?" Unable to remain conscious any longer, she gives us her last "Bon Appetit" and hits the floor, raising her head to remind us one last time to "Save the liver!"

The sketch was actually based on an incident that occurred on TV on Tom Snyder's *Tomorrow* show. Child was appearing with Jacques Pépin, and she cut her hand with the knife he brought before they started cooking. Proving to be unflappable in a crisis, Child went on with the segment.

Child appreciates all forms of flattery; she was sent the tape of Aykroyd's performance, and has been known to play it for friends. And it's a favorite of Aykroyd's fans as well. *Saturday Night Live's Best of Dan Aykroyd* compilation opens with this sketch.

Child's critics complained about the name of the show. After all, she was not French, nor was she a chef—though she always referred to herself as a home cook and a teacher, she never wore a chef's hat. The show's title was actually producer Russell Morash's idea. They hoped to persuade some French chefs to teach on air. Then, too, the series' creators wanted a short title that would be catchy in the TV listings. Other names they considered included "The Gourmet Kitchen," "Cuisine Magic," and "The Chef at Home."

Some viewers didn't know what to make of Julia Child, the TV personality. The *Boston Globe*'s first cover story about the show referred to her "charming French accent." There were those who were convinced she was sampling the cooking sherry, including British viewers who saw the BBC's trial run of her program and called the BBC network to ask who this "drunk" American was. The situation prompted the BBC to cancel her show.

Despite the BBC decision, *The French Chef* ran for almost eleven years in the United States, and forever changed the way Americans thought about food and public television. With cute episode titles like "Waiting for Gigot" and "Lest We Forget Broccoli," the mission of *The French Chef* was to demonstrate on air that if Child could do it, so could anyone at home. It was also okay to make mistakes, which Julia always handled with humor.

For example: one time, a bell could be heard from the freight elevator in the back of her TV studio. Child looked into the camera and remarked, "That must be the plumber. It's about time he got here!" On another occasion, she was trying to flip a potato pancake, but it didn't quite work and spilled onto the stove. With no hesitation, the enterprising host scraped up the pancake and put it back into the pan, saying, "Well, that didn't go very well, but you can always pick it up if you're alone. Who's going to see?"

For the record, this was the only time this pancake flip-flop ever happened. Child insists she has never dropped anything edible on the floor while in front of the camera. However, there are many stories like that circulating about Julia: that she dropped a whole chicken and put it back in the pan, or a fumbled piece of meat fell on the floor which she brushed off on her apron and plopped back into her casserole. None of these anecdotes are true, so why do these stories persist? Julia feels that "[The press has] exaggerated all of that. They don't know much about cooking and they want to have something to write about."

One of the most famous episodes of the long-running *The French Chef* opened in this fashion: An artichoke, shrouded in a piece of cheesecloth, is seen boiling in a pot of water. Suddenly, Child appears on camera, lifts the cheesecloth with heavy tweezers, and asks, "What's cooking under this gossamer veil? Why here's a great big, bad artichoke, and some people are afraid of it." This was really what was behind every episode: demystifying something that was new to so many at-home viewers.

"I think there was an awful lot of 'la-di-da, how smart I am,' like boning a chicken from the backbone, which is ridiculous because it's going to sit on its backbone, so who's going to know? A lot of silly things like 'I'm the only one who can do it.' My point is that anyone can do it. And it's worthwhile because it's so good to eat."

In 1965, the fifty-three-year-old Child was diagnosed with breast cancer, and suffered a radical mastectomy. In those days, reconstruction wasn't an option. With the support of her husband, Paul, she went back to work only six weeks after the operation and wore a prosthesis. She has been cancer-free ever since, and has not stopped working. Child cannot imagine having another occupation. "Once you're in it, this is a passionate profession. You love it. It's hard work but you're always learning something. It's wonderful to be with people who love what they're doing. It's almost like a big brotherhood.

"Now the culinary arts have become a real profession and discipline. For a long time they were just workers. In France they still are. They don't have the status of professors, and here, we have a lot of people who have Ph.D.s, and it's a real honorable profession, not the dumping ground it used to be. What concerns me is that you have to learn how to eat. If you have a family that doesn't really do any cooking, you don't grow up with an interest in good food, and if you're going to be a good cook, you have to know what good food tastes like. You're not going to get it from pizzas and hamburgers. A lot depends on how you were brought up or whether you've really become interested."

What is it about French cooking that makes it the basis of culinary studies? "French is the only cuisine that does have real rules and does have a history and does have certain things that you do because it has a classical background. It's very, very good training. You can learn it, and you can discard it if you want, but at least you have it in your background and you can know how to do it the right way. Of course, there are always continual changes, such as the sudden appearance of the food processor, which made so much difference in how to make foods. My feeling is if you have a thorough French background you can do anything."

After filming more than 200 episodes of *The French Chef*, Child branched out with additional TV series and cookbooks, listed at the end of this chapter. She was the first woman to receive La Commanderie des Cordons Bleus de France in 1980. She also received the Ordre de Mérite Agricole (1967) and the Ordre de Mérite National (1976), in addition to honorary degrees from Harvard University, Boston University, Bates College, Rutgers University, and Smith College.

With all of her TV experience, Julia is not an avid viewer of her genre. "I don't watch cooking shows, because I don't want to be influenced by others. It's easy to pick up someone else's habits." Why are others tuning in? "When you have arrived, you become interested in food and wine. It's kind of a status symbol. That may have something to do with it. And [the shows are] fun to look at. Children enjoy them whether they're going to cook or not."

Child can currently be seen on *Baking with Julia*, which is taped in the kitchen in her home, and features pastry chefs demonstrating how to make and bake various dishes. There are some who report feeling a bit uneasy watching the eighty-six-year-old Child observe as other people cook; they feel she should retire. But no one today is better qualified to ask questions of her TV show guests. She has no plans to retire, and on her new TV series, *Julia Child and Jacques Pépin: Just Cooking*, she is cooking on the air once again.

TV producer Geoffrey Drummond sums up Child's appeal this way: "Julia did the same thing in the 1960s that Emeril [Lagasse] is doing now. I'm sure that the cooking establishment, a lot of the French chefs with their tall white toques and pressed uniforms, were aghast at this woman who was having fun in the kitchen and sometimes she was a little sloppy and she said it's okay. She broke the mold; she pulled all these people into cooking and she gave people permission to come into the kitchen."

TV Series

The French Chef (PBS, 1963–74, Food Network, 1998–)
Julia Child & Company (PBS, 1978–79)
Julia Child & More Company (PBS, 1980–81)
Dinner at Julia's (PBS, 1983–84)
Cooking with Master Chefs (PBS, 1993–94)
In Julia's Kitchen with Master Chefs (PBS, 1995– *)
Baking with Julia (PBS, 1996–)
Julia Child and Jacques Pépin: Just Cooking (PBS, 1998–)

TV Specials

The White House Red Carpet (PBS, 1968)
Julia at 80: With Christopher Lydon (PBS, 1992)
Julia Child and Jacques Pépin: Cooking in Concert (PBS, 1995)
Julia Child and Graham Kerr: Cooking in Concert (PBS, 1995)
Julia Child and Jacques Pépin: Cooking in Concert (PBS, 1996)

Books

Mastering the Art of French Cooking by Simone Beck, Louisette Bertholle, and Julia Child (Alfred A. Knopf, 1961)

The French Chef Cookbook by Julia Child (Alfred A. Knopf, 1968)

Mastering the Art of French Cooking Volume II by Simone Beck and Julia Child (Alfred A. Knopf, 1970, 1983)

From Julia Child's Kitchen by Julia Child (Alfred A. Knopf, 1975)

Julia Child and Company by Julia Child with E. S. Yntema (Alfred A. Knopf, 1978)

Julia Child and More Company by Julia Child with E. S. Yntema (Alfred A. Knopf, 1979)

The Way to Cook by Julia Child (Alfred A. Knopf, 1989)

Julia Child's Menu Cookbook (One volume edition of *Julia Child and Company* and *Julia Child and More Company*) by Julia Child (Random House, 1991)

Cooking with Master Chefs by Julia Child (Alfred A. Knopf, 1993)

In Julia Child's Kitchen with Master Chefs by Julia Child with Nancy Barr (Alfred A. Knopf, 1995)

Videotapes/CD-ROMs:

The Way to Cook (WGBH and JC Productions, 1984)

Julia Child: Home Cooking with Master Chefs (A La Carte Productions, Microsoft, 1996)

Amy Coleman:
Home Sweet Home Cooking

Born: February 22, 1963.

Hometown: Wellsville, Pennsylvania.

Parents: Father, Donald Langstaff, salesman; mother, Irene Langstaff, registered nurse.

Siblings: Older sisters, Debbie and Karen; younger brothers, Tommy and Jimmy.

Schools: Pennsylvania State University (University Park, Pennsylvania), Culinary Institute of America (Hyde Park, New York), Columbia University (New York City).

Favorite Junk Food: "Anything with dark chocolate. The good stuff."

Always in the Pantry: "Cornmeal (I make a lot of polenta!), rice, chicken stock, jarred salsa, and pasta."

Always in the Fridge: "Grated cheese of several types, such as cheddar and jack; I always have Italian grated cheese. Also tortillas, lettuce, oranges, and skim milk."

Favorite Food Smell: "Stuffed artichoke. To me, that's the ultimate comfort food; that's my grandmother, my heritage. It's just a warm, thick, loving, hearty, comforting smell, with garlic, parmesan cheese, breadcrumbs, simmering on the stove for three hours, [making your] whole house smell [wonderful]."

Favorite Food Sound: "The sizzle of the grill."

Fantasy Last Meal: "Stuffed artichokes for an appetizer, spicy rubbed porterhouse steak smothered in onions and mushrooms for an entree, with the starch being risotto, and sugar snap peas for my vegetable. I think I'd have two desserts: mocha pots-au-creme with sour cherry compote, and my mom's cherry pie—the best in the world."

Amy Coleman (of *Home Cooking with Amy Coleman*, PBS) grew up in south central Pennsylvania where hearty family meals were a daily ritual. "Home cooked meals were a priority at our house. It didn't matter how many swim practices, wrestling matches, whatever, had to be juggled, we always had dinner together. My family laughs about it, but I had the quintessential Easy-Bake oven with the fifteen-watt light bulb; I started with one of those." Then she moved on to real appliances. "I remember my mom letting me, in the kitchen, take whatever ingredients and mix up whatever I want. I was always in the kitchen, setting the table before the meal, pouring the milk. As I grew up I got to make the salad; we made the homemade dressing right in the salad bowl."

Sometimes her penchant for cooking got Amy into hot water. "I remember getting in trouble because we had a brand new barbecue grill and my mom was always big on getting us out of the house to go out and play. It started to rain, and I made mud pies and thought I was making hamburgers. I put them on the grill, on the brand new grill, and left them there. My father found them a few days later! So, I was always cooking."

When Coleman was an adolescent, she was a certified scuba diver and wanted to be an oceanographer. "I was on a national swimming team for thirteen years when I was a kid, and won two junior Olympics, and had scholarships to college, but after thirteen years I figured it was time to hang up the suit and pick up the books. When I was in college [at Pennsylvania State] I changed my major like sixty-two times. I just wanted to make sure that I did something that made money and was entrepreneurial. I switched from law, journalism, oceanography, marine biology, and ended up with a hotel restaurant food business management degree."

Amy graduated from Penn State in 1985, then enrolled at the Culinary Institute of America (CIA) in Hyde Park, New York. She went there at first thinking she wanted to own her own restaurant; she had the management degree, and now wanted the culinary experience to understand both sides of the house. "That's why I went to culinary school, never thinking that I wanted to be a chef sweating behind a 110-degree [kitchen assembly] line every night, every holiday, and every weekend. That was never my intention." She graduated from the CIA in 1987, where she had particularly enjoyed the nutrition classes.

Coleman's defining career moment came at a CIA meet-the-alumni panel, where she asked, "If I have an interest in nutrition, do you think that's where the food service industry will be going? Would it be worthwhile?" The response was "If you know nutrition, and you know how to make food taste good and be healthy, you'll be worth your weight in gold." The next week she researched appropriate graduate schools. As a result, she attended Columbia University, graduated with a master's degree in nutrition education in 1993, and then did her residency there to become a registered dietitian.

Nutrition was a science-heavy degree. "It's funny, because I never liked science and was afraid of math. That's why I did more business-oriented things when I was a kid. I would have rather opened a vein than taken biochem or statistics. Oh man, did I hate that stuff. But it's like any job, you take the good with the bad."

Coleman then went back to the Culinary Institute of America to teach restaurant nutrition at St. Andrews Café, one of the four public restaurants at the institute. "I teach students how to develop and modify menus, how to take any recipe in a menu and do an analysis of it and then modify it so it meets nutritional requirements and guidelines, and so it'll still taste good." With more people eating out, or ordering in food more often than ever before, this has long-range effects. "When I was a kid, going out to dinner was a big deal. Someone got married, someone had a birthday, it was a special occasion. So from a nutritional standpoint, if you wanted the fettuccine Alfredo, then go for it, and if you wanted to back it up with a hunkin' piece of cheesecake, absolutely, because you didn't eat that way all the time. But now, people are eating out much more frequently, so they nutritionally and physiologically can't afford to be eating that way. We're eating out three to four meals per week; we're not making [meals], we don't have control over [them]. We're handing over so much control to chefs and the restaurant industry. Right now it's a need to eat differently, but hopefully it will develop into a want—wanting not to become overweight as children, wanting not to have the health problems our parents have, wanting not to be overweight if the rest of the family is."

If I Knew You Were Coming, I'd Have Baked a Tiny Cake

What do Amy Coleman (*Home Cooking*), Bobby Flay (*Hot Off the Grill*), and Mark Beckloff (*Three Dog Bakery*) have in common? They all had Easy-Bake Ovens when they were kids.

They weren't alone. Hasbro's Easy-Bake Oven was invented in 1963, and by February 1964 had sold more than 500,000 units at $15.99 each. As of its thirty-fifth birthday in 1998, more than sixteen million Easy-Bake Ovens have been purchased and more than 100 million baking mix sets used. Today, you can pick up an Easy-Bake Oven & Snack Center for about $20.

The price hasn't changed much, and neither has the heating element. The original oven cooked with two sixty-watt bulbs; today, it's a 100-watt unfrosted light bulb. However, the outside of the oven has been updated. It has gone from turquoise or yellow with a boxy oven look to pink and purple with a mod microwave design.

Over the decades, the Easy-Bake Oven has taken some flack. Some upper-level sociology courses explore how play ovens "separate domestic labor and play," and how this can place girls "on hold" or trivialize the domestic work that women do.

This criticism only goes to prove that the oven is a cultural landmark. It was even mentioned on the *Merv Griffin Show* episode of TV's *Seinfeld* when Kramer and the gang find one and make tiny cupcakes out of thirty-year-old batter. Don't try that at home.

Coleman is greatly attached to her two dogs, a sixteen-year-old Yorkshire Terrier named Soleil and a six-year-old Maltese named Truffles, both of whom she adopted after they were abused by their prior owners. Whenever she can, she spends time in the water, her first love. "My next house will be near the water—I want a view." She lives in a house full of antiques near the CIA Hyde Park campus, right on the Hudson River. This country setting provides Coleman plenty of opportunity to horseback ride and hike. Ironically, there aren't many good restaurants, another love of Coleman's, near the premier culinary school in the country.

Coleman's PBS series *Home Cooking with Amy Coleman,* which began in 1997, is her first foray into television. She was discovered by veteran producer Marjorie Poore who was shooting the series *Cooking Secrets of the CIA.* "We run it like it's my cooking school and I have a guest chef that's on it. We cook together, two professionals having fun and sharing our knowledge." The guests are people who have written cookbooks, which gives the show unlimited variety because of the hundreds of cookbooks written each year. Competition for air time and shelf space is fierce. A cookbook author who might not necessarily get or carry a show on one's own, gets exposure in a segment on *Home Cooking* by cooking with someone who knows what questions TV viewers might be asking. "There's good interaction between me and my guest, which is nice, instead of me just lecturing one-on-one to a camera."

Coleman sees her TV show as an extension of her teaching career. "I'm in the business of selling. As a teacher, I sell knowledge, and I have to pack it in a way that's educational and yet entertaining, and put it in a way my students are going to buy into and see what's in it for them. I can't sell anything unless I really believe in it. Some [cooking shows are] purely for entertainment. The foods that are being cooked, the techniques that are being used, and the time that it takes, and where you have to go for the ingredients, all of those things make some of the recipes and some of those shows almost unattainable. On the other hand, I like to think that the *Home Cooking* show is so popular because we go out of our way to make it so that it fits in with Americans' needs. The recipes have no more than twelve to fifteen ingredients, so you're not shopping all day, the ingredients are easily accessible, and the recipes only take about half an hour, because everyone has a half an hour, but not everyone has an hour."

Amy wants to be helpful in the home viewers' kitchens. "That is my personal philosophy for the show. I really hope that people will, I don't care if it's just once a week, get in the kitchen and cook for their families, fill their homes with smells that they'll always remember, because your olfactory sense, your sense of smell, is your strongest. If I say things to you like 'popcorn,' or 'roasted chicken,' or 'steaks on the grill,' if I just ask you to think about the smells of those things, your mouth starts to water. That's why I think 'home style' food [take-out food that is reminiscent of family-style fare and unlike fancy restaurant cuisine] will only have limited success, because they truly don't bring 100 percent satisfaction and satiety to people. Because you miss out on the stirring and the smells and the tasting as you go along, and the satisfaction of making something and presenting it to your family, the sense of pride and accomplishment and you get their appreciation, the fact of sharing things, you eat more slowly, you appreciate it, you have tabletop conversations . . . there's so much about home cooking that you can't get from restaurant take out food, no how, no way."

Coleman believes viewers truly want to learn to cook at home. "There's a whole, probably one, maybe even two generations that didn't learn how to cook. Not everybody grew up like I did with mom and grandma in the kitchen to be able to see how it's done. I think we've got lots of people that don't know how to cook that wish they did know how to cook, so I think that [watching cooking shows is] a way of holding onto nostalgia. They might not be doing it, but they like the idea of home cooking, they like the idea of family meals and I don't think they're willing to let that go, and I don't think that they will. Cooking on TV brings people closer to that. I think that's why they're tuning in."

TV Series

Home Cooking with Amy Coleman (PBS, 1997–)

Book

The Best of Home Cooking with Amy Coleman by Amy Coleman (Chronicle, 1998)

Dinner and a Movie: From Soup to Nuts

Paul Gilmartin

Born: June 29, 1963.

Hometown: Chicago, Illinois.

Parents: Father, Bill, semi-retired from insurance business; mother, Pat, charity work, involved in League of Women Voters, taught illiterate adults how to read.

Siblings: Older brother, Dave.

School: Indiana University (at Bloomington).

Favorite Junk Food: "Cinnabon. The first time I had one I thought, 'This is insane, I can't believe anything could be this good.'"

Always in the Pantry: "Flour, olive oil, garlic, and shredded wheat."

Always in the Fridge: "Milk, berries, pickles (the sandwich stackers!), and hot stuff; My wife and I are hot freaks, like olives stuffed with habañeros."

Favorite Food Smell: "Garlic cooking in olive oil. Or the bakery smell. I always get dessert in a restaurant."

Fantasy Last Meal: "Cinnabon. I'd eat them all day, slip into a sugar coma, and die."

Annabelle Gurwitch

Born: November 4, 1964.

Hometown: Miami Beach, Florida.

Parents: father, Harry, investment banker; mother, Shirley, small business owner.

Siblings: Older sister, Lisa.

School: New York University (New York City).

Favorite Junk Food: "I have a potato chip problem. If I eat a potato chip, I have to eat the entire bag. So the rule is, in my house, you just can't bring potato chips into my house. My one exception is if my husband keeps his potato chips in his desk drawer, I respect that privacy, I will not eat his chips. However, if they are in the kitchen or any general living area, it's fair game."

Always in the Pantry: "Olive oil, baby food, green peppercorns, sardines (we always have sardines in the house; my husband loves sardines!), and garlic."

Always in the Fridge: "Thai chili paste, we cook everything in a chili paste, chicken, and parsley. I love parsley."

Favorite Food Smell: "Baking bread, maybe with a little rosemary. It just smells comforting and warm, like your mother's kitchen, even though my mother never made bread. It's the way I would imagine my mother's kitchen would have smelled had she made bread."

Favorite Food Sound: "Frying—the frying of chicken."

Fantasy Last Meal: "I'd eat fried chicken all day. And I'd only eat the skin, because that's all I want anyway. Maybe I'd also go shopping for the thrill of going in and actually buying something at Prada [a fancy clothing designer]. It might be fun, since I wouldn't have to save my money and pay my mortgage, to buy a Prada dress, put it on, and eat fried chicken skin."

Chef Claud Mann, the TBS Food Guy

Born: August 10, 1957.

Hometown: Berkeley, California.

Parents: Father, Claud, television news journalist (retired); mother, Loris, musician.

Siblings: Two older sisters.

Schools: San Francisco State University (San Francisco, California); California Culinary Academy (San Francisco).

Favorite Junk Food: "I like crispy salty things, like pork rinds smothered with Tabasco. How are you going to operate in real life if you're taking a car trip and decide that you're not going to eat anything like that?"

Always in the Pantry: Olive oil. "Whenever I have a party and someone says 'What can I bring?' I always say, 'Extra virgin olive oil.' If you're having a big party you could end up with six bottles."

Favorite Food Smell: "The smell of barbecue, outdoors. I think it's genetically implanted that the smell of meat on a grill is the smell of security. It meant that our caveman forefathers weren't going to die of hunger that particular night. When you smell it from your neighbors' yard, you wish you were over there."

Favorite Food Sound: "I worked at a place where we would stand around the cutting board and chop all the herbs for that night and chop the garlic and [each] generally use two knives. I like the sound of ten people all chopping at the same time."

Fantasy Last Meal: "It depends on why you're dying, whether you're about to be executed, or pass away from natural causes with your family around. The most comforting thing would be chicken in a pot, but if I were going down in a blaze of glory, I'd probably want a whole beautiful pot of Beluga [caviar], and champagne."

Dinner and a Movie, TBS cable's unscripted Friday night cooking-around-a-movie show, has the kind of loyal following that goes beyond "cult." People are staying home on Friday nights to tune into a show in a time slot most adult shows would dread. Whatever good, bad, or even mediocre movie the programmers at TBS choose to air on Friday night, the *Dinner and a Movie* team comes up with recipes somehow related to the film, and cooks them in little segments before and after the commercial breaks.

The cohosts, actress Annabelle Gurwitch and stand-up comedian Paul Gilmartin, are not professional chefs, but regular folks who aren't foodier-than-thou. Folded into the mix are irreverent stories and improvised sketches based on the film du jour, and special guests like Kelsey Grammer, Kathy Griffin, and Randy "Macho Man" Savage. In 1997 Gilmartin and Gurwitch were nominated for CableACE awards as Best Entertainment Host. *Rolling Stone* listed the program as one of the "Top 100 Reasons to Watch Television."

But the food itself isn't a joke. It's real food, real recipes, and real techniques. So who is responsible for the recipes and the imparting of food knowledge? That job goes to professional chef and "TBS Food Guy" Claud Mann who has a total of fifteen years of hands-on experience in all aspects of food, wine, cooking, and restaurant operation. He served as head chef in numerous dining establishments in the United States and Mexico including the top-rated Nicola in Los Angeles and the four-star Hotel Palmilla in Los Cabos, Mexico.

The show's creator/producer, Kimberlee Carlson, has known Claud Mann for twenty years. Both were big TV food show groupies. "I think a lot of people in my age group watched the *Galloping Gourmet*," says Mann, "and I actually used to stay home from school if he was doing something very challenging that day or it was a two-part recipe. Mom was pretty good about that. I grew up in Berkeley, where food was becoming a big deal in the late sixties."

Carlson and Mann always talked about doing a TV cooking program. "We loved food shows," Mann explains, "but we thought sometimes they were too precious, almost untouchable. I'd watch someone do a recipe and my first response would be 'I could never do that!' My second response would be 'wait a minute—I know how to do that, it just LOOKS so hard!'"

When Carlson started working at TBS cable TV in Atlanta, the company didn't do original programming at that time, and was looking for some way to promote their Friday night movie showcase. Bingo! They got their inspiration from an unexpected place: *Car Talk*, the syndicated NPR radio show hosted by chatty brothers Tom and Ray Maliozzi, also known as Click and Clack. Mann explains: "They take what could be the most boring subject in the world, especially for people who don't care anything about cars, but you don't have to care about cars to listen, and they really make it approachable and fun by approaching it with humor. And so we said, 'Wouldn't it be fun to do a cooking show that was more along the lines of *Car Talk*?' And, of course," he quips, "we never did that. But we did do *Dinner and a Movie*."

At first, the higher-ups at the cable network wanted someone to fumble around the kitchen with "joke food," such as funny-colored Jell-O molds. However, Carlson, who had insisted on bringing a pro like Mann into the mix, protested, saying the joke would wear thin, and the series would never build an audience. So they gave Mann five movies and told him to come up with recipes. He created recipes like "Whoopi's B-Flat Flatbread," for *Jumpin' Jack Flash*, "May the Borscht Be with You" for *Spaceballs*, "*Urban Cowboy* No Bull Tequila Fajitas," and "*Blues Brothers* Funky Chicken."

"Claud came up with great ways to work in food tips," said Carlson, "and keeps it grounded in some sort of cooking philosophy to really give added value to the viewer. [TV watchers] might not know *how* to truss a chicken, but now they would know *why* you truss it." So why not have Mann host the show? "If there was just a chef, people might have the feeling they were being lectured. This way there's an extra way you can teach, because the hosts are being taught along with you. If the hosts look inept, it's more user friendly. Both Paul and Annabelle have a certain intelligence; even though Annabelle does the 'dingy' thing, she's well-read and can put things in context. Paul plays the Everyman. Then we started bringing Claud in as a character. We wanted him to seem prissy, to come in and cry 'What have you done?'—to be a foil which allows them to overexplain."

"Claud is such a great cook," says Gilmartin. "He so enjoys teaching people about food and cooking. He never intimidates you. He's not a snob. He never says, 'Why are you asking me what blanching is?' after we've already done eight recipes with blanching."

It's also helpful to have a cohost. "I can't really chop the way you're supposed to," Gurwitch admits. "You have to hold onto your object and bend your hand in a certain way. They can never shoot me chopping because I cannot master the technique. I also cannot chop onions. My eyes really water, and it's been a problem on the show a couple of times; my makeup smears and we have to wait fifteen minutes to redo the whole thing. It sounds silly but it's been disastrous for us. Paul doesn't cry, so he has to chop the onions on the show."

The first *Dinner and a Movie* aired in September 1995 and it caught on quickly with the public. "All the press we got in the beginning was really about the food," said Carlson, "because that's what makes it stand out as a prime time show. People felt some kind of comfort level. Cooking shows are like porn. You can't stop watching a cooking show, even if you're not cooking along, because you want to see what will happen. People who thought it was going to be boring really underestimated that, like porn, when you turn on a cooking show, you know what you're looking at, and you feel really grounded, unlike watching sitcoms, which you turn on and are, like, 'What?' You've seen cooking shows all your life. There is reality there."

Mann agrees with that analogy. "People aren't necessarily cooking more. . . . I think people don't have time, but with our show I think we get people cooking along with us, at least according to some of the mail. But sometimes people aren't even sitting down together any more, so they're like culinary peeping toms. It's fun to peek in and watch somebody else do it even if you know you'll never do it yourself."

Gilmartin and Gurwitch also see the fantasy aspect of TV cooking. Says Gilmartin: "A lot of people, myself included, fool themselves into thinking that they're either going to make that [dish] some day, or they're going to have the opportunity to order it in a restaurant. They want to know exactly what it is. It's fantasy." And Gurwitch: "It's like people watching [TV's] *Lifestyles of the Rich and Famous*—'Oh, I could have that one day.' But I know I'm never going to make it, so I don't watch."

~~~

Claud Mann was immersed in cooking from the beginning. His mother insisted each of her children cook one night per week. "We'd consult with her or make it up but it had to be interesting, taste good, and the colors on the plates had to be right." She thought of it as an extension of their education. Mann and his two sisters weren't officially home schooled, but it was the sixties, and Berkeley, California, was experimenting with its public schools. It was possible to get through four years of high school without taking English, so the Manns taught their kids about literature and the arts, and they considered cooking a natural extension. "I was asking for cooking stuff as birthday and Christmas presents when I was twelve years old. I was a freak."

If you're from the West Coast, you may recognize the name Claud Mann. Mann's father, also named Claud, is the Emmy-winning in-the-trenches reporter and newscaster who broke the Patty Hearst story back in the late 1970s. Or you might recognize Claud the chef from his days as an actor. He appeared on TV in a *Love Boat* episode and in some commercials.

Mann went to San Francisco State for six years. He was interested in so many things, he kept changing his major. However, he knew the restaurant business was calling him. "It was something I always wanted to do ever since I was a kid. [I was] the way some people are about theater. I thought it was just the coolest business. Whenever I was in a restaurant I knew something was going on back there, something sexy and really alluring. Then, of course," he quips, "once I got in the business, I found out I was wrong."

Mann decided it was a good idea to work in several restaurants on both sides of the house (the kitchen and the dining area), to learn the whole restaurant experience. He has served as head chef in restaurants in both the United States and Mexico. He was also employed as a wine buyer, and then attended the California Culinary Academy. As a result, he has experience in all aspects of food, wine, cooking, and restaurant operation.

However, Mann really was looking for a more settled job. "I really wanted to be there when my daughter [Emma Leone] was born, so I started consulting, helping restaurants that were having a hard time, with stuff like having a standardized recipe book, so in case your chef gets hit by a car, you can still go back in and make the same dishes. And then I was ready for something else, and that's when *Dinner and a Movie* called. I had no idea it would be this popular."

This experience has created a little cottage industry for Mann. Warner Home Video has him cooking four recipes for their video series—similar to a miniature cooking show at the beginning of movie videos (look for Dearly Departed Sole if you rent *Beetlejuice*). He's also doing six recipes for shows on the six major networks for *TV Guide*.

Mann has another talent: he backs up his wife, singer Perla Batalla (who used to sing backup for Leonard Cohen) by playing drums and percussion. Claud and Perla produced *Mestiza*, their latest CD together. Perla's brother, Rick, is a writer/performer on *Dinner and a Movie*. Recently, Mann has developed Telechef, a national culinary consultation phone line that can be accessed by calling 1-800-62-CHEFS. He has assembled a group of professional Los Angeles chefs to create a culinary think tank, which anyone can call (at $1.49 per minute) for help with specific cooking questions.

~~~

One person who probably never thought he'd call that number is a man who, as a semi-finalist on *Star Search* in 1994 in the comedian category, once told Ed McMahon that he had a guest spot on *Baywatch* as "Jojo the Lotion Boy." Stand-up comedian Paul Gilmartin was twelve years old when he decided he wanted to be the next Johnny Carson. He grew up in the south suburbs of Chicago, and graduated Phi Beta Kappa from Indiana University at Bloomington, with a bachelor of arts in theater and drama. He performed in several plays in the Chicago theater scene, and graduated from the Second City Training Center, at the famed Second City Theatre in Chicago.

Gilmartin has written for the *Emmy Awards* and the *Dennis Miller Show*. He has been on *Caroline's Comedy Hour* on A&E, MTV's *Half-Hour Comedy Hour*, Showtime's *Comedy Club Network*, HBO *Comedy Showcase* on NBC, and Comedy Central's *Short Attention Span Theater* and *Comics Only*. Gilmartin has a Web site, www.paulgilmartin.com, where fans can learn more about him and his CDs. His wife, Carla Filisha, also a stand-up comedian and writer, contributes to the site as "Live Nude Girl."

Five Classic Food Scenes (in Non-Food Movies)

Five Easy Pieces (1970). Written by Adrien Joyce and Bob Rafelson; directed by Bob Rafelson; starring Jack Nicholson and Karen Black. While at a coffee shop, Robert Eroica Dupea (Nicholson) keeps trying to order wheat toast until he gets so fed up with the no-substitution rules that he trashes the table and tells the waitress what she can do with his order.

Monty Python's Meaning of Life (1983). Written by Graham Chapman, John Cleese, Terry Gilliam, Eric Idle, Terry Jones, and Michael Palin; directed by Terry Jones; starring the writers. Like it or not, you can't forget the image of Mr. Creosote (Jones), the world's most obese man, eating one more bite and paying the grotesque price.

National Lampoon's Animal House (1978). Written by Harold Ramis; directed by John Landis; starring John Belushi and Tim Matheson. Two words: food fight.

Tom Jones (1963). Written by John Osbourne; directed by Tony Richardson; starring Albert Finney and Susannah York; Oscars for best picture, director, screenwriter, and composer. Tom (Finney) and Mrs. Waters (Joyce Redman) eat a pre-coital meal that's pretty coital. If you don't know how to eat an oyster, rent this British film classic. For a 1980s variation, check out *Flashdance* (1983). Directed by Franca Pasut; starring Jennifer Beals and Michael Nouri. Welder/dancer Alex eats lobster in a way that's supposed to be erotic, and takes off her bra without removing her carefully torn sweatshirt.

When Harry Met Sally... (1989). Written by Nora Ephron; directed by Rob Reiner; starring Billy Crystal and Meg Ryan. Sally fakes an orgasm in a New York deli, Harry and the rest of the customers stare in amazement, and Rob Reiner's mother utters an oft-repeated punchline.

Annabelle Gurwitch was born in Alabama, but primarily grew up in Miami Beach. Both of her parents worked outside the home so she didn't have a lot of home cooking. "We occasionally had housekeepers who cooked for us, and we ate a lot of catered food. My mother does have a few things that she's sort of famous for making. She makes Beef Wellington, and a three-colored Jell-O mold, which is very Fifties. My dad makes fried chicken because he's from Alabama. Basically the only thing I ever learned to make at home was fried chicken, and I made a lot of fried chicken at every dinner party I had, for many years. I've only recently branched out."

There was a cognitive food moment in young Annabelle's life. "When we moved from Wilmington, Delaware, to Miami Beach when I was in fifth grade, it was as if we changed centuries. I don't remember fresh fruit in Delaware. It was a lot of canned food. In Florida it was fresh fruit, fabulous food. Just having the freshness which we didn't really have before was really extraordinary and mind-boggling. Also, with the different cultures in Florida, we did eat a lot of Cuban food, which I still love. It was a really big food awakening."

Gurwitch always wanted to be an actress, and never really considered anything else. "One of my favorite roles... was when I was twelve. I played Linda in *Death of a Salesman* at my community theatre. Just the thought now of how I was trying to evoke 'We're free at last...' at twelve years old. I wish they had video cameras then. If I had a copy of that I would laugh myself to sleep every night."

Annabelle attended New York University and has worked in theater off-Broadway, including her participation in the recent revival of Wendy Wasserstein's *Uncommon Women and Others*. In addition, Gurwitch wrote

Hope, a one-act play, described as a "meditation on sex and salty food," which was performed at Naked Angels in New York City. She has written pieces for *Premiere* and *Buzz* magazines, and her essay "Getting in Touch with Your Inner Bimbo" recently appeared in *Los Angeles* magazine.

As far as movies go, Gurwitch has appeared in films such as *Masterminds* with Patrick Stewart, *Mousehunt* with Nathan Lane, *The Cable Guy* with Jim Carrey, and *One Night Stand* with Wesley Snipes. In the TV medium, she anchored two award-winning seasons on HBO's *Not Necessarily the News*. She starred in the ABC movie of the week *Encino Woman* with Jay Thomas and guest starred in more than thirty series, including *Seinfeld* (she was Katy in "The Cadillac, Part One"), *Murphy Brown*, *Tales from the Crypt*, *Dream On*, *The Last Frontier*, and *L.A. Firefighters*. In the comedy arena, Gurwitch has been a guest and sketch contributor to numerous TV shows, including *Women Aloud, Into the Night, The Midnight Hour, Sunday Night Comics, Fools for Love, Hosted By*, and *Bad Date Diaries*. She has emceed *HBO Entertainment News* and VH1's *Inside Music*.

Then *Dinner and a Movie* came along in 1995. "They didn't care if we had cooking experience, otherwise I wouldn't have gotten the job! They were looking for the chemistry between two people. Everyone thinks [Paul and I are] married. I think it's that our relationship reflects a more natural relationship than you see sometimes between people who are hosting a show. We disagree with each other. We don't go out of our way to gloss over our differences. We're different people, we have different opinions, and I think personally, that's what makes the show fun for me to do."

Gilmartin agrees. "Mostly I get, 'What's the deal with you and that girl? Do you hate each other, do you like each other, are you married?' This really says something about the state of marriage in this country; you know, 'You guys seem to hate each other—are you married?'"

"No one ever [directs us to] act more 'lovey dovey,'" says Gurwitch, "and I enjoy that freedom. On the show we sort of let that fiction [that we're married] stand, and I've always been a supporter of that, I think that's fun. Because we're not exactly playing ourselves, there's freedom. It's a fictionalized version of reality."

The freedom of the show gives Gilmartin and Gurwitch a place to stretch. "What's fun about the show," says Gurwitch, "is that we improv[ise], and that keeps the spark alive for me, and, I think, for all of us. When we get to work we really don't know how the day is going to turn out. Because of the nature of our show, we're able to, at the very last minute, come up with crazy ideas, and then execute them. Another show couldn't necessarily adjust to that kind of thing, but because we're improv, and because we're sort of on the outer fringes of Ted Turner's [cable TV] empire, and people aren't looking at us and saying, 'Well, perhaps you shouldn't do that,' we just do it." They can also abandon ship pretty quickly if it doesn't work out. Each segment is only about three minutes long, depending how long the movie is running.

Still, the focus of the show is food. "Cooking was never really a passion of mine till I was out of college, in my late twenties," says Paul Gilmartin. "It also had a lot to do with how much money and time I have. When we were poor and had a lot of time I cooked a lot more. Now that we're not poor and I don't have as much time, I don't cook as much. My favorite thing to do is buy a cookbook of a cuisine I know nothing about, and then make it three times a week for a month and then never make it again. I really, really love to eat, and I like to create stuff too. That sounds kind of pompous, but whether it's writing a joke [or cooking a meal], I like the feeling of sitting back and saying, 'Wow, I made that.' I think there's something very basic and human about feeding other people and bringing pleasure by giving them food. When I have people over and they bite into something I've made and say, 'This is fantastic!' it's the greatest feeling in the world. I'm happy when I'm around food."

"I did a little bit more cooking before *Dinner and a Movie* than I do now," admits Gurwitch. "It's sort of like a busman's holiday. I spend so much time in the kitchen on the show. When we're shooting the show I don't set foot in my kitchen for a week. Don't even get me near the kitchen. For instance, if I played a doctor on television, I probably wouldn't do a lot of brain surgery in my spare time." Gurwitch's fan mail includes invitations from guys who want to cook her dinner. "I just wonder where they were when I was single. No one wanted to cook me dinner before, except my husband."

A typical dinner for Gurwitch and her husband, Emmy award-winning comedy writer Jeff Kahn (they have a baby son, Ezra, born in 1998), is likely to consist of open containers of garlic-flavored hummus, wheat-free toast, and eggplant caviar. They're trying to avoid meat and eat lower on the food chain. But that wouldn't necessarily describe the food she cooks on *Dinner and a Movie*. Does she eat it anyway? "The problem is it all tastes really good, so even things I don't normally eat in my life, I eat on the show. I can't help myself, I must eat it. You're cooking it, you're smelling it all day, and it's right there. What can you do?"

She did draw the line. "There was one thing I didn't eat on the show. We made Bite Your Tongue Tacos for *Look Who's Talking Too*. I did not eat tongue sandwiches. The whole idea of the show was to demystify organ meats, and I failed miserably. I just can't get over the tongue aspect."

"I wanted to do tongue for Bite Your Tongue Tacos," explains chef Claud Mann, "and [Gilmartin and Gurwitch] did not want to touch the tongue. That was one of the shows I had to go on. So we wrote that in, that they didn't want to touch it and I came in. I wanted to address the fact that people aren't honest about their food, that they don't come to terms with where food comes from, and that to me is not healthy, so we turned that into the arc of the show."

"Neither of us [hosts] is a professional chef," explains Gurwitch, "or claims to know what were doing in the kitchen, and viewers will say, 'If these two boobs can cook something, maybe I can too. So, perhaps [cooking] will move from fantasy to actually executing—not necessarily a recipe, but one of the techniques. Maybe we can just elevate and enliven the palates of a few viewers out there, but I do think the appeal is the nonprofessional element of the two cohosts."

Mann agrees. "Part of [the appeal] is the fact that Paul and Annabelle are not cooks, and before we do a segment I talk them through it so they'll synthesize it and articulate in a way that makes sense to them." Says Gilmartin: "People think I do know what I'm talking about because Claud tells me exactly what to say thirty seconds before the camera rolls."

"If you watch the show," says Mann, "even if you don't think it's funny, even if you just like that particular movie and don't like the recipe, if you walk away remembering, 'if you sauté something, heat the pan up first before you put in the fat, don't crowd the pan,' [we've done our job]."

TV Series

Dinner and a Movie (TBS, 1995–)

Book

Dinner and a Movie (recipes by Claud Mann) by Kimberlee Carlson, Claud Mann, and Robert Taylor (Turner Publishing Co., 1996)

Web Sites

www.tbssuperstation.com/d_and_m/
www.electricearl.com/batalla
www.paulgilmartin.com

Susan Feniger and Mary Sue Milliken (Too Hot Tamales): The Real Spice Girls

Susan Feniger

Born: May 8, 1953.

Hometown: Toledo, Ohio.

Parents: Father, Yale, in steel business; mother, Ruth.

Siblings: Older brother, Bill; older sister, Kris.

School: Culinary Institute of America (Hyde Park, New York).

Favorite Junk Food: "Cheetos and popcorn."

Always in the Pantry: Virgin olive oil, sherry vinegar, popcorn, crackers, and sesame oil.

Always in the Fridge: Cheeses (St. Andre, morbier, feta), edamame, cranberry juice, olives, and artichokes.

Favorite Food Smell: "Chicken soup, or pork roasting."

Fantasy Last Meal: "St. Andre cheese, tapanade with black or green olives, avocados and artichoke in olive oil, and a great bread, mushrooms, a great cabernet [wine], some sort of delicious apple, maybe throw in a delicious lamb chop, and some just-picked corn. Then I would probably want a great chocolate dessert, but something simple, like our chocolate scooters."

Mary Sue Milliken

Born: February 21, 1958.

Hometown: St. Clair, Michigan.

Parents: Father, Jake, principal and Superintendent of Schools in Illinois and Michigan; mother, Ruth, retired to Arizona after teaching second grade, selling real estate, and working as pastry chef at her daughter's restaurants.

Siblings: Older sisters, Christine and Julie.

School: Washburn Trade School (Chicago, Illinois).

Favorite Junk Food: Häagen-Dazs ice cream.

Always in the Pantry: Black peppercorns, extra virgin olive oil, Maldon sea salt, basmati rice, and lemons.

Always in the Fridge: Blue cheese, whole milk, plain yogurt, mayonnaise, farm fresh eggs, and pale ale.

Favorite Food Smell: Basmati rice or fresh ground pepper.

Fantasy Last Meal: "I'd want to cook it myself, and it would depend on the season, because everything would have to be perfectly ripe. The whole thing would take about a week to make. I'd want to shop for it. I'd have a big salad with arugula and fennel and toasted sesame seeds, an assortment of cheeses, and lots of cocktails."

George Burns and Gracie Allen. Heckle and Jeckle. Wayne and Garth. Mary Sue Milliken and Susan Feniger have been compared to all of these teams. What makes a team work is the way the members interact. The "Tamales" cheerful, sisterly jabs at each other, and their ability to finish each other's sentences, all bespeak nearly two decades of knowing and caring about each other. Their lives and livelihoods are so tied to each other that it must be hard for the two Midwesterners to believe they had lives before they met.

~~~

When Mary Sue Milliken was a fifth grader in Michigan, she found a recipe in *Redbook* magazine for a Danish dough coffee cake and was drawn to it. "It was a weird recipe with dough and butter, and I thought,

'What could this possibly be?' So I got up really early in the morning to make it for my family. It had all these layers and it became flaky and beautiful. I've always been fascinated with the science of food, like, why it happens."

A few years later, when she was sixteen, she decided cooking was to be her career. "I met a guy who was a chef. He was really impressive, a really fast cook. Good with a knife. Made dinner in five minutes. I decided that's what I want to do. And my sister, who had just graduated from Northwestern University, was in a rebellious period, burning her bra and her degree, said, 'Oh yes, don't go to college, go to cooking school.'" Following that advice, Milliken attended the Washburn Trade School in Chicago.

~~~

Susan Feniger was in college when she made the decision to cook for a living. She was studying economics and business, first at Goddard, in Vermont, then at Pitzer in Claremont, California. "I worked in the cafeteria for this incredible man named Perry who was a cook in the army. He had this unbelievable spirit, and I just loved working for him. He said, 'Hey, why don't you go to cooking school? Why are you here?' and it was like, 'I don't know, I have no idea.' It was the first time I had really considered it. And that's exactly what I did." She went to the Culinary Institute of America, in Hyde Park, New York. Her classes and Milliken's classes were both filled primarily with men.

"We were both drawn to [cooking] as kids," Feniger says. "My mom is a really good cook. We always had really great food, and she cooked a lot for parties. When I was in high school, I worked at Smith's Cafeteria in Toledo [Ohio], we [Milliken and I] both worked in donut shops, and Mary Sue worked at a pizza place. We were food-connected. But for me, it was the environment. I loved the environment of being around people in the food business because it has such a family feeling to it. That part of it had a lot of appeal."

~~~

Soon it was time for the paths of Mary Sue Milliken and Susan Feniger to cross—the first time. "We met so long ago," Milliken says to Feniger. "I was about twenty, or twenty-one, and you were a much older twenty-five." Such is their banter off the air as well as on; Feniger gets ribbed for being older, and Milliken gets it right back for being larger. They met in 1978 at Chicago's distinguished Le Perroquet restaurant, as the first women ever to work in that prestigious kitchen. Mary Sue got the ball rolling, pioneering in the all-male domain where it took her a year to land a job. The owner told her she was too pretty for the kitchen and, offered her a job as a hat-check girl. She just kept nagging him until he finally gave in. "I was hired for minimum wage, after I'd already worked in Paris and Chicago, to peel garlic. After he saw that I was working circles around everyone else in the kitchen, he gave me more and more responsibility, until finally he thought, 'Oh, this is great deal, I'll hire another one!'"

Southern Hospitality

The first woman since Julia Child to cook on PBS, Nathalie Dupree is sometimes called the "anti-Martha" because of her relaxed approach and penchant for using easy-to-find ingredients. "I don't have time to keep running miles and miles to the farmers' market," she said in *People* magazine. "My mission is to get people to relax and enjoy their friends."

Born in 1940, Dupree received her culinary training with an advanced certificate from London's Cordon Bleu. After cooking in Italy and France, she worked as a restaurant chef in Majorca, Spain, and then returned to the United States in 1972 to open her own country restaurant in Social Circle, Georgia. In 1975, Dupree founded Rich's Cooking School and served as chef, teacher, and director for almost ten years with more than 10,000 students. Dupree also served two years as president of the International Association of Culinary Professionals, which has more than 1,000 members in fourteen countries.

New Southern Cooking debuted on the PBS network (and was shown on The Learning Channel) in 1986. She followed that TV series with *Nathalie Dupree's Matters of Taste, Nathalie Dupree Cooks for Family and Friends, Nathalie Dupree Cooks,* and her latest program, *Nathalie Dupree Entertains.* Her books include the companion books to these series, as well as *Nathalie Dupree's Southern Memories* (which won the 1994 James Beard award), *Nathalie Dupree Cooks Everyday Meals from a Well-Stocked Pantry, Nathalie Dupree Cooks Quick Meals for Busy Days,* and *Nathalie Dupree's Comfortable Entertaining.*

Dupree has also written columns for the *Los Angeles Times,* the *Atlanta Journal-Constitution,* and currently provides a monthly food feature for *Atlanta* magazine; she also has a syndicated radio show, *Home Cooking.*

That "other one" was Susan. "At that point," Feniger adds, "we were just happy to be working in kitchens, so [the sexism] was not even an issue." They both came to work early, stayed late, and worked relentlessly.

The best teams naturally complement each other's talents, so they don't need to consciously divvy up the work. Like the little girl fascinated by the coffee cake she made, the tall, blond, and serene Mary Sue still likes the science of food, and can often be found making pastry, a more precise, solitary act. Always drawn to theater and pressure, and the familial feeling of the food business, the shorter, brunette, and more intense Susan still prefers the fast-paced action of the hot, busy kitchen.

Despite her experiences with sexism, Milliken maintains her optimism about the culinary world. "In retrospect, we've become aware of women's struggles in this profession and others. I believe that people really want to do the right thing. I don't think men have tried consciously to keep women down in that way. I don't think the solution to the problem is to not figure out a way to work together. I think women bring a whole different thing to the kitchen in the restaurant industry than men do and it's been really exciting to see the change because now, cooking schools are graduating 50-50 [ratio of men to women]."

Feniger adds, "The reality of this profession is that it's an extremely wearing, demanding profession. You have to be really passionate about it. Anyone who goes into it to make a bunch of money... that's totally the wrong way to go into it. It takes so long to get to that place, you have to be in it for the long haul. It's so 'hands on' in so many ways, stuff like when the dishwasher breaks down and you have to do the dishes. Women or men, you have to be really passionate, because the rewards are in the everyday satisfactions, like the great food you're serving, the relationships you develop, and your passion about food."

"We were just able to set [the sexism] aside," says Mary Sue, "in order to do what we thought we had to do, to achieve success in a man's world. I have no doubt that we both chose this profession for many rebellious-type reasons."

"I chose it because I got to wear a uniform every day to work," jokes Susan. "It's such a waste of time to figure out what to put on!" So she'd be just as happy working at a gas station? "That's true, I could still have the relationship with people...." Both Tamales have put their own spin on the conventional chef's jacket, which you rarely see them not wearing. Both eschew the traditional white for colors such as pink and green; Milliken gets the sleeves tapered and likes to wear decorative pins, while Feniger gets her jackets shortened and accessorizes with many earrings.

After her tenure at Le Perroquet, Feniger went on to California to work with Wolfgang Puck at Ma Maison in Los Angeles. She met up with Milliken again in France, where Mary Sue was working at Restaurant d'Olympe in Paris, and Susan was at L'Oasis, a three-star restaurant on the French Riviera. It was in France that the idea of working together began to take form.

"We were just sort of drinking one night," explains Feniger, "and there had been a big rainstorm and a big rainbow and we both sort of said, 'Why don't we open up a restaurant together?' We didn't have one cent, but we thought, 'Wouldn't this be great?' We didn't think this would be a partnership forever. We didn't really get that far—we just got busy."

"Then we both went back to where we came from," Milliken adds. "Susan went to California, and she kept telling me to move out here. She is very persistent, so I said, 'Okay, for a couple of months,' and four years later I hadn't even left the kitchen."

They opened the tiny City Cafe on Melrose Avenue in West Hollywood in 1981, with only enough kitchen space for a hot plate. They quickly outgrew the little facility and opened the more spacious City Restaurant in the same vicinity. This was followed by the 1985 opening of Border Grill in Santa Monica, which was named one of forty best restaurants by the *Los Angeles Times*, and one of the best restaurants in America by *Gourmet* magazine. It was one of the first restaurants with an Internet Web site. Another restaurant of theirs, Ciudad (Spanish for "city"), opened in downtown Los Angeles in 1998. It offers food from all over the Latin world, including Argentina, Cuba, Brazil, Chile, Portugal, and Spain. In contrast, the chefs at Border Grill serves up authentic food from Mexico and Central America.

Milliken and Feniger are active board members of many culinary associations, including a founding role in the development of the International Association of Women Chefs and Restaurateurs, which cultivates the careers of women in restaurants, and Chef's Collaborative 2000, which supports the use of sustainably grown (i.e., organically grown, socially responsible, and environmentally sound) products in the food service industry. They work with the U.S. Department of Agriculture on the school lunch programs. They're involved with numerous charities, including the Scleroderma Research Foundation, for which they spearheaded a dinner/comedy event for the last fourteen years, repeatedly attracting the likes of Robin Williams, Lily Tomlin, and Ellen DeGeneres.

Together they have authored four cookbooks, including *City Cuisine* (1994), which was nominated for best cookbook by *Cooks* magazine. In 1988 they were the first women to receive the California Restaurant Writers' prestigious Chef of the Year award. And in 1993, they were two of only sixteen chefs worldwide to be invited to cook with Julia Child in her PBS-TV series *Home Cooking with Master Chefs* and are featured on the CD-ROM of the same name. From 1995 to 1998, they hosted their own weekly radio show, *Good Food*, on NPR station KCRW. The Tamales have been featured in *USA Today*, *People* magazine, *Entertainment Weekly*, and on such TV programs as *Oprah*, *Maury Povich*, *Sally Jessy Raphael*, and the *Today* show. They even appeared as themselves on an episode of ABC-TV's *Sabrina, the Teenage Witch*.

Milliken and Feniger are entwined in each other's lives in and out of work. Their closeness has prompted some to speculate that they are a couple. Feniger is an out lesbian (a profile in the December/January 1994 issue of *Out* magazine was her first in the gay press) and involved in a relationship. Milliken is wed to architect John Schweitzer, who is Feniger's ex-husband from a long-ago marriage. Feniger and Schweitzer remained friends, and later, she thought he'd be perfect for Milliken. Schweitzer also designed their restaurants. He and Milliken have two children: Declan, born in 1990, and Kieran, born in 1998. Feniger is godmother to both children. When she and Milliken lived closer to one another, even their dogs (they each have two) frolicked together regularly.

Feniger and Milliken think of themselves as teachers as well as chefs. "We started teaching in 1981," says Milliken, "because people were interested in what we were cooking, and we wanted them to have a fuller experience. [For example], why [do] onions caramelize? Because they have the most sugar of any vegetable in the kingdom. [Knowing that] just made their experience a little bit more fun. Teaching them about what they're eating is a way to enrich that experience."

In a move that seems a precursor to their cooking shows, Milliken and Feniger were the first to show surveillance-camera footage of their restaurant's kitchen on the bar's television. But it was time to let more than one night's customers watch the Tamales create their rustic Latin American fare. After a stint on the Food Network's *Chef du Jour* in 1995, the Tamales got their own TV show. So, who thought of the name? "Food Network came up with the 'Border Girls,' or 'South of the Border,'" says

Milliken. "We came up with *Too Hot Tamales*. Now [when they see us] people yell out, 'Hey, it's the Tamales!' Particularly businessmen in Manhattan."

Men do watch, and so do little kids and college students. Fans of all ages enjoy the enthusiasm the hosts clearly feel about their subject. They are not Puritans, they are sensory junkies. And it's fun to watch people who are comfortable enough with each other that they can tease and disagree one minute (such as judging each other's chopping styles), and be warm and familiar the next. It's impressive that they manage to be so alert, given their taping schedule. Because they are first and foremost chefs and restaurateurs, Milliken and Feniger can't spend too much time away from their restaurants. They take three to five days at a time to travel to the East Coast and tape five or six daily shows in succession.

Besides being called the Tamales everywhere they go, there's another by-product of being on TV that Feniger mentions. "I can't tell you how many people say to us at the restaurant ,'You look so much thinner and so much younger [in person].' I can see why people get complexes."

Too Hot Tamales did get a little too "hot" early in 1997, to the extreme dismay of its hosts. Due to a technical snafu, a hardcore pornography video appeared on the screen for a few minutes as the audio of Milliken and Feniger narrating directions for Latin risotto continued to run during the broadcast.

Although *Too Hot Tamales* introduced millions to the nooks and crannies of the Latin American food landscape, their second show, *Tamales World Tour*, with a funky, colorful set like that of its popular predecessor, presents an eclectic mix of food with Asian and European influences. The opening to *Tamales World Tour*, featuring their heads floating about in a cartoon spaceship, says it all; they are ambassadors, gathering up foods we might not know about, and might not be able to get in restaurants (yet), foods from the streets or from family kitchens, and they're teaching us about them.

"I think we're really attracted to rustic food," says Mary Sue. Susan agrees. "We have a real respect for different cultures and their origins. What's most interesting for us is not to take food from different cultures and make it our own. I think our challenge has always been to learn about other cultures and their food and what they've done for centuries, and be able to recreate that in our own kitchen; to respect it like someone growing up in that culture would."

Mary Sue and Susan take seriously the responsibility of presenting foods from cultures other than their own. Says Milliken, "I think my responsibility is to feel passionate about it. We get a lot of feedback at the restaurant and the Web site, and 90 percent of the mail from Hispanics is, 'Wow, this is so fabulous, thank you for showing what I've been doing all my life.'"

"When someone does make a comment," Feniger continues, "it's usually, 'You did this wrong,' and that's good. We don't want to give misinformation."

Their goal is to build a bridge between what they call "peasant" foods and the classic French technique they both studied so assiduously. Feniger explains: "Having been trained in pretty strict French kitchens, we both learned a huge amount about technique and understanding food combinations. It just kind of got beat into us. Then, we went to Mexico, and our background gave us the tools to look at food and understand combinations in ways that we may not have been able to do without that background, even though the cuisines were totally different. Techniques that we learned in the French kitchen could maybe even improve a dish. We'd see an inspired dish, take our technique, and not change it, but make it better than a home cook would because we have professional skills. For cuisines that are daunting to people, we're able to get in there, explore it a little, and break it down, so someone will say, 'Look, this isn't so daunting.'"

The purpose is to present the similarities of dishes from different cultures, not the differences. "[For example], with lamb curry, we always make the point that this is no different than making a lamb stew if you're in France, because it's the exact same technique; it's the same as brisket. Instead of this spice it's that one. That's a lot of what we do, is teach technique, where our passion is, and we pour it into the different areas of food that we're passionate about."

In fact, the Tamales aren't as concerned with people trying out their recipes as they are with TV viewers picking up a new technique or two. "Our main goal is to get people cooking," says Milliken. "Even if they use a bottled salad dressing, if they pop [the salad] in a big oversized bowl, and understand the difference between shaking [the dressing] on at the table and putting it on the whole salad beforehand so every leaf has flavor, we've just enriched their lives a little bit, and they're going to have more fun."

Mary Sue believes times have changed regarding food. "People ask at the restaurant, 'Is that balsamic vinaigrette?' Five or ten years ago no one would have said that. People are so much more interested in [food] . . . which I'm so happy about, because I've always been obsessed with that!"

TV Series

Too Hot Tamales (Food Network, 1995–98)
Tamales World Tour (Food Network, 1997–)

TV Specials

Days of Mescal & Roses (Food Network, March, 1997)
Cooking Treasures of the Maya (Food Network, April, 1997)
Border Grill (Food Network, October and November, 1998)

Books

City Cuisine by Mary Sue Milliken, Susan Feniger (Hearst Books, 1994)
Mesa Mexicana: Bold Flavors from the Border, Coastal Mexico, and Beyond by Mary Sue Milliken, Susan Feniger, and Helene Siegel (William Morrow & Co., 1994)
Cantina: The Best of Casual Mexican Cooking (Casual Cuisines of the World) by Susan Feniger and Mary Sue Milliken (Sunset Pub. Co., 1996)
Cooking with Too Hot Tamales: Recipes and Tips from the Television Food Network's Spiciest Cooking Duo by Mary Sue Milliken, Susan Feniger, and Helene Siegel (William Morrow & Co., 1997)

Web Sites

www.bordergrill.com
www.foodtv.com

Bobby Flay:
Full of Flay-vor

Born: December 10, 1964.

Hometown: New York City, New York.

Parents: Father, Bill, lawyer/restaurant manager; mother, Dorothy, paralegal.

School: French Culinary Institute (New York).

Siblings: None.

Favorite Junk Food: "Ice cream, my total weakness. Häagen-Dazs, anything vanilla."

Always in the Pantry: "Olive oil, balsamic vinegar, and eighteen kinds of mustard, my favorite condiment."

Always in the Fridge: "Milk, orange juice, and ginger ale."

Favorite Food Smell: "I like the smell of smoke, things that are being smoked."

Fantasy Last Meal: "Dinner at [famous Brooklyn, New York, steak-house] Peter Lugers. A porterhouse steak, creamed spinach, and home fries. [Cook it myself?] No way."

Bobby Flay of Food Network's *Hot Off the Grill* can remember his first and formative cooking experience. "When I was about seven or eight, I asked for an Easy-Bake oven, and I got it. I was amazed by the way you could make chocolate pudding, like My-T-Fine chocolate pudding, and how it would start to get thick all of a sudden. I was always fascinated with cooking, amazed that I could make that happen, that I could take some brown powder and some milk, heat it up, and in about eight minutes it would get thick; it would actually change. I remember wanting to cook in the kitchen a lot, like making deviled eggs, stuff like that."

Bobby Flay was raised in the Yorkville (Upper East Side) section of Manhattan by divorced parents, Dorothy, a paralegal, ("My mom's food was very American, lamb chops, pork chops...") and Bill, a lawyer-cum-manager of the Manhattan restaurant Joe Allen's. The athletic Flay had childhood fantasies of becoming a baseball or basketball player. "You get a very rude awakening that about one-tenth of a percent even get close. But I was always the best [athlete] in my neighborhood, so to speak. In high school, I was still playing sports but I was playing on the street, and was sort of a tough kid, hanging out in some tough neighborhoods." He bounced in and out of parochial educational institutions before graduating in 1982 from a now-defunct Manhattan private high school.

"I didn't know where I was going. My father, who's this very scholarly guy and continues to go to school as we speak, he said to me, 'Well, you've graduated high school, do you want to go to college?' I said 'Yeah, sure,' I just figured that was the next step. He said, 'You know what, Bobby? Don't go. You don't want to go, and don't waste my money. Go to work.' Two days later he called me and didn't ask me, but told me to be at the restaurant because there was a busboy who needed two weeks off. When I was there I became friendly with the chef and he asked me if I wanted to work in the kitchen after I was done, and that's how I started."

Flay was only seventeen years old. "For the first four or five months, it was just discipline and I didn't want to have it. I was late for work. I still remember coming to work an hour and a half late, and the chef trying to cover for me, and my dad waiting on the steps of the restaurant. You just want to die. He knows I'm late; what am I going to say to him? And my dad said, 'Look, you have to work harder than anyone else in this restaurant because you're my son.'"

Suddenly, things came into focus. "One morning I woke up and I couldn't wait to go to work. You know, it just happens. I became really inspired." Deciding he'd found his calling, Flay worked in and around the restaurant's kitchen, and one day his father and Joe Allen came to him and told him about a new school opening up in Manhattan called the French Culinary Institute, and if he wanted to go, they'd pay for it. Joe Allen thought Flay could be an asset to him down the line, and was betting on him for the future. Allen wrote Flay a check, and he enrolled in the very first class of the Institute. "I was the youngest in the school, and there were only nine of us; they were still building the walls."

Though he now had a direction, Flay still lacked the intense discipline necessary for culinary school. "My father would get the phone call, 'How come Bobby's not here today?' I thought, is this ever going to end? It was a very intense school. I think that eighteen, nineteen years old is too young for culinary school, for most people. You're not ready to be an adult yet, you're just not, and it's really an adult world there. Lots of discipline and a lot of knowledge to know and a lot of respect for a career, as opposed to just going to school."

From his time at Joe Allen's, where he continued to work while attending the Institute, Flay had more experience than most of the other people in the class. "I sort of had the attitude that I knew more than they did, which was the wrong attitude to have, obviously." Despite all of this, Bobby considers culinary school a great experience; he thinks of things even today that he learned there.

After completing the two-year program, Flay worked full-time at Joe Allen's for a time, and then its owner told him: "'You know Bobby, you gotta get out of here. You've learned everything you're going to learn here, good-bye. Maybe one day you'll come back and we'll do something but if you don't that's okay too. Get outta here and go learn.' He was a mentor in a very quiet way. He just helped direct me without my even knowing it. It's one of those things that you realize later."

So, at the age of twenty, Bobby aligned himself with the Brighton Grill and experienced what he calls a "classic restaurant story." It was a new restaurant on Third Avenue in Manhattan. The first night there were lines around the block for no other reason than that it was new, and people had watched it being built in their neighborhood on their way home from work. Flay was hired as a sous-chef, and the chef was a man from New Orleans. He was a little older than Flay, but had a very real problem. "He had an incredible drinking problem. I don't mean 'one too many.' I mean I can't even describe how many tequilas he would have in the stretch of an evening—like thirty shots. [The owners] knew he had a problem but they were trying to look past it, because they really liked him, and he was talented. Then one morning about a week into it I got to work and he was sleeping in the laundry room from the night before on top of the dirty laundry! Finally the owners realized he couldn't do it so they gave me his job. So here I am, culinary school, time at Joe Allen, and about a week there, and now I'm a chef at this restaurant that's packed every single night, and I'm twenty. It was a very long year."

He held it together, thanks to an innate managerial skill he credits his father for passing on to him. Flay characterizes himself at that time as both inexperienced and immature. "I didn't want to hire people better than me, I was always at the restaurant because I didn't trust anybody else. I was afraid that someone else would be better than I was and take my job. I was insecure. So, after about a year, my body collapsed and I said 'I can't do this anymore,' and I left. It was the classic chef story."

After a short break, Flay went to work for restaurateur Jonathan Waxman at the Manhattan-based restaurant Buds. "That was where I really learned good food at a different level than I had ever experienced." He worked at different New York City establishments for Waxman for about three years, during which time he met Wolfgang Puck and Alice Waters. Bobby got a lot of exposure during the 1980s, when restaurants became extremely popular, and chefs became celebrities. But soon, the twenty-three-year old chef, who was always the youngest in the kitchen, burned out again. So he walked away.

After he quit, Bobby went to Aspen, Colorado, for six weeks to ski. "All the guys I was with were just so rich, they were making all this money, doing nothing on Wall Street. They'd buy, they'd wait, they'd sell, they'd get rich. This was the eighties, this was a piece of cake. So I said, 'Why don't you guys get me a job? I just want to work for somebody and learn the business, and see if I like it; I don't even have to get paid.' So some guy hires me and I was making $230 a week, before taxes." Flay figured it would be a "get rich quick" proposition.

He spent six months at the wires on the American Stock Exchange, surrounded by phones, a quotron machine, paper, and pencils, screaming across a stadium-sized room to his broker, and then flashing hand signals that must have brought him back to his days as a baseball pitcher. According to Bobby, "I loved the action, but hated the people. To me the great thing about the restaurant business, besides loving what I do, is the people. I could have stayed there [in the stock market] and made a fortune, but I didn't have any interest in getting up and going there every morning. It just did not interest me in the least, and the whole 'every Friday at four o'clock everybody goes to the [South Street] Seaport and gets drunk' thing, it was not my scene. So, I walked away from it, but I'm glad I did it. It was great experience, and now I know a lot about the market."

For the Defense—Jack McDavid

Your favorite baseball-cap-and-overalls-wearing chef could have represented you in the courtroom. That was Jack McDavid's (Food Network's *Grillin' and Chillin'*) career goal before the cooking bug bit.

McDavid, in his thirties, was raised on a small farm in Clinchport, in the western tip of Virginia. He studied accounting at the University of Virginia and planned to go to law school. Then he took a job in a sandwich shop in Charlottesville, doing the accounting. He wound up in the kitchen and fell in love with cooking.

When nearby Monticello needed a chef, it was McDavid to the rescue. There he cooked for Queen Elizabeth II, Jimmy Carter, Anwar Sadat, and Menachim Begin.

Later, when McDavid decided a career as a chef was the way to go, he left school and started working at restaurants around the area, which provided him with superior vocational training. He learned how to sauté from a Greek short order cook. He studied the use of knives and the art of presentation from Chiang Kai-Shek's ex-chef, Charlie Yu. He learned the rudiments of French technique from Marriot's top chef Dietmar Salat, Jean-Pierre Goyenvalle of Washington's Lion D'Or, and Georges Perrier at Le Bec Fin in Philadelphia.

Today, McDavid is the owner of Jack's Firehouse in Philadelphia, and is a perpetual boy of summer in reruns of Food Network's *Grillin' and Chillin'*. It's just as well—if McDavid had become a lawyer, he probably wouldn't have been able to wear his "Save the Farm" hat in the courtroom.

Flay probably always knew he'd return to the restaurant business, and that's exactly what he did in 1987. He became the chef at Miracle Grill in New York City, and returned to his familiar role as the youngest guy in the kitchen, which often irked others around him. "When I was at

Brighton Grill, it was just about insecurity, but once I became better at what I did and got more confidence, it was up to them whether they wanted to like [my youthfulness] or not." It was at Miracle Grill that Flay developed his talent for his signature cooking style, Southwestern. "Jonathan [Waxman] brought California cuisine to the East Coast. Chili peppers, fresh corn, beans, using limes instead of lemons, blue corn tortillas, the colors and the textures of all those ingredients are incredible, and the flavors are even better. Nobody was really doing a focused, contemporary Southwestern restaurant in New York at that time. I decided that's what I wanted to do. I really honed my skills at Miracle Grill."

Flay had never visited the Southwest, but his take on its cuisine drew a cult following, including restaurateur Laurence Kretchmer, who helped create the financing for Mesa Grill, which he and Flay opened on January 15, 1991. Food critic Gael Greene wrote, "the sassy fare at Mesa Grill surpasses anything of its kind elsewhere in New York." The *Zagat Survey* voted Mesa Grill the number one American regional restaurant, as well as one of the top twenty restaurants in New York. Also that year, Flay married fellow chef Debra Ponzek but the marriage ended in 1993.

In May 1993, Flay was voted the James Beard Foundation's Rising Star Chef of the Year, an award that honors the country's most accomplished chef under the age of thirty. Also in 1993, the French Culinary Institute, his alma mater, honored him with its first ever Outstanding Graduate Award, an annual award that recognizes the school's most accomplished alumni. Bobby Flay (Bo), along with partner Laurence Kretchmer (Lo), opened their second restaurant, Bolo, in November 1993, geared to exploring Spanish cuisine. Bolo was awarded two stars by the *New York Times* in 1994 and continues to be voted the top Spanish restaurant in New York City by the *Zagat Survey*. In May 1994, he published his first book, *Bobby Flay's Bold American Food*, which won the 1995 IACP (International Association of Culinary Professionals) award for design. A third restaurant, Mesa City, debuted in 1996 and was sold in 1998. Flay also owns a catering company, and Mesa sauces, condiments, and apparel are available through mail order. His second book, *From My Kitchen to Your Table*, appeared in 1998, and his third, *Boy Meets Grill*, is a 1999 release. Flay is also active in food industry–related charities, such as City Meals on Wheels.

"I really like where my life is right now," says Flay, who resides in lower Manhattan. "I have two very manageable restaurants that are very successful and are being run well, which is so important. I used to think I wanted eighty restaurants. I don't. I just don't." He also has a two-and-a-half-year-old daughter named Sophie. He shares custody of the youngster with her mother Kate Connelly, from whom Flay is separated. She is the former cohost of the Food Network's *Robin Leach Talking Food*.

"I was a little scared about being a dad, but now I think I'm really good at it," Flay told *People* magazine. "She's already developing a taste for things like capers and lobster." There must be an Easy-Bake Oven in her future.

Flay's first television appearance was in 1987, while he was at Miracle Grill, when he was a guest on *Live! with Regis and Kathie Lee* and made southwestern potato salad oncamera. "I was not nervous until [producer] Michael Gelman walked up to me thirty seconds before the segment while we were in commercial and said 'Don't be nervous, only two and a half million people are watching.' He did it just to [play] with me. But Regis made me feel very comfortable, he said, 'Don't worry, I'll take care of you. Say what you need to say and if you need to skip a beat, I'll be right in there.' He's a pro."

Bobby did *Live!* three or four times, the *Today* show about ten times, plus other morning TV outings, as well as *Late Night with David Letterman*. Then, in the mid-1990s, the Food Network contacted Flay. He did eight episodes of *Chef du Jour* (a week of Mesa Grill recipes, and three episodes of Bolo dishes).

The Flay-named show, *Grillin' and Chillin'*, came about in 1996. It was the network's idea to pair him with his friend Jack McDavid in a 'city versus country' theme. Reruns of that show still have a cult following. Bobby and Jack filmed about forty shows in seven days in Clearwater, Florida. "It was 100 degrees out, and we shot six or seven shows a day. I don't remember doing the [first] shows. I had just had a daughter ten days prior and then I had to go shoot the shows, so I was delirious."

In 1997, Lifetime cable was auditioning candidates to take over their cooking show, *The Main Ingredient*. It was hosted by a soap opera actress, and now they wanted a real chef. Flay got the job, but he wasn't always happy with the showcased food, which he described as "a lot of really simple homestyle stuff. Also, they were directing me in a very heavy way. But I really learned a lot about television." Production values were higher and staffs were bigger than they were on *Grillin' and Chillin'*. However, *The Main Ingredient with Bobby Flay* has stopped airing, and Flay believes the Food Network has had such an impact that networks like Lifetime no longer can compete in the area of cooking programming.

Flay returned to the Food Network for his latest show, *Hot Off the Grill with Bobby Flay*, where he feels more like himself (he thought he seemed "hyper" on his Lifetime outing). Food Network wanted Bobby grilling on air again, and they wanted him to have someone to talk to. "Basically they wanted someone who is into food, not necessarily a professional, likes to cook, and kind of understands what it's all about, but someone who can be funny and keep the action going and has a good oncamera presence." Seventy people auditioned for the cohost position, and network executives chose actress and stand-up comedian Jacqui Malouf, whom Flay liked immediately. *Hot Off the Grill* is filmed in Old Brookville, on Long Island, and Flay has a lot of input for whom his oncamera guests are. His favorite guest so far is James Carville, apparently a real foodie, with whom he made soft-shell crab sandwiches. "James Carville was always my dream guest. I love him."

Today, the Food Network's official Grilling Boy of Summer, Flay fondly remembers grilling lobster and corn outside with his parents at the New Jersey shore. "I love the culture of grilling," he told the Web site StarChefs. "It creates an atmosphere that is festive but casual. Grilling takes the formality out of entertaining. Everyone wants to get involved. The process and the great smells it produces make everyone hungry and get everyone's mouth watering. And it gives men a chance to cook."

Bobby Flay's message to his TV viewers is simple. "Enjoy cooking, and have fun with it. Don't take it so seriously. Don't use cookbooks as bibles, use them as guides." And why are so many people watching? "Everybody can relate to food. That's the common denominator, whether [the show is] entertaining or boring, whether it's good or bad food, whether the cook is good or not, it doesn't matter—people can relate to it. 'I'm a bad cook.' 'I'm a good cook.' 'I want to know how to make that.' 'That reminds me of my mother.' It's got this great common thread."

 TV Series

Grillin' and Chillin' (Food Network, 1996– *)
The Main Ingredient with Bobby Flay (Lifetime, 1997)

Hot Off the Grill with Bobby Flay (Food Network, 1998–)

Books

Bobby Flay's Bold American Food: More Than 200 Revolutionary Recipes by
    Bobby Flay and Joan Schwartz (contributor) (Warner Books, 1994)
Bobby Flay's from My Kitchen to Your Table: 125 Bold Recipes by Bobby Flay
    and Joan Schwartz (Clarkson Potter, 1998)
Boy Meets Grill by Bobby Flay (Hyperion, 1999)

Web Site

www.foodtv.com

CHAPTER 12

Mollie Katzen:
Still Life in Vegetables

Born: October 13, 1950.

Hometown: Rochester, New York.

Parents: Father, Leon, attorney; mother, Betty (Heller), former social worker, homemaker.

Siblings: Older brother, Joshua; younger brothers, Daniel and Ezra.

Schools: attended Cornell University (Ithaca, New York), San Francisco Art Institute (San Francisco, California).

Favorite Junk Food: "Breakfast cereal. I feel like Seinfeld."

Always in the Pantry: "Grains, beans, olive oils, vinegars, and dried fruit."

Always in the Fridge: "Spinach, broccoli, carrots, zucchini, shitake mushrooms, celery, tofu, breads, cheeses, leftovers, and apples."

Favorite Food Smell: "Baked bread, and caramelized onions."

Favorite Food Sound: "The really really hot pan. One of my favorite things on my show is having a mike over the stove. I'd get the pan really hot and hear a really loud sizzle sound when I put stuff in."

Fantasy Last Meal: "A Burmese feast with ginger salad, garlic noodles, and tomato curry."

If you look in the kitchens of people in their sixth or seventh decade, a copy of *The Joy of Cooking* will most likely be found. In contrast, in the kitchens of their offspring, a copy of the perennial bestseller, *Moosewood Cookbook*, will most likely be discovered. Owned by both hardcore vegetarians, hippies, and college students, *Moosewood* is the classic veggie cookbook. Neither the book nor its author, Mollie Katzen, who is not strictly a vegetarian, advocates vegetarianism as a morally or economically superior way of life.

"I don't think everyone should be a vegetarian. I want to include as many people as possible. I don't want them to be scared away. I mention options on my [TV] show for meat eaters. To tell you the truth, I get a lot of teasing because I'm not a vegetarian. I eat fish, and free-range chicken. I'd rather eat a very beautifully prepared light chicken dish than a yucky vegetarian one. My kids eat burgers. It's about loving food, not about thinking other foods are bad. I hope that comes across. I want people to enjoy it, too."

Mollie Katzen's Rochester, New York, childhood was fairly vegetable-free. She ate meat practically every day until she was eighteen. Like most 1950s moms, Katzen's mother used convenience foods such as Minute Rice, except on Friday Sabbath meals. Katzen helped with the cooking at an early age, partly because she got to spend more time with Mom that way. When she was still a toddler, Mollie cooked with invisible ingredients, mixed with grass, flowers, and mud.

When she was seven, Katzen began making coffee for her parents every morning. "I felt very special, very useful, which children don't often get to feel," she told Mary MacVean for the Associated Press. When she was nine, Mollie tested and wrote her first recipe for a chocolate dessert that leaked out of the oven door and across the floor. She and her mother named it "Creeping Australian BooBoo." Inspired by Julia Child and Graham Kerr on TV, she continued to experiment in the kitchen and wrote down recipes, including several chocolate desserts she invented when she was still a teenager.

"I hadn't tasted a fresh green vegetable until the age of twelve," Katzen writes in the prologue of the 1992 revision of the *Moosewood Cookbook* (first published in 1977), "when I was invited to dinner at the home of a friend whose mother had a vegetable garden. She picked fresh green beans for dinner and served them lightly steamed in bowls, with a little warmed milk poured on top. I went wild! This was a radical new discovery for me.... I kept thinking about those green beans long afterwards."

Katzen studied oboe and piano at the Eastman School of Music in her hometown of Rochester, New York, then enrolled at Cornell University in Ithaca, New York, as a fine arts major. Perhaps because of the "questionable" sources of the dining hall's meat, she soon found she hadn't consumed any in quite a while and felt fine. She wrote, "I wondered if this made me a vegetarian, although at that time I didn't know anyone who was. To be one was looked upon as a cross between an eccentricity and an affliction."

After two years at Cornell, Katzen transferred to the San Francisco Art Institute's honors program in painting. She held several food-related jobs in high school and college. As she detailed in her *Moosewood* book, "I saw cooking as a trade that could be a source of income until my paintings were hanging in the Metropolitan Museum, my concerts sold out at Carnegie Hall, and my prize-winning novels and poetry published in many languages."

While Mollie was on the West Coast, her brother Joshua and his friend decided to start a restaurant in Ithaca, New York, patterned after the natural foods establishment in San Francisco where Katzen worked. They asked her to join the enterprise and she agreed, thinking it would be for about three months. She ended up staying for years. In January 1973, the now-famous Moosewood Restaurant (named after a type of maple tree) opened its doors in Ithaca, with Mollie in the kitchen as one of the seven owners. She worked full-time for the first five years of the restaurant, which was operated as a collective.

Like its cook, Moosewood's customers were not solely vegetarians. They were people looking for homecooked meals. Soon people started asking for recipes, so Katzen hand-lettered her own little cookbook, and sold out her 800 copies in a week. It was clear it was time to find a publisher. One major New York City publisher showed interest, but requested that Katzen get rid of her pen-and-ink drawings, such as a duck saying "No duck in here" above the recipe for Chinese duck sauce. However, Ten Speed Press offered her complete artistic and editorial freedom, so she chose them as her publisher.

The *Moosewood Cookbook* sold very well, and it still does—it's one of the best-selling cookbooks of all time. The recipes are simple and use ingredients easily found in supermarkets. By 1980, there was demand for a sequel. However, Mollie had left the Moosewood restaurant and was about to begin graduate study in piano. Just days before her conservatory audition, she had an epiphany. "I hate performing the piano," she explained in the *San Francisco Chronicle*. "I can barely play with my friends in the room. I can't stand performing; I'm very shy about it. 'Am I crazy? Why don't I write the cookbook?' So I took the contract and never played the audition."

In 1982, *The Enchanted Broccoli Forest* came out. It was followed up with *Still Life with Menu* (1988), the revision of the *Moosewood Cookbook* (1992), and *Pretend Soup and Other Real Recipes* (1994, written with her son's nursery school teacher). A complete list of Katzen's cookbooks appears at the end of this chapter. As an artist, vegetables and fruits appealed to her sense of color. You normally don't see a still life of a rump roast. However, pictures of vegetables and fruits abound in her cookbooks.

In 1992, Katzen saw a vegetable salad at a food stand at a Pittsburgh airport that looked pretty familiar—it was one of hers. She decided it was time to explore the potential of television. "[The TV show is a] really nice way to teach more people. Because I'm primarily a visual artist, I loved the whole visual aspect of the television medium—the colors, the production—it excites me. I really enjoy it. It's a three-dimensional creative experience. I've never had the ambition to be a celebrity or to have people recognize me personally. So the goal of the TV show was to work in another medium, like an artist." Ironically, the woman who despised performing music in front of people had no problem in front of the camera. "Piano is private, for me. This is totally different. To me, this is just talking to people."

Katzen became the executive producer of her cooking show, appropriately named *Mollie Katzen's Cooking Show*. Debuting in 1995, it was public television's first vegetarian cooking program shown nationally; not surprisingly, it's sponsored by anti-gas remedies such as Beano and Prerelief. "Even PBS has been very leery about vegetarianism. But at least two or three of the top ten best-selling cookbooks are veggie; the trick is to have it be inclusive."

The vegetarianism of the 1970s was quite different from that of today. Back then, the big fear of going meatless was the lack of protein and sacrificing that "filled up" feeling. So, veggies were often mixed in with high-fat dairy products, such as cheese and eggs. A typical meal at the

Moosewood restaurant included a heavy cheesy casserole, along with the soup, vegetable salad, and fresh fruit salad. Today, spices are replacing dairy, which Katzen's next series will reflect. She wants to bring vegetarian cooking into the new century.

But Mollie is not a fanatic. In fact, she has very little patience for such obsessed individuals. "See why so many people are starving," she has said, "instead of worrying about whether your cooking has honey or sugar in it."

Katzen insists on having artistic control of her TV series. "I know what I don't know about, and I'll hire the best person I can find. I spend months collaborating with the set designer. I think that paying attention to every little visual detail gives the show qualities that you might not be able to put your finger on, but add up to the sum of a certain kind of look. I hate to sound like 'the cover of a book is more important than the book,' but the look of a cooking show is absolutely critically important. A person is sitting in their house with a remote control in their hand and 5,000 channels they can click to, and you have to hold their attention so they won't turn the channel." Illustrations from her books appear as graphics between scenes on the show, and she performs the theme music on piano (French Suite #5 in G major by Johann Sebastian Bach). "I've incorporated all the things I love. I'm so happy about that."

Presenting whole balanced vegetarian menus, including dessert, is the priority of the show, especially because no meat is prepared on camera. In addition, Mollie likes to pack her show full of vegetable trivia, partially to fill "dead air." On one episode viewers learn that the ancient Egyptians thought the onion symbolized the universe. The concentric layers were thought of as heaven, hell, and in-between, and the onion was worshipped for centuries. On another show, it is noted that the word "lentil" is derived from the Latin word for lens, and the optic glass lens comes from "lentil" and not the other way around. Proving she's not a puritanical health nut, Katzen admits she agrees with the botanical name for chocolate, which means "food of the gods."

"Lots of times when I watch other people's shows, even shows that I like, I feel like a little old lady talking back to the TV set, and I'll say, 'Okay, you have dead air right now!' Like they'll say, 'Soften the butter instead of melting it,' and I'll say, 'Why?' People on cooking shows tell you what to do, 'Do it this way and not that way,' but they don't tell you why, and to me, the 'why' is the most interesting part." Fans of her show enjoy her mellowness and low-key sincerity. People looking for flash aren't likely to find it here.

Katzen has been married since 1986 to clinical psychologist Carl Shames. Their daughter Eve was born in 1991. Katzen's son, Samuel, born in 1984, is from her first marriage. Katzen and her family live in northern California, where Mollie likes to hike, read, and do her artwork in her home studio. "I'd be writing and illustrating children's books, or just painting [if not for the cooking career]."

Katzen says that feedback from her Web site indicates that people really go off and cook the food she showcases. "This is really the best thing anyone can tell me. In fact, my tag line at the end of every show is some variation on 'I hope you'll really cook this food.' I don't want to go over their heads. I don't want to impress them. I want to show them that they can do it."

How does she explain the popularity of cooking on television? "If you rub up against something, you feel like you've done it, like reading a book review and thinking you've read the book. The *New York Times Book Review* is the Cliff Notes of the millennium. Time has really collapsed for everybody, and you feel like you've cooked and eaten that food if you've watched it [on TV]."

TV Series

Mollie Katzen's Cooking Show (PBS, 1995–)

Books

The Moosewood Cookbook by Mollie Katzen (Ten Speed Press, 1977, revised 1992)

The Enchanted Broccoli Forest by Mollie Katzen (Ten Speed Press, 1982, revised 1995)

Still Life with Menu Cookbook by Mollie Katzen (Ten Speed Press, 1988)

New Kosher Cuisine for All Seasons by Ivy Feuerstadt, Melinda Strauss, Mollie Katzen (editor) (Ten Speed Press, 1993)

Pretend Soup and Other Real Recipes: A Cookbook for Preschoolers & Up by Mollie Katzen and Ann L. Henderson (Tricycle Press, 1994)

Moosewood Cookbook Classics by Mollie Katzen (Running Press, 1996)

Mollie Katzen's Vegetable Heaven: Over 200 Recipes for Uncommon Soups, Tasty Bites, Side-by-Side Dishes, and Too Many Desserts by Mollie Katzen (Hyperion, 1997)

Food, Sex, & Relationships by Susie Bright, Harriet Lerner, Mollie Katzen (contributor) (Cassette edition: Sounds True, 1997)

Web Site

www.molliekatzen.com

Food Pop Quiz

Remember when you were a kid and you learned that the origin of spaghetti is not really Italian, but Chinese (the noodle was introduced to Italy by Marco Polo on his return from China)? You were never the same, were you? Well, brace yourself:

QUIZ QUESTIONS

1. The croissant is originally from
   (a) France
   (b) Austria
   (c) U.S.A.
   (d) Belgium

2. Where did sauerkraut originate?
   (a) Germany
   (b) Austria
   (c) USA
   (d) China

3. Bananas are classified as a
   (a) fruit
   (b) vegetable
   (c) berry
   (d) herb

4. Peanuts are
   (a) nuts
   (b) legumes
   (c) vegetables
   (d) fruit

5. French fries originated in
   (a) France
   (b) USA
   (c) Belgium
   (d) Haiti

6. Russian dressing is from
   (a) USA
   (b) Canada
   (c) Poland
   (d) Russia

7. Asparagus, garlic, and onions are all
   (a) vegetables
   (b) fruit
   (c) berries
   (d) flowers

8. Which of the following are ingredients found in canned whipped cream?
   (a) hydrogen sulfide
   (b) potassium chloride
   (c) sodium nitrate
   (d) nitrous oxide

9. Chop suey is from
   (a) France
   (b) Italy
   (c) USA
   (d) China

10. The Jerusalem artichoke is
    (a) from Israel
    (b) an artichoke
    (c) Both
    (d) Neither

Quiz Answers

1. (b) The croissant is Austrian and was brought to Paris from Vienna by Marie Antoinette in 1770. The word "croissant" is French for crescent. Austria was at war with Turkey about fourteen years earlier, and the pastry is in the shape of a crescent, a symbol found on the Turkish flag.

2. (d) Yes, the Chinese have been eating sauerkraut for more than 2,000 years. The name sauerkraut is German for "sour cabbage," and when it came to Europe, the Germans adopted it.

3. (c) and (d) Bananas are not technically fruit: botanically the edible part is classified as a berry, while the plant itself is considered an herb.

4. (b) Peanuts are not nuts, they're legumes, which are plants with seed pods.

5. (c) They're called French fries because they are "frenched," which means cut into lengthwise strips.

6. (a) Russian dressing is another American creation. The name is thought to come from the fact that earlier renderings of the dressing contained caviar, which is always associated with Russia.

7. (d) Asparagus, garlic, and onions are all members of the lily family.

8. (d) It's used to expand the cream into a puffy form.

9. (c) Though technically a Chinese-American dish, chop suey is non-existent in mainland China. And no, Swiss steak isn't Swiss—it's American too. And so are English muffins!

10. (d) The Jerusalem artichoke is neither; it's part of the sunflower family and it's American. The name is derived from the Italian word for sunflower, "girasole."

Graham Kerr: Intensive Kerr

Born: January 22, 1934.

Hometown: London, England.

Parents: Father, John D., hotelier; mother, Marjorie (Howard), hotelier.

Siblings: None.

School: Manager-trainee program at the Roebuck Hotel (England).

Always in the Pantry: "Rice wine vinegar, sea salt in crystal form, tomato paste, peppercorns (black and white), de-alcoholized wines for cooking, and Cross and Blackswell branston pickles."

Always in the Fridge: "Yogurt, parmesan cheese in a block, and six very fresh vegetables."

Favorite Food Smell: "When my wife Treena passes the blade of a knife through fresh basil leaves. I can smell it the moment that basil is incised; it breaks its marvelous fragrance out and I begin to salivate at the idea of lunch."

Fantasy Last Meal: "Vine-ripened tomato salad with my wife's vinaigrette, slow-roasted chicken with a curried coconut sauce, and an almond meringue sponge with creme de cacao."

Graham Kerr (rhymes with "rare") grew up in London, where both of his parents were hoteliers. Young Graham ate from an a la carte menu and never had to make his bed. "I had this very strange upbringing. My mother never cooked for me. I don't remember anything my mother cooked." However, the service business got into his blood.

"At ten years of age I was chatting up customers at the bar. I mean, it's illegal! So my dad took me into the kitchen and said, 'Look, the boy's got to play somewhere, and there are no other children around, and chef, do you think you could teach him to cook?' The chef was from Provence and said words to the effect of, 'My father taught me how to cook; it would be a great pleasure for me to teach the little master,' at least I think that's what he called me." The chef stiffened a special orange crate, and Kerr stood on it, just tall enough to reach the kitchen bench. He was given a little paring knife and something to chop. "I played for years, five, six years. I could fillet fish just like anybody could. They'd say, 'Come and look at him, look what he can do now!' Plus, I smelt the smells, heard the language, and saw the theater of it all. At six o'clock the dining room would open and it was always a panic. It's vaudeville."

As he grew up, Kerr's goal was to be the managing director of the Dorchester Hotel in London. He went through the manager-trainee program at the Roebuck Hotel in England, finishing in 1949. He wound up, at the age of twenty-three, as general manager of the Royal Ascot Hotel in England. "I was always a gross early achiever."

From 1952 to 1957 Kerr served as a captain in the British Army, and then was off to Wellington, New Zealand, to be chief catering adviser for the New Zealand Air Force from 1958 to 1963. "It wasn't until we left for New Zealand in 1958 that I actually got to be in a country which didn't have a food style of any kind; there was only one restaurant that had a wine license in the whole country." When the well-trained Kerr arrived, he was suddenly an expert. "I did a radio program and was forced onto television by the Air Force. I was on the first day of television in New Zealand in 1959."

Kerr, who cooked tableside when he was fourteen years old, wasn't nervous on camera. He was an immediate hit. "It got a marvelous write-up, 'best live show to date,' which wasn't surprising because it was on the first day, and there were only fifty television sets in the country." Kerr purposely used terms like "bash" this and "wap" that, because he was talking to people who didn't know anything about food. And he encouraged them to have fun.

Kerr was on radio and TV in Australia when he entered the cookbook world. His 1964 *Graham Kerr Cookbook* won a Gold Medal from the International Culinary Olympics. TV cooking became his career in Australia; then he relocated to Ottawa, Canada, to begin his second TV cooking show.

The *Galloping Gourmet*, which was produced by his wife Treena, whom he married in 1955, ran from 1968 to 1971 in thirty-seven countries. It was actually named for Kerr's habit of searching the globe for rare gourmet recipes, not the way he bounced around the set. The program was a huge success, due largely to the fact that Graham was probably the best-looking chef on the tube. Kay Gardella of the *New York Daily News* swooned over the thirty-five-year-old in 1969, calling him "a combination of Dick Van Dyke and William Buckley, Jr."

Kerr didn't think of himself as a teacher, like confrere Julia Child did, but as a liberator of sorts. He told Gardella, "What I am trying to do is to 'turn on' women who don't like to cook and free them from 'the hamburger syndrome'—not by teaching, but by showing the preparation of a dish entertainingly."

Another difference was that Child's cooking show ran on PBS-TV, which wasn't yet what it is today. Most markets had only three networks and one public television station. "When I went on, I went on between *As the World Turns* and *Secret Storm* at twelve noon on CBS in New York. I mean, how can a guy fail, come on? It'll never be done again, it can't be. It's a completely different world. I used to get a seventeen rating in New York City; that's unheard of." An estimated 200 million viewers tuned in each week.

Though Graham Kerr obviously knew what he was doing in the kitchen, he liked it when he dropped utensils and made messes, because it was more natural that way. He'd flirt with the camera, and the ladies in the studio audience, and nip at the old cooking sherry and anything else in the cabinets. He made risqué jokes about chicken breasts. He once described the trimming of mushroom stems as "a small circumcision." Two decades later in a *People* magazine interview, Kerr described his attitude at that time as "Look at me—aren't I funny, pouring brandy over everything!" Today, he describes it this way. "People love to see indulgence. It's like the old program *Lifestyles of the Rich and Famous.* We love to look in on something that is way over the top. I didn't look deliberately for that. I just looked for the very best there was in the whole world. We'd done a total of twenty-eight trips around the world in that search for great experiences."

Production of the *Galloping Gourmet* came to a sudden halt in 1971 when Kerr and Treena were injured in a serious car accident. The reruns ran until 1974, when Kerr himself wanted them pulled from the airwaves. He thought the episodes inappropriately emphasized conspicuous consumption and off-color humor. The Kerrs would never be the same after the accident. Graham was temporarily paralyzed on his left side and Treena required major surgery, which required partial removal of a lung. Their recuperation process included sailing around the world from 1972 to 1974 on their seventy-one-foot yacht, with their three children, Theresa, Andy, and Kareena. It was on this trek that Kerr made a practical discovery: to take the bite out of seasickness, you should eat simpler, lower-fat foods. Mr. Cream Sauce had seen the "lite," but no one in the family was happy about it at first. Meanwhile, another type of light was heading the Kerrs' way.

The Happy Homewrecker

Portraying a Galloping Gourmet of a different kind, Betty White won two Emmys (1974–75 season and 1975–76 season) for Outstanding Continued Performance by a Supporting Actress in a Comedy Series for her role as Sue Ann Nivens on the TV sitcom *Mary Tyler Moore Show* (1970–77). The character of Sue Ann was first introduced on the 1973 episode "The Lars Affair," in which Phyllis (Cloris Leachman) suspects her husband Lars is having an adulterous relationship with the star of WJM's *Happy Homemaker Show* and enlists Mary's help in saving her marriage. After the success of Sue Ann's appearance she was featured more and more regularly, popping by the newsroom to exchange quips with Murray the newswriter and hit on Lou Grant (Ed Asner), whose one-night-stand with Nivens had him promising to give up drinking forever.

Sue Ann, the man-hungry cooking show host, was narcissistic, sarcastic, self-absorbed, cynical, self-promoting—pretty much everything Mary wasn't. But when the cameras were rolling, the "Happy Homemaker" was as wholesome and cheerful as Katie Couric picking daisies.

Marital and financial troubles had plagued the couple, and Ruthie, their maid, suggested Treena "give her problems to God." Treena did just that, and, soon Graham followed. He described the day that Jesus "welcome(d him) aboard" in the *New York Post* as only a born-again cooking show host could: "He was just like a giant can opener and He rolled back the ceiling."

After a three-year absence, Graham Kerr returned to television in 1975 with *Take Kerr*, a series of five-minute cooking spots. With no more risqué jokes, butter, or tippling, the spots were comprised of healthy, sober cooking tips and each one ended with a Biblical passage, for which Kerr received flak from the producers. Eventually, the Kerrs quit TV, as Graham said in a *People* magazine interview, "because we had to be silent about the thing that was most life-changing about us."

Treena, who hadn't shared Graham's new love of healthy eating, suffered a heart attack in 1986. Kerr became even more married to the healthy food idea and refined his recipes by adding more flavor. He invented the "Minimax" method—*min*imize risk but *max*imize pleasure from ingredients with aroma, color, and texture. However, without a public forum, the Kerrs couldn't affect people's lives the way they desired. Their mission became clear: a new TV show featuring really healthy low-fat low-cholesterol cooking. The Kerrs again returned to television with several different offerings, all listed at the end of this chapter. His newest PBS series, *The Gathering Place*, is a TV talk show about food.

Although some viewers say a sober, health-conscious Kerr isn't as much fun on camera anymore, he still calls himself a sensualist. His goal is to break people out of the reliance on outdated classic ways of cooking and eating, which emphasize huge portions heavy in saturated fat and salt. The key, he says, is not to compare a new, healthier version of a dish to the old one. He points out that though we've developed a taste for fat and salt, they were used as preservatives in an earlier time and aren't really necessary today. "I'm constantly on the lookout for the great foods that have pleased people and those great flavor combinations, and seeing how I can reinterpret those and lose the original names, but pay homage to the root."

In a time when TV cooking shows are more popular than ever, providing a new outlet for fantasy for most people who don't have time to cook or eat well, Kerr's old show *Galloping Gourmet* might make more sense to some than his newer shows. Many people don't want to be constantly reminded how unhealthy everything is, and are tuning into cooking shows to vicariously enjoy cream and butter-filled dishes. Kerr is aware of this. "I did that. I have absolutely no right to sit in some sepulchral setting casting epithets of blame at these [chefs]. They know what sells, and it's not the kind of food that is necessarily ever cooked. The television thing is still fantasy to a great degree. Just to look at something sautéed in half a pound of butter and drowned in cream has a certain vicarious [thrill]. [But I'm not] the food police. It's just that some of the people who have a vested interest in what I would call classic food, have a way of saying with some legitimacy that a light Alfredo sauce doesn't taste as good, and invite comparison. It's nice to hear Beethoven's Fifth [Symphony], but now and again its kind of refreshing to hear someone take a twist on it."

What is TV veteran Kerr's take on the popularity of cooking programs? "There is a brilliant generation of women who, released from the presuppositions about sexuality that have admittedly been grossly unjust for many years, broke out of the norm. What they did in the process of doing that, as a gender, is they dropped the wooden spoon and for a whole generation or two, young people were raised without tuition at the kitchen stove. Because of that there is an element of kindness in the kitchens of today which is missing in real life. Now, the whole thing about today's food [shows] is showing things that just don't happen that often at home. And it's a sort of hankering of, 'Oh, I wish someone would go to that trouble for me, and do something from scratch for me.' We have turned the table into a trampoline and we bounce off it on route to something that we think is more important and we're missing out on a great deal of life. We're getting our fix on television."

TV series

Entertaining with Kerr (New Zealand and Australia, 1959–68)
Galloping Gourmet (syndicated, 1968–71)
Take Kerr (CNN, 1974–75)
Simply Marvelous (PBS, 1988–92)
The Graham Kerr Show (Discovery, 1990–96)
Graham Kerr's Kitchen (PBS, 1992– *)
Best of Kerr (PBS, 1996– *)
Swiftly Seasoned (PBS, 1997– *)

TV special

Julia Child and Graham Kerr: Cooking in Concert (PBS, 1995)

Books

Entertaining with Kerr by Graham Kerr (AH&AW Reed, Wellington, New Zealand, 1963)

The Galloping Gourmet by Graham Kerr (AH&AW Reed, Sydney, Australia, 1965)

The Graham Kerr Cookbook by Graham Kerr (Doubleday & Co., 1970; originally AH&AW Reed, Wellington, New Zealand, and Lion Publishing, London, England, 1964)

The Television Cookbooks by Graham Kerr (Seven Volumes) (Fremantle International, 1970-72)

The Complete Galloping Gourmet Cookbook by Graham Kerr (Grossett and Dunlap, 1973)

The New Seasoning by Graham Kerr (Simon and Schuster, 1975)

The Love Feast by Graham Kerr (Simon and Schuster, 1977)

Step by Step Cookbook by Graham Kerr (David C. Cook, 1981)

Graham Kerr's Smart Cooking by Graham Kerr (Doubleday & Co., 1991)

Graham Kerr's Minimax Cookbook: Illustrated Step-by-Step Techniques Plus 150 All-New Minimax Recipes to Guarantee Minimum Risk and Maximum Flavor by Graham Kerr (Doubleday & Co., 1992)

Graham Kerr's Creative Choices Cookbook (A Minimax Book) by Graham Kerr (Putnam Publishing Group, 1993)

Graham Kerr's Kitchen by Graham Kerr (Putnam Publishing Group, 1994)

Graham Kerr's Best: A Low Fat, Heart Healthy Cookbook by Graham Kerr (Putnam Publishing Group, 1996)

Graham Kerr's Swiftly Seasoned by Graham Kerr (Putnam Publishing Group, 1997)

The Gathering Place: Informal International Menus That Bring Family and Friends Back to the Table by Graham Kerr (Putnam Publishing Group, 1997)

Video/CD-ROM:

Mastercook 4.0 / Swiftly Seasoned by Graham Kerr CD-ROM software edition (Doug Siebert, 1997)

Look & Cook with Graham Kerr: Stocks by Graham Kerr VHS Video edition (Charles H. Kerr Publishing Co., 1995)

Look & Cook with Graham Kerr: Seasoning by Graham Kerr VHS Video edition (Charles H. Kerr Publishing Co., 1995)

Look & Cook with Graham Kerr: Desserts by Graham Kerr VHS Video edition (Charles H. Kerr Publishing Co., 1995)

Look & Cook with Graham Kerr: Protein by Graham Kerr VHS Video edition (Charles H. Kerr Publishing Co., 1995)

www.grahamkerr.com

Emeril Lagasse: He Gives a Bam

Born: October 15, 1956.

Hometown: Fall River, Massachusetts.

Parents: Father, John, retired textile worker; mother, Hilda.

Siblings: Older sister, Delores; younger brother, Mark.

School: Johnson & Wales University (Providence, Rhode Island).

Always in the Emeril Live Pantry: Garlic, Steen's 100% Cane Syrup, Bayou Blast (a.k.a. Essence), Southwest Spice, Rustic Rub, and Vegetable Dust.

Always in the Emeril Live Fridge: The Trinity (Pepper, onions, celery), pork, beer, and frozen Oreo cookies.

Favorite Portuguese Dish: Kale Soup.

Favorite Cooking Sound: "Bam!"

If food were rock and roll, and the Food Network were MTV, Emeril Lagasse would be filling stadiums with wild fans. Maybe you love him, and maybe not, but Lagasse has changed the cult of chef celebrity forever. A chatty, down-to-earth, blue collar gourmet who enjoys a good cigar in his limited spare time, Lagasse is also a world class chef who's got a vibe with women, men, and children. You can't stop him—you can only hope to contain him.

"It's amazing how many people TV touches," Lagasse told *People* magazine in 1996. "I have children cults! I have firemen, thirty at once, watching in firehouses around the country. Now I walk down a street in New York, and a taxi driver will say, 'Hey, Essence!'" which refers to the signature spice mixes that he likes to slam-dunk onto his dishes while yelling his trademark, "Bam!" That's only part of the "Emerilized" vocabulary ("Emerilized" means to add more flavor and spice to something), which includes "Bam!" "Kick it up a notch!" "Notches unknown to mankind!" "Happy happy!" "You wanna talk about good?" and "Pork Fat Rules!"

This "Engagin' Cajun" . . . isn't a native of New Orleans. Emeril Lagasse was born in Fall River, Massachusetts. That's why you hear "ahsk" instead of "ask." His father is French Canadian and his Portuguese mother loved to cook. She ran the house, so Lagasse grew up Portuguese. But you already know about Big John and Hilda if you're an Emeril fan; they've been on his TV show many times.

Lagasse began cooking when he was seven years old, helping his mom make vegetable soup. "I was kind of viewed as a weird kid because I liked food," Lagasse told *People*. "I used to play around with dough." Not many other Fall River kids shared his enthusiasm. Lagasse credits his mother and her Portuguese heritage for his love of food, and his father for his hardworking side. John Lagasse recently retired after thirty-five years of dyeing suits at a textile company. He often worked the second shift, and moonlighted as a cab driver and security guard to provide his family with more than he had while growing up.

The future rock star of the cooking world entertained childhood rock star fantasies. Starting at age eight, Emeril played drums in a local forty-five-member Portuguese band that toured locally on summer weekends. Needless to say, Lagasse was the youngest band member. He taught himself to play the trombone, trumpet, and flute, but his first love was still percussion. He also drummed in a trio that played at local weddings, and in a band called The Crowd. This was the first band to perform ZZ Top songs on the deck of the U.S. battleship *Massachusetts* in 1975, according to the extant band's Internet Web site.

Lagasse has said that music is playing in his head all of the time. However, ultimately, he chose the kitchen fork over the tuning fork. After winning a scholarship to the New England Conservatory of Music in Boston, Lagasse attended for only a few weeks. He transferred to vocational-technical high school to study cooking, and then worked sixty hours a week at a banquet-style restaurant to pay his way through the three-year culinary program at Johnson & Wales University in Providence, Rhode Island. "I was a whiz kid at music," Lagasse told the StarChefs Web site, "and cooking was more of a challenge." Since graduation, Lagasse has gone back to give cooking demonstrations to students, and received an honorary doctorate from his alma mater. He also provides two six-month internships a year to Johnson & Wales students at his New Orleans restaurants.

After finishing culinary school in 1978, Lagasse worked at the Sheraton Hotel in Philadelphia and realized he needed to experience quality time in the cuisine capital of the world, Paris, France. He lived there for three months working as an unpaid apprentice. That accomplished, he returned to the United States and worked at the Berkshire Place Hotel in Manhattan, joining a team headed by Wolfgang Puck. Then it was off to the Parker House in Boston, where he began keeping a wine record book. Once a week he'd buy a bottle for under ten dollars and analyze it. He also went to fine restaurants to study each of them. He knew he'd own one someday, and he was, in effect, continuing his education.

Lagasse moved on to two Dunfey Hotel restaurants, one in Portland, Maine, and one on Cape Cod. It was on Cape Cod where the twenty-six-year-old got the call to take over for Paul Prudhomme at Ella and Dick Brennan's historic Commander's Palace in New Orleans. He was the head chef for seven and a half years. During Lagasse's stint at Commander's, Ella Brennan became a mentor and friend, helping to smooth out his rough edges and calm the somewhat combustible style of management he had acquired from working in kitchens supervised by hot-tempered chefs. Emeril made a name for himself at Commander's Palace, fitting in well with New Orleans' unique food atmosphere and its "live to eat, not eat to live" philosophy. Eventually it was time to branch out on his own.

Emeril's opened in the New Orleans' Warehouse District on March 24, 1990. By then, Lagasse's style of cuisine evolved from traditional Creole and Cajun to what he calls "new New Orleans cooking." The roots are Creole, but he incorporates other styles, including regional American, Asian, and Italian. His cooking style is lighter than the traditional New Orleans fare. In a precursor to his TV career, Lagasse included a chef's food/bar at the establishment, originally conceived as a more comfortable place for people dining alone to watch him in action. In 1993, Lagasse opened NOLA (which stands for New Orleans, Louisiana) in the French Quarter. At present, he owns Emeril's New Orleans Fishhouse, in Las

Vegas' MGM Grand Hotel and he recently took over Delmonico's in New Orleans. Lagasse convinced his parents to move to New Orleans, where they help at the restaurants.

As a rising star in the New Orleans food world, Lagasse appeared on local New Orleans television programs, but never really imagined TV in his future. In 1993, after Lagasse's first cookbook, *Emeril's New New Orleans Cooking,* was published and it was time for promotional events, his publisher suggested he take a media-training course to learn the finer points of appearing on television. Lagasse's TV image continued to be refined, and soon he caught the eye of the Food Network. In 1994, he was asked to host *How to Boil Water,* a show meant for true beginners in the kitchen, which was later taken over by stand-up comedian Sean Donellen. "We sort of made a trade," Lagasse told Phillip Silverstone for the Internet's Restaurant Report Online. "I learned a little bit about the TV world and I hope I gave them something good about the food world." Lagasse became more at ease on camera, and learned to talk to the camera instead of looking down at the food, an occupational hazard of chefs. However, the show wasn't really right for him. "After the first series, [Food Network] said, 'I think we have a little problem here. You are a little over-qualified for the job. Maybe you should consider your own show.'"

And so, later in 1994, *Essence of Emeril* reached the airwaves, and Lagasse's comfort level on camera continued to increase because he was cooking his own recipes. "I started doing TV," he explained in *The Web* magazine, "because I was trying to influence the dinner tables in American households. I felt that I could make a small impact on the yuppies of today, who can't even boil water. They missed something along the way, which is called 'cooking' and 'food.'"

Essence, still in reruns on the Food Network, is relatively tame, and more traditional in format—no live audience, no house band. In its 1996 year-end issue, *Time* magazine named *Essence* one of the top ten Best Television Shows of 1996. Lagasse became weekly Food Correspondent for ABC News' *Good Morning America* in 1997. That same year *Emeril Live* debuted on the Food Network, and Lagasse finished evolving into the creature known only as "Emeril."

Emeril Live is more of a pop culture casserole than a true cooking program. The audience gets warmed up ("Is anyone here from out of town?"), Lagasse runs onto the set and shakes hands like Jay Leno. The music from musicians like C. F. Steaks and Bouillabaisse, Doc Gibbs,

Dr. Strings, or the Jammin' Queen could very well usher out a talk show host. Lagasse has Arsenio Hall's noisily rabid type of audience. He changes into his chef jacket like Mr. Rogers switches into his sweater at the beginning of his TV show. During breaks, at least five assistants run onto the set, moving, arranging, and plating the food as if it's a patient on *ER* while Lagasse throws frozen Oreos and Snickers bars at the audience like a vendor in a baseball stadium. In his first season, he was on a quest to buy the famed Partridge Family's multi-colored bus, something that Rosie O'Donnell would do. He raises his caterpillar-like eyebrows and says, "Hey now!" like Hank Kingsley from *The Larry Sanders Show*. He refers to the other late-night shows as if they are competition; both Lagasse and David Letterman (whose "I've been hyp-mo-tized!" he has borrowed) have had their cooking moms on their respective shows.

Gar-on-teed Gumbo

Although *Emeril Live* owes much to *Yan Can Cook's* live TV shows, Justin Wilson is the actual archetype for Emeril Lagasse. For many people, Wilson's was the first cooking show in which the actual cooking mattered little; he was usually making gumbo in an immense vat in his backyard, anyway. It was the personality of "Joost-ain," whose program *Louisiana Cookin'* can still be seen in reruns on some PBS stations, that lured his fans.

Half Louisiana French, Justin Wilson was born in Amite, Louisiana. The son of the Commissioner of Agriculture of Louisiana, Justin was a safety engineer for more than forty years. He was working as a warehouse examiner along the Bayou LaFourche when his job took him to the heart of Cajun country, in Crowley. He fell in love with the people and the culture, and traveled up and down the bayous for years telling Cajun stories. People liked hearing them, so Justin recorded them. His first album sold more than a million copies.

Wilson released a total of twenty-seven albums of stories, including *Hunting with Justin Wilson* (1972), *Shot Dem Duck and Hunt* (1980), *Justin's Pick: Justin Wilson's Personal Favorite Cajun Stories* (1980), and a disc of Christmas songs with a jazz band. He also composed ten songs, not to mention the background music for his cooking show.

Wilson is a member of the American Society of Safety Engineers, has written five best-selling Cajun cookbooks, two volumes of Cajun stories, served as an instructor on human relations at six police academies, and was a political commentator on radio for eleven years. He also has a Web site at www.justinwilson.com.

And then there was the TV show. Justin created the Cajun classics on air, notably huge barrels of gumbo. He told stories. He cracked up the TV studio staff around him. He wore red suspenders. He said "I gar-on-tee," "on-yon," and "glad for you to see me." And he introduced thousands of home viewers to Cajun culture.

So, what's the difference between Cajun and Creole cuisine, anyway? Cajun cuisine is a combination of French and Southern styles of cooking in a robust, country fashion, using plenty of roux and animal fat (think "country"). Creole cooking combines French, Spanish, and African influences in a more refined style, emphasizing the use of butter and cream (think "city"). Creole is said to rely more on tomatoes (a common Creole dish: Gumbo) where Cajun uses more spices (a common Cajun dish: Jambalaya). Both use what Lagasse and Wilson might call "The Holy Trinity": chopped green pepper, onion, and celery.

Emeril Live...isn't. Because 1997 CableACE award-winning Lagasse is still involved in all aspects of his restaurants every day, he tapes the unscripted *Live* three shows a day, with up to twelve shows in a week. He had a similarly grueling taping schedule for *Essence*. His critics might say that this unbelievable pace explains the repetitive nature of his banter. They may also be wondering where the backlash is; anyone this popular usually gets some, whether deserved or not. So far, it's nowhere in sight. His fans are fanatic. They "bam" when he "bams" and sometimes before. They cheer when he dumps a whole bottle of hot sauce onto something. They howl when he throws thirty-five cloves of garlic into something. They scream when he pours beer into a pot, and then takes a sip for himself. They even laugh when he mangles a joke, and blame themselves if they cook one of his recipes and it doesn't come out right.

How does Lagasse explain his enormous and growing acclaim? "I think it's because I'm a real person," he told *Restaurants USA*. "We're all just trying to put our pants on in the morning. I'm just trying to do it a little better than yesterday. Mine is not like a typical cooking show. I don't throw gorillas across the set, but I think I have a very vibrant, uplifting, passionate cooking show."

No chef has ever attained this level of hysteria before. His Food Network colleague Bobby Flay (*Hot Off the Grill*) was at a recent *Book and the Cook* event in Philadelphia. "I did a demonstration right before him," said Flay, "and it was full, fully sold out, and I walked away and went to do my book signing, and then [Emeril] came on stage, and it felt like the building was going to shake and fall down. I mean, it was just amazing. He doesn't even have to do the demonstration. [His fans] could do it from their seats. They know every line. They know when he's going to say 'Bam,' and they say it with him. He's the franchise of the network."

Many of Lagasse's enthusiasts are men; many are kids who wear makeshift T-shirts and aprons bearing the phrase "Pork Fat Rules!" Many fans are women who say he's a bonafide sex symbol, while others insist that he's the son any mother would love. Lagasse's first marriage, to a schoolteacher named Elizabeth, ended sixteen years ago, and produced two daughters. Jillian has worked as an apprentice at one of her father's restaurants, and Jessica attends Cornell University. Lagasse married again in 1989 to actress and fashion designer Tari Hohn, who did public relations to help launch his restaurants. That relationship ended in 1996.

The real Emeril Lagasse is soft-spoken and sincere, even when chatting directly after his amped-up show. He's serious, quiet, and humble. Says Bobby Flay, "He's nothing like his television persona. It's not even that he's serious. He's very low key. [When] Emeril talks to you, he's, like, whispering in your ear." Flay credits Lagasse's media training with the fervor of his TV alter ego. When he was told to project his voice, "[Emeril] took the note." Michael Lomonaco (*Michael's Place*, Food Network) points out, "Emeril is a musician. He has tremendous instincts for entertainment, people, audience, and timing."

Flay also has something to say to those who think Lagasse isn't for real. A critical article in the *New York Times* called "''ere's Emeril!' Where's the Chef?" accused Lagasse of poor cooking skills, sloppy presentation, disregard of tradition, and having nothing behind his "façade." Flay says, "I hear people say, 'Well I don't really think [Emeril] cooks.' I'll tell you right now, he can cook his ass off. He's a really great chef."

Geoffrey Drummond, producer of *Baking with Julia* (PBS, 1996–), compares him to that famous host: "Julia did the same thing in the 1960s that Emeril is doing now. With Emeril it's 'notched up,' to use his expression. He personalizes his cooking. I think a lot of food people have a difficult time with him, especially ones who know him and say, 'That's not really the Emeril we know, he's kind of quiet, and real serious about his food.' But he's entertaining and personalizing, and what he's doing, which is terrific, is he's bringing lots of people in. He's really entertaining with food as the medium.'"

"I look at cooking the way other people look at theater or music," Lagasse told the Mr. Media Web site. "Food is definitely an art form. I'm just fortunate that now I have an audience of people on the show who don't have to pretend they have smell-o-vision. We're actually feeding these people." Plates with samples do get passed around the studio, adding to the party atmosphere for which the *Emeril Live* crew is aiming. With a visit to his Internet Web site, you can order his four cookbooks, his "Essence" spice mixtures, T-shirts, baseball hats, plates from one of his restaurants, and a Cajun Cooking music CD to complete your "Emerilization" at home.

When asked what he'd like to be remembered for, Lagasse replied, "That I was a sincere and honest guy, and that I didn't bastardize anything in this profession." The "Emeril" persona would probably answer, "That I kicked it up a few notches!"

TV Series

How to Boil Water (Food Network, 1994)
Essence of Emeril (Food Network, 1994– *)
Emeril Live (Food Network, 1997–)

TV Specials

Creole Christmas (Food Network, November and December 1997)
TV Dinners (Food Network, October and November 1998)

Books

Emeril's New New Orleans Cooking by Emeril Lagasse, Jessie Tirsch (contributor), Brian Smale (photographer) (William Morrow & Co., 1993)
Louisiana Real and Rustic by Emeril Lagasse, Marcelle Bienvenu (contributor), Brian Smale (photographer) (William Morrow & Co., 1996)
Emeril's Creole Christmas by Emeril Lagasse, Marcelle Bienvenu (contributor) (William Morrow & Co., 1997)

Emeril's TV Dinners: Kickin' It up a Notch with Recipes from the Food Network's Emeril Live and Essence of Emeril by Emeril Lagasse, Marcelle Bienvenu, Felicia Willett, Brian Smale (photographer) (William Morrow & Co., 1998)

Web Sites

www.emerils.com
www.foodtv.com

Emeril Worship Web Sites

garnet.acns.fsu.edu/~ceb7499/emeril.htm
www.netaxs.com/~jeric/eric/emeril.html
www.net1plus.com/users/keithl/jody/bam.htm
www.via.ayuda.com/~rabbit/emeril/
www.viser.net/~driggs/emeril_s_page.html

Mario Batali: "Cooking is the leisure of the next millenium." Courtesy of Mark Ferri

The Three Dog Bakery: Mark Beckloff, Dan Dye, Sarah, Dottie, and Gracie. Courtesy of Mark Beckloff

Sissy Biggers: "Watching cooking shows is guilt-free television." Courtesy of Edie Baskin

Amy Coleman: "There's so much about home cooking that you can't get from restaurant take out food, no how, no way." Courtesy of Darla Furlani

Annabelle Gurwitch and Paul Gilmartin, hosts of TBS's Dinner and a Movie. *Courtesy of Chris Cuffaro, © 1997 TBS, Inc.*

Claud Mann, the TBS food guy. *Courtesy of Janet Van Hamm, © 1998 TBS, Inc.*

The Too Hot Tamales, Susan Feniger and Mary Sue Milliken: "We always wanted to do a cooking show; we were teaching from the first day we started working together." Courtesy of R. Dickerson

Bobby Flay: "Don't use cookbooks as bibles, use them as guides." *Courtesy of Tom Eckerle*

Mollie Katzen: "It's about loving food, not about thinking other foods are bad." *Courtesy of Terence McCarthy*

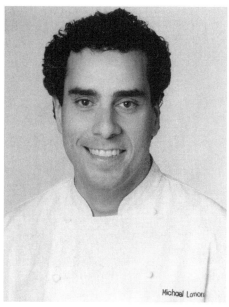

Graham Kerr: *"One of the most important things to a cook is an audience."* Courtesy of West 175 Enterprises, Inc., © 1998

Michael Lomonaco: *"It is a good and nurturing act to cook for someone else."* Courtesy of Lou Mauna, © 1995

Emeril Lagasse: "Mine is not like a typical cooking show." Courtesy of AP Photo/Jim Cooper

Jacques Pépin: "I love to cook and teach. Doing television enables me to inform people." Courtesy of Bill Lyle

Molly O'Neill: "The less people cook, the more they fantasize about cooking." Courtesy of West 175 Enterprises, Inc., © 1998

Martin Yan: "Many people still believe that cooking delicious meals is something for the professional chefs. Not true at all." Courtesy of George Sellano

Ming Tsai: "Don't be scared of a cuisine that you may not be familiar with." Courtesy of Ming Tsai

The Two Fat Ladies, Jennifer Paterson and Clarissa Dickson Wright: "It's a cookery show with anarchy and a motorbike." Courtesy of Jason Bell

Bob Blumer, the Surreal Gourmet: "More of all the tasty things." Courtesy of Patricia Bilawke

Julia Child: "My point is that anyone can do it, and it's worthwhile because it's so good to eat." Courtesy of AP Photo/Douglas C. Pizac

Michael Lomonaco:
Brooklyn Boy Scout Makes Good

Born: January 2, 1955.

Hometown: Brooklyn, New York.

Parents: Father, Frank, a barber; mother, Mary, a homemaker.

Siblings: Older brothers, Salvatore and Anthony.

Schools: Started City University of New York (New York City; Brooklyn College (Brooklyn, New York; later, New York City Technical College's Hotel and Restaurant Management Program.

Favorite Junk Food: "I love pizza, though pizza is not junk food. I like snack cakes. I have a sweet tooth. I like a good Ring Ding every now and then. And a good candy bar, even though I also have a taste for very high-end chocolate. I love potato chips. I know my way around a vending machine, and I'm not afraid of them. Also, a hot dog at the ballpark. Not a street hot dog. I like being in the ballpark and having a hot dog. You gotta have one."

Always in the Pantry: "Pasta and canned Italian plum tomatoes, parsley, garlic, olive oil, and whole grain cereal. I love cereal when I come home from work. I don't eat that much at home."

Always in the Fridge: "Olives, cheeses, anchovies, and orange juice. I drink a lot of orange juice."

Favorite Food Smell: "Onions frying. That's a real sensory thing. Sweet onions caramelizing are beautiful, and they make a house smell great. Even if you can't cook, fry some onions up, and you can convince anyone you're a great chef."

Favorite Food Sound: "The sound of a busy restaurant kitchen is really a turn on to me. Food being ordered, the sound of the communication between the waiters and the kitchen, pickup, order, pickup, that's like symphonic. It means the restaurant is busy and people are enjoying themselves. A noisy kitchen is a cook's link to someone else's pleasure."

Fantasy Last Meal: "I would want it to be with the woman I love, my wife Diane. It wouldn't matter what I was eating. The company is more important to me."

Michael Lomonaco (*Michael's Place*, Food Network) was raised in Brooklyn and grew up "in a house that spent a lot of time eating." Marketing and cooking were a daily part of life in those days. "We ate every meal at home. I did my homework in the kitchen. I grew up in the kitchen. That was the center of life; the daily focus of life was around the kitchen table. I grew up watching my mother cook and being curious about some things, and helping her. I learned how to shell beans, and really learned about food products. I probably learned how to clean squid when I was ten years old." Because his nearest sibling is fourteen years older, Lomonaco was the only child in the house. "So I saw my mother shop and cook and do all those things that later had significance."

Just as significant to his culinary future was scouting. "I was a Boy Scout, so I started cooking when I was ten. You had to cook out on the weekends. So by the time I was eleven, I was learning how to do stuff in Dutch ovens, marketing, bringing food, and making breakfasts from raw ingredients." Each patrol, which was a group of five or six kids, was responsible for its own meals, including bringing, finding, buying, shopping, and cooking and cleaning up. "Some of it was baking burgers in aluminum foil and stuff like that, but at Boy Scout camp you had to cook real food."

Lomonaco was becoming interested in cooking, but not enough to consider it a possible career. "Cooking was something I felt very comfortable with from the time I was a boy, so I really watched Julia Child and the *Galloping Gourmet* religiously as a twelve- , thirteen- , fourteen-year-old." One of Michael's brothers worked in a restaurant during college and brought home an appreciation for dishes like duck á la orange. He had a friend who owned a meat market, so he gradually learned how to cut meat. "Cooking was really growing to be a fascination with me. I was reading cooking and restaurant columns in the newspaper." This would serve him well later, but it wasn't yet time.

As a teenager, Lomonaco had another idea for his future—acting. Starting in junior high, he covered all the bases: high school, community theater, college theater, off-off Broadway, improvisational theater, confrontational theater, bit parts in films (he was an extra in a few Woody Allen movies, including *Broadway Danny Rose*, and was in the cult classic *The Warriors*), touring companies, national tours, bus and truck companies, you name it. Then during college, at Brooklyn College and City University of New York, he was a speech and theater major, and worked as a stage manager, lighting technician, and prop technician. Actor Jimmy Smits is one of his colleagues from his acting days. Lomonaco supplemented his acting/theater studies with standard jobs for aspiring actors: a little bartending and driving a cab. However, he did something a lot of people aren't able to do—earned a living in the theater, for about nine years. Here's an acting tip from an expert: "The whole secret to making a living as an extra is never to really be seen on camera. I did that for about a year and half, where I worked a lot because I was just a body."

Lomonaco's interest in food did not wane during his acting career. When he was twenty he left college to try theater full-time and explore the country by embarking on national tours. He played Caiaphas, bass baritone high priest, in *Jesus Christ Superstar*, and was also in *Hair*. During these treks he spent a lot of time cooking because the troupe stayed in cities for long stretches in hotel efficiency units. "I cooked because it was more economical, and also because I wanted to taste my mother's food. So I re-created things that I remembered my mother cooking. I was becoming a self-taught home cook."

Traveling throughout the United States added to Michael's unofficial culinary education: "The minute I left New York, I wanted to experience the foods of the region, so down south I was looking for the best barbecue, in New Orleans I looked for gumbo, and out west, I was looking for authentic Mexican food. It was the beginning of an awareness of American regional cooking."

He also honed his business skills on the road. "I'd ask a local restaurant to stay open for us. Restaurants close early outside of New York. At ten o'clock they're closed, and our shows wouldn't end till eleven. We'd have no place to eat, so I'd make deals with the restaurants: 'Look, please, stay open—I guarantee you there'll be twenty-five of us at dinner.' I'd ask the bus driver or stage hands, 'Where do you eat? What's the best?' It might be the local donuts, or fried chicken, or regional soda pop. I was developing into a true food maniac, only I didn't know it. I got the bug bad."

Back in New York, Lomonaco's intensive study of the food press paid off in 1982. He was struggling as an actor, driving for a private car service, and one night the job was to pick up the chef at Odeon, who was Patrick Clark. "I knew who the chef at Odeon was because I was reading about him; he was famous, and I wanted that job, and I picked him up. It was late at night, around one in the morning, and I took him home." In that forty-minute ride, the chef and the actor/cabby talked about what Clark did, how he learned, where he went, and Lomonaco told him how much he loved food and cooking, and how he noticed that the restaurant business seemed to be growing. Clark said that if he truly felt that cooking was something he loved, maybe he should pursue it. "He told me about New York City Technical College [and the Hotel and Restaurant Management Department], how it shaped his life and gave him the tools of the career. Sure enough, six months later I enrolled, to follow that advice but also to follow through on something I really felt strongly about." Lomonaco figured he'd learn as much as he could, and see what happened. "If I wound up two years later back in acting, [at least] I would be a much better cook than I'd been before."

Many ex-actors frequently admit the best advice they ever got was this: if you can find anything else you like to do as much as acting, do it. Was this part of Michael Lomonaco's decision? "There's some truth to that. It's a tortuous life, going from job to job, or no job to no job, audition to audition, it's pretty tough. I certainly felt frustrated by the slowness with which an acting career can move, and wanted to take control of my life, and have more input into my own creative life. An actor needs a play, a theater; an actor needs to be engaged, hired by a director or producer. It's difficult to act alone."

Being a chef would also prove to be an outlet for his frustrated creativity. "I certainly felt that there was a creative instinct that I was trying to follow. By being a chef, I'd have a better opportunity to have some control over my output." It was also the early 1980s, and the restaurant culture was about to explode. "It was 1983 when I started in school, and I definitely felt there was something new about American cooking and the restaurant business, and the idea of American chefs having the stage of a restaurant to work in was a very attractive and compelling idea—and it was a new idea. It was really just getting started as a lifestyle, as a career choice for Americans."

The phrase "the stage of a restaurant" is not accidental. "I really felt that I wanted to cook to be able to reach people and give to them and communicate with...the audience, alright, I'll call it the audience. [Being a chef] has its artistic side to it, certain aspects where you can really be creative and you have control over it and you can express yourself. And it has a very practical business-like side to it also, which I excelled at in theater, such as being a stage manager, working in props and electrics, which were practical things that had artistic expression to them. There was overlap for me, and I felt very comfortable learning a new technical craft."

Michael was actually no stranger to the restaurant business. The father of one of his oldest friends from grammar school had been a professional captain (waiter) all his life, in some of the great New York restaurants, such as The Colony and Le Cirque. "I heard Renato telling stories, as a twelve-, thirteen-, fourteen-year-old, about working at Le Cirque, and I heard of Le Cirque opening before anyone had heard of Le Cirque. I had a very direct link to the top end of New York dining from the time I was fourteen years old, really almost all my life. By extended family I knew very intimately what Le Cirque was about, and I wasn't even in it yet."

Lomonaco graduated from the eighteen-month educational program at New York City Technical College in 1984. He worked in restaurants while in school and was employed in a private club after graduation. Then his old family friend Renato introduced him to the chef at Le Cirque, Alain Sailhac. Lomonaco presented the chef with his resume, and three months later, when the chef needed someone, he called Lomonaco. Michael went to Le Cirque as an apprentice cook in 1986. By mid-1987 he followed Sailhac to The "21" Club after remaining at Le Cirque for about eight months with another big New York chef, Daniel Boulud, who went on to open Daniel. Over the course of a year and a half, Lomonaco worked with two talented chefs in one of New York's great dining establishments. This put to rest any remaining doubts he had about his career change.

As a sous-chef at "21" in 1987, Lomonaco "just flew right through that experience." He left "21" in mid-1988 to become executive sous-chef at

Maxwell's Plum, and in 1989 "21" asked him to come back and be the executive chef. Food critics credit him with polishing the menu at the seventy-five-year-old former speakeasy. The James Beard Foundation named him one of "New York's Great Chefs"; *Gourmet* magazine proclaimed that The "21" Club's "now admirable kitchen" was due "in great measure to the talents of Michael Lomonaco"; *Food & Wine* magazine's John Marinani reported that with Lomonaco at the helm, "'21' Club hasn't just regained its luster, it has also become one of this country's great American restaurants."

The Prototype New York "Foodie"

Felix Unger (Tony Randall) of TV's *The Odd Couple* (1970–75) probably ate at every restaurant where Michael Lomonaco has worked. Unger was a New York "foodie," arguably the first recognizable member of that species on television. Besides being an opera, classical music, art, and theater buff, and an award-winning photographer (portraits are his specialty), he was a gourmet chef. We've seen him make all kinds of meals on camera, from birthday cake to fondue, most of which his roommate Oscar Madison (Jack Kleigman) was late for (without calling to apologize). We're talking about a guy who carried vichyssoise in his thermos when he was a soldier in the Korean War.

It was during the Korean War that he met Yamata (Pat Morita), as revealed via flashback in the episode "Partner's Investment." Felix convinces Oscar to co-invest in Yamata's Japanese restaurant, but finds himself in trouble when he ends up doing all of the cooking.

In another episode, "The Moonlighter," the tables turn when Felix finds Oscar moonlighting as a cook in a dingy diner after Oscar backed the wrong horse with money Felix advanced him.

On a Garry Marshall–penned segment called "They Use Horseradish, Don't They," Felix enters a cooking contest, but when his arms suddenly go stiff (one of his many nervous conditions), Oscar helps him prepare his famous roast beef. It's in this episode that Felix utters this battle cry of all gourmets: "In a world of lying, cheating, and stealing, can't we at least be honest in the kitchen?"

Lomonaco stayed at "21" until 1996, when the challenge of the huge Windows on the World restaurant atop the World Trade Center in lower Manhattan beckoned. "I came to Windows for a reason: to try to have some impact on what should really be a major part of the dining scene in New York because it's an icon in the New York skyline." He's still there today, and is credited with revitalizing that menu, too.

Between his stints at Le Cirque, "21," and Windows on the World, you'd be hard pressed to name a famous person that Lomonaco hasn't cooked for, including every U.S. president since Richard Nixon. He was invited in 1994 to cook for the Clinton family with two other chefs, and trained some of the White House staff. However, for Lomonaco, that didn't pack the biggest wallop. "I cooked for [Frank] Sinatra a number of times, and that was a big thrill for me. I'm a Sinatra fan, how could I not be? Italian-American, you know?"

As an actor, Lomonaco never performed on TV. As a chef, it's a different story. He started turning up on local New York television in the early 1990s, beginning with a show titled *Nine Broadcast Plaza* on the former WOR (now UPN), hosted by a not-yet-well-known Matt Lauer. "I did *Nine Broadcast Plaza* so many times that they had to stop inviting me because the union wanted me to have a SAG card, even though I have all those, I still have my SAG and Equity cards." And speaking of *Today* show hosts, Michael was on the first of Katie Couric's broadcasts. He did several appearances on *Late Night with David Letterman*. (New Yorkers know the *Letterman* studio is just blocks away from "21"—Lomonaco was often called to fill in if a guest couldn't make it at the last minute, and he'd run down the street loaded down with foodstuffs.) Michael appeared on the PBS-TV series *Great Chefs of the East* and *In Julia's Kitchen with Master Chefs*.

Enter the Food Network. Lomonaco did the usual TV fare (which served as audition tapes) on *In Food Today, Ready...Set...Cook!,* and *Chef du Jour*. The network talked to him about doing his own show, but it wasn't till he left "21" that it became a reality. He filled in for Sara Moulton on the Food Network's *Cooking Live* for two weeks, and appeared on the Election special in 1996. The concept for *Michael's Place* was developed in late 1996 and it started taping in February 1997.

As Lomonaco's TV show is about cooking at home, he purposely doesn't wear a chef's jacket. "[I want viewers to feel] that they can do this, that they can cook, too. If they do cook, I want them to feel like we've communicated with each other, that I've shared something of my passion and my enthusiasm for food and wine and cooking and dining with them. I want them to feel that cooking is genuinely a really creative release and can be for all of us, that it's not just the high profile chef in the trendy restaurant that can artistically communicate their soul through food, but that is accessible and available to anyone. I would be privileged to inspire people to go into the kitchen and do something where they can learn how to express themselves in much the same way as people who learn how to draw learn how to express themselves. Not everyone is going to be a Matisse, but it's available for everyone to do."

Michael's acting background put him at ease in front of the cameras, even under stressful conditions. "Sometimes we tape four shows a day. It's almost like guerrilla theater. I had a background in street theater, avant garde, off-off Broadway confrontational theater, and it was exciting to do that kind of television." Fans of his show point to his ability to be natural, and not just a persona.

Why does he think people are tuning in? "I believe that cooking is real the way sports are real. The person doing it is cutting, dicing, chopping, slicing, sautéing—they're doing something real. They're not involved with a fourth wall of a drama or comedy. Even if [the viewers] don't know how to cook, they know what they like and if it looks good they relate to it instantly. There's live action, it's real action, it's not staged or phony, [just like] sports are not made up. People love to eat and drink in this country. We're a country of armchair experts and specialists. We like to watch someone do something who may do it better than us, who might have greater skill, and it's fun to watch that. It's also fun to watch cooking because very often a home cook sits there and says 'I can do that. I've done that. I know how to do that,' and feels good about themselves for the very fact that they share something in common with a total stranger. So it's a real connecting thing." Michael is a supporter of such charities as Meals on Wheels, City Harvest, Share Our Strength, and the March of Dimes.

Lomonaco has been married for eighteen years to his wife Diane, whom he's known since high school. His spouse, who works in publishing, also cooks, but *not* if her husband is home. "When I'm home, I really do all the cooking. That's mutually agreed. When I'm home, she's happy to have me cook. I like to cook at home. I know some chefs don't at all, but I like to go to the market. I could spend hours in the supermarket just going up the aisles and looking at everything."

Besides surveying the supermarket aisles, Lomonaco also unwinds through music. "I've been playing the guitar since I was fourteen. I don't have the time to play enough . . . to be good enough, but someday I'll do it." Michael occasionally plays guitar on his show.

But music isn't what fuels Michael Lomonaco. "I became a chef so I could be an insider. I think this is a great business. I was so fascinated by being a diner that I wanted to see the other side. And it's a privilege to be able to cook for people and have them come back. See, they voluntarily come to the restaurant. They choose. It is a good and nurturing act to cook for someone else. That's what we do in restaurants."

TV Series

Michael's Place (Food Network, 1997–)

Book

The "21" Cookbook: Recipes and Lore from New York's Fabled Restaurant by Michael Lomonaco, Christopher Baker (photographer), Donna Forsman (contributor) (Doubleday & Co., 1995)

Web Site

www.foodtv.com

Sara Moulton: Live, from New York

Born: February 19, 1952.

Hometown: New York City, New York.

Parents: Father, Henry, Executive VP of Fiduciary Trust; mother, Elizabeth, writer (novels, poetry, articles).

Siblings: Older sister, Anne; younger brother, Peter.

Schools: University of Michigan (Ann Arbor, Michigan); Culinary Institute of America (Hyde Park, New York).

Favorite Junk Food: "Potato chips, if I had those bad habits."

Always in the Pantry: "Pasta, organic tomatoes, rice, hot sauce, extra virgin olive oil, vinegars, and, I'm ashamed to admit, canned soups."

Always in the Fridge: "Milk, orange juice, carrots, cheddar, mozzarella and Roquefort cheeses, and my once-a-week organic grocery order."

Favorite Food Smell: "Bacon. You get happy. It's like burning leaves. It's fall. You get cozy."

Favorite Food Sound: "The crackling of sautéing or pan frying."

Fantasy Last Meal: "Sautéed fresh foie gras with cherry sauce, confit of duck, some sort of rich mashed potatoes, spring vegetable ragout with favas [beans], asparagus, wild mushrooms, and cherry pie."

Who has the top-rated *live* cooking show on the Food Network? Nope, not Emeril Lagasse. It's Sara Moulton of *Cooking Live*, the cooking/call-in show. *Cooking Live* is about as spontaneous as it gets, complete with unrehearsed callers and a seat-of-our-pants atmosphere. Moulton's show is happening as you watch it, and she handles everything with an alertness you might not expect from someone with three jobs plus a family.

Although native New Yorker Sara Moulton attended high school, cooking was one of her hobbies: "My mom and I would make these fancy dinner parties. I also used to play around with leftovers and create my own concoctions. My grandmother was a fabulous 'Ye Olde New England' cook, who went to the Fanny Farmer school [in Boston], so she would teach me how to make roast beef and Yorkshire pudding and bread pies."

Moulton never thought cuisine would be her career, even though she always cooked as a hobby. After graduating with a B.A. from the University of Michigan in 1975, she cooked in a bar in Ann Arbor, waiting for career inspiration. Her mother wrote letters to food writers Craig Claiborne and Julia Child to learn about a career in cooking for her daughter. Sara would meet Child later in life, but it was Claiborne who wrote back with advice on cooking schools.

So, cooking school it was, but it was actually a tough decision. Moulton was living with her future husband and didn't want to leave him. Still, upon Claiborne's encouragement, she went off to The Culinary Institute of America (CIA) in Hyde Park, New York, and realized food was destined to be in her life.

"I'm completely driven by my love of food. I love to eat." This love, combined with talent, led Moulton to graduate second in a class of 450 and with high honors from the CIA in 1977. After receiving a scholarship from Les Dames d'Escoffier, she moved to France for a few years to immerse herself in classic technique. Back in the United States, Moulton was a working chef, first as a chef/manager of a catering house in Cambridge, Massachusetts, then as a chef at Cybele's, a Boston restaurant. Then she moved back to New York, where she was sous-chef at Cafe New Amsterdam, and then chef at La Tulipe.

Sara honed her teaching skills as an instructor at Peter Kump's New York Cooking School between 1983 and 1985. In 1984, she became one of *Gourmet* magazine's staff of food editors, and four years later became *Gourmet*'s executive chef, a full-time position she still holds today. It was also in 1984 that she began as an off-camera chef for food demonstrations on ABC-TV's *Good Morning America*, something she still does today. In 1997, Moulton joined the on-air *GMA* family as Food Correspondent.

It wasn't always smooth sailing for Sara. There were those critics who tried to make her believe she was in the wrong profession. "I always feel like I have something to prove, but I think in some ways it helps me. I'm short, blond, and female. The blond thing especially makes people take you less seriously."

Sexist doctrine may dictate that a woman's place is in the kitchen, but that's the home kitchen, not the professional one. Men told her "Women do not belong in kitchens. You can't lift the pots."

"The pot-lifting issue is absurd. Use your brain, guys, all you need is a pivot. Get a buddy, pivot a stock pot into another stock pot together, or get a guy to do it for you for ten seconds. This is hardly a reason to quit the business!"

Moulton's cooking school class had a six-to-one ratio of men to women, and she did experience sexism at first. "After a while they were coming to me for the answers because I was a good student. I went to school [CIA] with all these kids who were just trying to have a good time, and I was very intense, and a lot of the female students were doing better than the males because [the women] were just better students."

Her experiences with sexism in the culinary world led Moulton to co-found in 1982 what she calls an "all-gals network," the New York Women's Culinary Alliance, designed to help women in the food industry. The atmosphere is improving in the culinary world, but there are throwbacks. For example, Moulton had a male guest chef on *Cooking Live* who seemed genuinely surprised that she was handling her own sautéing duties.

Moulton keeps her cool no matter how much the chauvinist attitude frustrates her. She remembers the advice her husband once gave her: "Don't go out singing your own praises. Just keep doing a great job, and those people you care about will notice. Those who don't, well, screw them."

Moulton dipped into the oncamera television pool by appearing on *Good Morning Boston* in 1979 to demonstrate Cybele's Cornish Game Hen. However, her real entrance into TV came earlier that year in Massachusetts when she became a behind-the-scenes associate chef of Julia Child during the production of the WGBH-TV program that became *Julia Child and More Company*.

At the time, Sara was chef/manager of a catering operation in Boston and was a fan of Julia's cookbooks. One of her employees was volunteering on Julia's TV program. "I said 'Wow! I love Julia, do you think they'd let me volunteer?'" Turns out that after hearing about Moulton, Child wanted to hire her. "I called [Child] from the corner drugstore because I didn't want to jeopardize my job, since I didn't know where this was going. Julia got right on the phone and said," and here Moulton does her impression of Child, "'Oh yes, dear, I've heard all about you. Can you style food?'"

Moulton said yes, though she didn't really have the kind of experience to which Child was referring. Every chef styles food every time they place it on the plate, but Child was talking about serious food styling for camera purposes. Moulton was needed to fill in for Child's regular food stylist for the first month of tapings. This all happened at the same time that Moulton was transferred to be the chef at Cybele's. So, for these months, she was working seven days a week—two with Julia and five at the restaurant. However, it was worth it to work with Julia Child and Moulton later became executive chef of Child's segments on ABC-TV's *Good Morning America.*

"Julia is one of the nicest people ever to walk this earth, and one of the funniest. She says what's on her mind. She has no problem being honest. She's extremely self-effacing; she's not interested in talking about herself or her accomplishments. She's very interested in people, and not just people in the food business. She's a very nurturing, caring, loving woman."

Sara's own show, *Cooking Live,* came about after she appeared on Food Network's *Chef du Jour.* She was a hit, and asked to fill in on a TV show then hosted by Michele Urvater. It was called *How to Feed Your Family for $99 a Week.* Sara substituted for five episodes. The first four were taped, and the last one was a live call-in format. "I liked that the best because I love talking to people." It proved to be so popular that the Food Network added Moulton to their schedule about two months later with a weekly live call-in show in the evening.

In April 1996, *Cooking Live* began on the air, but it was not without its kinks. "In the beginning, I'd be cooking hamburgers and someone would call in about cheesecake. But since then we've honed that. We got smart about that real fast. Now we only take questions about what we're doing, for the most part."

Silence of the Lamb Chops

If you were born in the 1960s or later, or have children who were, you've been to *Mister Rogers' Neighborhood*. And you know probably the most famous TV cook for kids, Chef Brockett, who could usually be found in the back of his bakery, making vegetables into dinosaurs and a lake out of Jell-O.

The raspy-voiced Don Brockett, who died May 2, 1995, at the age of sixty-five, was also a film actor. Highlights of his film career include sharing Hannibal Lecter's cellblock as a deranged prisoner in *The Silence of the Lambs* (1991), playing a construction boss in *Flashdance* (1983), and portraying the good-ol'-boy police chief in the Chevy Chase vehicle *Fletch Lives* (1989). He was also a police chief—"Buzz Saw" Ryan, to be exact—in a 1991 flick called *Bloodsucking Pharaohs in Pittsburgh*.

Brockett, one of the only independent producers of theater in Pittsburgh, was also the director of *Forbidden Pittsburgh*, a series of annual year-in-review spoofs of that Pennsylvania city where *Mister Rogers' Neighborhood* is produced. He began playing Chef Brockett when *Neighborhood* started airing nationally in 1968, and continued in the role until March of 1995.

Also, the man who showed Presbyterian minister Fred Rogers and millions of children how to make tapioca pudding was Anthony Hopkins' prison mate in *The Silence of the Lambs* (1991). Wonder if he helped Hannibal Lecter whip anything up....

The show does have screeners, but it doesn't have a delay, which means someone can call up and tell the screener he's going to ask about lamb chops, but once he's on the air, he's free to bust Moulton's chops and all they can do is cut him off. As any Howard Stern fan knows, there are those who enjoy taking advantage of these on-the-air situations, and Moulton says that her prank callers always seem to be male.

"Very early on, like my second week," recalls Moulton, "I was cooking eggplant rollatini, and this guy called in and said 'how do you make eggplant a la penis?' I just said I'd never heard of that region of Italy before, and we got rid of him." Moulton also gets her share of well-meaning, but just plain foolish questions. Her favorite was when a woman wanted to know how to transport her Jell-O mold from New York to Chicago. "I said, 'Just make it when you get to Chicago!' When they're dirty phone calls, I don't get flustered. I just say, 'Gee, some people just have too much time on their hands.' They'd love it if they thought they were getting to me. These dirty phone calls are on the caliber of, 'Is your refrigerator running?'"

Distractions aside, Moulton is very clear on her TV show's mission. "I want to get us all back to the table and eating together. I want people to consider the community of cooking and dining. I like to do dishes that are technically ridiculously simple, but by the time you get them on the table, look complicated. Kids are watching, and that to me is extremely hopeful. I want to empower more people to cook."

The live aspect of her show is all part of the empowerment. If something goes wrong, Moulton can't stop the tape. So, have there been any disasters? "Nightly! Are you kidding? Nightly! And I don't cover. One time I was making pancakes. The stovetop on the set has a mind of its own, and I knew the burner was too hot. So I said, 'I'm not sure I should flip these because I know they'll burn,' and I flipped them anyway. Or another time, the blender wouldn't go on, so I said, 'Lets pretend it's blending [and made a sound effect like] blend blend blend.'" She learned this from the master, Julia Child. "The whole purpose of this show is to say, if I make a lot of mistakes, it's okay. I show [viewers] how to fix the mistakes, and they feel better, particularly if I'm doing it on national TV. And that's something that Julia used to do all the time."

Are cooking shows more popular these days? "I think we lost a couple of generations in terms of cooking. I think part of it is Americans' need for an outlet. And there are people like me who have too many jobs and a family and no down time [for whom] this is a fun hobby. You just click on the TV and whether you cook or you don't cook, it's pretty entertaining. It's a hobby for those people who are overworked."

If cooking shows can be put on a spectrum from informative to entertaining, she'd put hers well on the informative end. "I don't think my show is entertainment. I mean, I hope people are enjoying themselves, but my show is completely informational and technique-driven. But some of the shows are meant to be entertainment—that's the point of *Emeril Live*. For a while there, the network said 'It's all got to be entertainment,' and then the *[Two] Fat Ladies* came on board, and I thought, 'Oh God, I'm going to be kicked right out of there' because that's not me." There's definitely room for Moulton and her popular show on a network devoted to food.

Judging from the diversity of those who call in, she has all kinds of fans. These enthusiasts include youngsters, who are especially likely to call in when Moulton has her own children, Ruthie and Sammy, on the program. To make sure she and her husband, Bill Adler, spend quality time together, they started having Thursday night dates. "One week it's my job to plan it, and of course, we just go out to dinner. The next week it's his turn and we always go to a movie or something cultural." Adler, who represented rap artists for years, has his own record label, called Mouth Almighty, which specializes in spoken-word recordings. They put music behind the poems of Alan Ginsburg, William Burroughs, even Edgar Allan Poe, as well as those who are lesser known.

With three food jobs, Moulton's hobby is . . . cooking? "When we go on vacation I purposely take along a couple of cookbooks that I've been dying to try out. I enjoy just reading cookbooks." It's a good thing, too, because when you're hosting a live cooking show, you have to be ready for anything.

TV Series

Cooking Live (Food Network, 1996–)

Web Site

www.foodtv.com

Molly O'Neill: Fare Commentary

Born: October 9, 1952.

Hometown: Columbus, Ohio.

Parents: Father, Charles, excavating contractor with own business (O'Neill Excavating's slogan is: "We Dig Columbus"); mother, Virginia.

Siblings: Five younger brothers, Mike, Pat, Kevin, Robert, and Paul.

School: Denison University (Granville, Ohio).

Always in the Pantry: "Everything. If we couldn't leave the building tomorrow, I could probably cook for a year. I've got a real bomb shelter mentality, so there's tons of staples and specialty products and spices and herbs."

Always in the Fridge: "There's condiments on the door, always milk and seltzer and a cheese or two, salad stuff, and whatever we're going to cook that day, or the leftovers from the day before. But I don't fill up the refrigerator; live food, I don't hoard."

Favorite Food Smell: "I don't have a favorite. I like to smell things cooking. I like smelling chicken soup as much as I like smelling apple pie or roasting garlic. But I love to smell things and I love it when the house smells like something's cooking. It says that something is alive."

Fantasy Last Meal: "I don't know what I want it to be because I don't know what the weather will be the day that I die. I don't know what I'll want to taste, but I would just want something that was really good and simple that was prepared with care by someone who really loved me."

Molly O'Neill, *New York Times* food columnist and host of PBS-TV's *Great Food*, grew up in Columbus, Ohio, where her mother cooked three meals a day and the family ate out once a week. A typical childhood meal was roast beef or roast chicken, lima beans, corn on the cob, potatoes, and milk. "I started helping my mother in the kitchen when I was really little, but it didn't become a big deal until I was probably in early adolescence, when I started really cooking things. I did it because I had five younger brothers and they really liked my cooking and I like to please people. I'm not sure it was as much about cooking as it was about pleasing." Her first culinary venture, fried chicken, was very popular with her brothers, one of whom is New York Yankees right fielder Paul O'Neill.

O'Neill studied painting and writing at Denison University in Granville, Ohio, and graduated in 1975. She went on to the University of Vienna in Austria to study Jungian psychiatry and literature. "I read Jung and the existential philosophers for a year, and then decided against becoming a psychiatrist in favor of writing." O'Neill taught writing and women's studies at Hampshire College in Amherst, Massachusetts, for two years. During that time she was very active in the women's movement and, along with eight other women, opened a women's food co-op and a health food restaurant in Northampton, Massachusetts. "I could see that I wasn't really cut out for academia. Working in a college setting made me realize that I would never write and I would never paint if I continued that. But I could cook for a twelve-hour day and then go home and still write a poem, and that was really cool. So I decided to get serious about cooking." O'Neill would perfect her craft spending the winters in France and Italy. She studied at La Varenne in Paris and did about six apprenticeships in different restaurants throughout Italy and France.

Molly continued to work as a chef until she was twenty-seven. "At that point I realized that if I didn't stop doing what I was doing, I

would be doing it when I was fifty—I'd be doing it for my whole professional life. I was no longer writing, I was no longer painting, and the
reason that I'd started to [cook professionally] was no longer valid. I had
a feeling that I was sautéing my brains out and that I was starting to hide
out in the profession."

O'Neill had never thought about food writing until 1980, when she
was asked by playwright Lillian Hellman to help with her culinary
memoir. "At the same time, the *Boston Globe*—I was living in Boston at
the time—asked me if I'd ever thought about food writing and I hadn't,
but at that point it sounded interesting. I wrote one story for them and
got a job at *Boston* magazine, where I worked with [Don Forest], the best
editor of my life. I became their food columnist as well as their wine
columnist, but he also made me report straight news every issue, so I got
an incredible kind of training from him."

When that editor became part of the start-up team for *New York Newsday* in 1985, O'Neill went to Manhattan to be their restaurant critic and
write features. After about four years, she moved over to the *New York
Times*, where she remains today, writing for both the newspaper and her
weekly column for the *Sunday Magazine* section. She has also been a
columnist at *Food and Wine* magazine, and has contributed to all of the
major food magazines. She has been nominated for the Pulitzer Prize
twice. Her first cookbook, *The New York Cookbook* (1992), took her five
years to complete. "For me it was finishing my Ph.D. in food, because it
was so heavily, heavily researched—such a big work." This book won
both the Julia Child/IACP and James Beard Awards, and was made into
a ninety-minute PBS special, *Molly O'Neill's New York—A Taste of the City*
(PBS, 1998).

O'Neill lives in a loft in the Hell's Kitchen section of midtown Manhattan with her second husband, Arthur Samuelson. He is a book publisher at Random House to whom she's been wed since 1992 (her first
marriage, lasting ten years, ended in 1987). Also living with her is her
seven-and-a-half-year-old stepdaughter Ariana, and three champion
bearded collies: "Herschel is nine, Betty Lou, his wife, is seven, and their
daughter, Field of Dreams, called Phoebe, is three." O'Neill is an avid baseball fan, often grabbing a hot dog at Yankee Stadium while watching her
brother Paul play. She also writes fiction, paints, hikes, and does a great
deal of traveling.

Molly's first forays into television weren't always fulfilling. "I'd
done a lot of TV promoting books and I had not enjoyed it. I didn't have

very much respect for the medium. When you're promoting something they put you in this fake kitchen, and you pretend like you're making something, and you try to be clever and make people want to buy your book. I'm not the kind of person who learns by watching something on TV. I'm really bull-headed and I learn by doing, so watching a talking head on television doesn't teach me how to cook. In fact, I don't even get ideas from that. My interest in food is basically an interest in American culture." However, she did want to find a way to use television to that end. "The medium is a really powerful one and [I wanted] to be able to reach the American audience using food as a metaphor for our life and our times. But I couldn't do that standing in a kitchen chopping things. It just was not going to work."

Culture Vultures

Food can teach us a lot about other cultures, so the combination of food and travel is a natural one, and usually the domain of journalists. The king of the food travelogue is Burt Wolf.

Burt Wolf doesn't cook on television, though he's often seen in international kitchens. He reports on the history, folklore, food, and attractions of destinations around the globe. Born in Manhattan in the 1940s and reared in the Bronx, Wolf has redefined "gallivant"; he's been everywhere from Patagonia, to Singapore, to the Yukon, to Las Vegas. Wolf has hosted five internationally syndicated television series dealing with food, travel, and cultural history, including *Origins*, his most recent PBS network offering. He also reports on food, travel, and business for CNN cable and is a mainstay on the Travel Channel. In addition, he's got a Web site: www.burtwolf.com.

The endurance and evolution of foods can also educate about a specific culture, which is the domain of journalist Joan Nathan, host of PBS' *Jewish Cooking in America* (she also wrote the book of the same name). She takes her TV viewers on a tour of Jewish cuisine and culture by crisscrossing the country and visiting Jewish cooks, such as Cuban Jews in Miami, originally from Poland, who bake mandelbrot with guava.

Along came *Great Food* in 1998, a TV show put together by the BBC and PBS via West 175 Enterprises featuring the following BBC chefs: Madhur Jaffrey, an international authority on Indian cooking; Ken Hom, master of Asian wok cookery; Delia Smith, the best known cooking expert in the United Kingdom; Gary Rhodes, a punk-coiffed British chef; Antonio Carluccio, presenting Italian feasts; and Nick Nairn, a self-taught, down-to-earth chef from Scotland.

"I really loved the group of people," says O'Neill. "They're visionary and they're risk-takers and they like to have fun. They're not food precious, but they're food smart. It was just a really good fit." In addition to hosting another season of *Great Food*, O'Neill will also work with West 175 Enterprises on a forthcoming show called *Masterchef*, in which she searches for the best amateur cook in America. "It's really fun and it's really ambitious and it's about real people. It's not about chefs, it's not about status, it's about an affair of the heart, really, and that's what interests me."

Although it doesn't work for her, a lone figure cooking in a studio kitchen talking to the camera is still commonplace on television. Why is it so popular? "My sense of it is that the phenomenon is very similar to one in print. The less people cook, the more they fantasize about cooking. I think that my readers of the *Times* magazine clip those columns loyally and they pledge to themselves, 'One day I'm going to make this.' And they put it away and they never do. Cooking is about good intention, and it almost doesn't matter whether it's realized or not. I think most of the time it's not realized. It's voyeurism. It allows us to look at a way of life that we fantasize about but who has the time to do it. There's something very consoling about the notion that somewhere, somebody is cooking dinner."

Is the current popularity of food an indication of a revolution? Not exactly. "There's been a consciousness-raising about food, but our country was built on the notion of revolution. It was built on the notion of the perfectabiliy of humans, and anyone who's grown up in this culture always needs to believe they're getting better and better every day. And what's the cultural expression of that? Revolution. Food's just a part of it, and it always has been.

"I think there's a whole food 'machine' that would have us believe that America has suddenly awakened, but there's always been fine food in America among the elite, and there's still fine food in America, among the elite. Fine food has always been co-opted by the mass market and moved downscale, and the same thing's happening. It's just that it's happening within generations. My generation, the baby boom generation, exists in such large numbers with so much more disposable income than has ever occurred before in the history of the country, and food is one way we do it. That's a jaded, non-romantic way of looking at food and the whole explosion. I think there's some wonderful, delightful, dear parts of all of this, but I don't think that it has to do with some sort of enlightenment. It has more to do with good will and desire and an underlying panic that we're losing private life, and cooking is the heart of private life. So, what do you do when you feel like your life has become completely public and run by a calendar and a clock? You have that sort of paroxysm of grabbing for something that can make you believe that there's such a thing as a private life. There you have cooking."

Molly feels one thing definitely has changed about the world of food and cooking. "I hear from as many men as women, in reader and viewer mail. It's not a woman's world any more. In the chefly realm, it has never been a woman's world, but in the quotidian of it all, it's always been a woman's world, and so there's been some kind of shift there. I would suspect, jadedly, that it's because everybody's working so hard, and so many women are working outside the home. Maybe it bespeaks some sort of change in the marriage contract, as we move from coupling to partnership as a social institution.

"It could also just be looking for a common denominator. Our lives have become so shattered that common denominators have become exaggerated in their importance. I'm not scorning it, I make a living this way, but once in a while I think we need to look a little bit beneath the surface and try to put ourselves in a larger context than believing, 'Oh my goodness, we invented great food in America.' Baloney. Or [believing that] this has changed things forever. Hey, wait till we have a depression, or a war, or suddenly the economy realizes that it can't bear this number of women in the workforce. Anything like that that happens, anything that changes our economic or social institutions, will immediately be reflected in what we eat and how we view it. And that's what I love. When I talk about writing about food as a cultural thing, or getting out there on TV, talking to people about culture through food, that's the kind of thing that I'm talking about."

TV Series

Great Food (PBS, 1998–)

Books

New York Cookbook by Molly O'Neill (Workman Publishing Co., 1992)

A Well-Seasoned Appetite: Recipes for Eating with the Seasons, the Senses, and the Soul by Molly O'Neill (Viking Books, 1995, reprint, Penguin USA, 1997)

The Pleasure of Your Company: How to Give a Dinner Party Without Losing Your Mind by Molly O'Neill (Viking Books, 1997)

Great Food (companion cookbook), introduced by Molly O'Neill (West 175 Enterprises, 1998)

Web Site

www.greatfoodtv.com

Jennifer Paterson and Clarissa Dickson Wright (Two Fat Ladies): Women Behaving Badly

Jennifer Paterson

Born: April 3, 1928.

Hometown: London, England.

Parents: Father, Robert, army major; mother, Josephine, home-maker.

Siblings: Older brothers, Charles and James.

Always in the Pantry: "Olive oil, anchovies, salt, pepper, and saffron."

Always in the Fridge: "Butter, milk, salad, water, and white wine (for guests)."

Favorite Food Smell: "Roasted coffee."

Fantasy Last Meal: "Caviar, a fine dressed crab, grouse, and lots of bread sauce."

Clarissa Dickson Wright

Born: June 24, 1947.

Hometown: London, England.

Parents: Father, Arthur, surgeon; mother, Molly (Bath), Australian heiress.

Siblings: Older brother, Anthony; older sisters, Heather and June."

Junk Food: "I don't believe in guilt and I don't eat junk food."

Always in the Pantry: "Piri piri sauce, garlic, packets of noodles, Worcestershire sauce, and anchovies."

Always in the Fridge: "Butter, milk, smoked salmon, filet steak, and goose fat."

Favorite Food Smell: "Ginger."

Fantasy Last Meal: "Lobster, Won Ton soup, and Beef on the Bone."

If Judith Stone of *Mirabella* magazine told you to "emulate the stars of what may be the best show on television," would you roll your eyes and reluctantly picture Jennifer Aniston and Courteney Cox of the TV series *Friends*?

Well, try again. Stone was refering to Jennifer Paterson and Clarissa Dickson Wright, the British hosts of the BBC network's *Two Fat Ladies*, which airs on the Food Network. These are the Shakespeare-quoting poster children for the health food backlash who have the nerve in this squeamish age of political correctness and health scares to use the unholy trinity of bacon, cream, and butter (according to Dickson Wright, more vegetarians relapse on bacon than on any other substance). *Rolling Stone* magazine called them hedonists; when was the last time you heard that word in the 1990s? This is the country that created fat-free fat. "'Add more cream' is my adage!" says Paterson.

"If anyone had said, 'You're going to be a media star late in your life,' I'd have said 'yes dear, put more water with it,'" claimed the forthright Clarissa Dickson Wright in the *Washington Post*.

Always the self-sufficient free spirit, she once put a mugger in intensive care, and knocked out an Alsatian dog with a right hook. Paterson smokes on camera, wears black-rimmed glasses and rolls her phlegmy "r's" in the ultra-plummy English style.

~~~

Jennifer Paterson, born into an army family, was conceived in China, and born in London; then her family returned to China from the time she was three months old until she was four years old. When they returned to England. In China she used to "bother the cook and make disgusting little cakes." She also lived in Portugal, Italy, and Libya, gathering recipes at each locale.

Paterson never really liked her mother, whom she felt favored her brothers. However, she was quite fond of her dad. Always rebellious, she attended English convent schools until she was expelled at age fifteen. "They said if I left, the school might settle down," she told *People* magazine. She was a beautiful young woman who did a lot of traveling, and met her "first great love" in Germany. "He died last year but we always remained friends," she informed London's *Weekend* magazine, "and his seven children all dote on me, but I don't think his wife does."

Fans of *Two Fat Ladies* know Jennifer loves to sing. When she was younger she longed to go onstage but her mother forbade it. Over the years, Paterson held many jobs, but was typically fired for insubordination. When she was a school matron, for example, she gave girls gin for their menstrual pains.

"I've no qualifications," Paterson admitted to *People* magazine. "I get jobs by mistake." She was editor for a mystery magazine, assistant to a hermaphrodite sculptor, a regular on TV's *Candid Camera* in the early 1960s, and boardroom cook at *The Spectator* magazine for eleven years. There she cooked for Prince Charles, but was eventually told to leave when she lost her temper and threw lots of crockery out the window. Instead she became a columnist for the magazine, a job she still holds.

Top chefs devour Jennifer's regular columns in *The Spectator* and *The Oldies*, because in the stiff culinary world, she's a breath of fresh air. She's also enlivened the radio world, on BBC Radio 4's *Questions of Taste*, and BBC2's *Food and Drink*.

Paterson lives in a London flat with her deaf uncle, who's in his eighties and looks after the poor. If you visit that city, you might see her zooming around on her Honda 90cc scooter. She's been riding motorcycles since 1965. For *Two Fat Ladies*, however, she travels in a Triumph Thunderbird 900cc with a Watsonian scooter for her cohost, ex-barrister Clarissa Dickson Wright.

~~~

Clarissa Dickson Wright was born into considerable poshness. Her father, Arthur Dickson Wright, was surgeon to the Queen Mother when she was Queen, and a gourmand from whom she picked up much kitchen knowledge. Clarissa's mother, Molly Bath, was an Australian heiress. The household had six servants, a regular caviar stock, and pigeons brought in from Cairo to supplement the range of foodstuffs.

Dickson Wright chose the life of a barrister, and became a trial lawyer at the age of twenty-one. Why? "I hated my father, and he hated lawyers," she informed *People* magazine. (One episode of TV's *Ladies* has the duo picking mushrooms and Clarissa quipping that she used to look for the poison ones for her father.) She was very fond of her mother, but cites her parents' marriage and her brilliant, violent, alcoholic father's abandoning of the family in 1968 as the reason she's never married herself. "If the happiest moment of your life is when your father leaves your mother," she said in *Weekend* magazine, "it rather puts you off marriage." She doesn't regret not having children, either; it was a decision she made when she was ten and a half. "I just thought that as far as my family were concerned, we had come to the end of our genetic usefulness," she told London's *Spectrum* in 1997.

After her father left, the family had a brief financial crisis so Clarissa Dickson Wright took over some of the cooking. The witty, attractive Clarissa continued to live at home, and one day in 1975 when she came home to find her mother dead. She went to her then-boyfriend's flat and he offered tea, but she wanted a drink. That was the beginning of twelve years of alcoholism, something she has been quite open about in interviews with such publications as *People* and *London Weekend*, in the hope of helping others.

At the peak of her drinking, Clarissa was reportedly up to two bottles of gin, not to mention 100 cigarettes, a day. She carried forty-ounce bottles of gin in her handbag. She was also squandering a lot of her considerable inherited fortune, soon spending a million pounds. Although the drinking did not cause her career to suffer, after a while she didn't feel the urge to practice law anymore. She sailed around the world, dabbled in pheasant farming and catering, then took over a drinking establishment in London, called Wildes after Oscar Wilde, and turned it into a luncheon club.

Around the time the lease on her club expired, she had been living with Clive, a man she loved, for about six years. He died the day the Falkland War was declared in 1982. These events sent her into an emotional tailspin that lasted another year and a half; by the time she emerged from her funk, the war was over.

By this time, Clarissa had lost everything, except a few books, the clothes on her back, and her knives. She had been cooking in other people's homes to keep a roof over her head. She started to cook privately for a London tycoon, a job she lost in 1987. She checked into an alcoholism recovery and detox program when she was forty and she's been sober ever since.

Fat Ladies-Speak

Oscar Wilde once said, "The English have really everything in common with the Americans except of course for language." The following is a glossary of food terms, British-to-American. Refer to this list next time you watch *Two Fat Ladies*.

aubergine = eggplant
bangers = sausage
bap = hamburger bun
biscuit (sweet) = cookie
biscuit (unsweetened) = cracker
black treacle = molasses
bridge roll = hotdog bun
broad bean = lima bean
butter muslin = cheesecloth
candy floss = cotton candy
chicory = endive
chips = French fries
corn flour = corn starch
courgettes = zucchini
cream cracker = soda cracker
crisps = potato chips
desiccated (as in coconut) = shredded
endive = chicory
essence = extract
fish slice = spatula
icing sugar = confectioners or powdered sugar
joint (meat) = roast
kipper = smoked herring
liver sausage = liverwurst
mince = hamburger meat
poor knights of Windsor = French toast

lolly (iced) = popsicle
pudding = dessert
rasher (bacon) = slice
semolina = cream of wheat
spring onion = scallion
stone (fruit) = pit
sultana = raisin
swede = rutabaga (turnip)
Swiss roll = jelly roll

Dickson Wright feels very lucky that the alcohol didn't do permanent damage to her physically or mentally, but ironically, the tonic water that she drank with the gin, did. The quinine in the tonic water damaged her adrenal glands and permanently slowed her metabolism. That's the reason she's overweight today, and the reason she doesn't bother dieting.

Dickson Wright soon became known in London for running Notting Hill's Books for Cooks. She also established a book store "up north" in Edinburgh, Scotland, devoted to cooking. Henrietta Green, the author of *The Food Lovers' Guide to Britain*, has called Dickson Wright "the world's leading authority on cookery books." Clarissa is now a columnist for *Decanter* magazine and a regular contributor to *House & Garden* magazine. She has also turned up on BBC Radio 4's *Curious Cooks*. She lives in Edinburgh, Scotland, in a rented seventeenth-century lodge and still operates the Cooks Book Shop.

~~~

Jennifer Paterson and Clarissa Dickson Wright met briefly in Tuscany in the 1990s. However, it was BBC producer Patricia Llewellyn, creator of the show *Two Fat Ladies*, who had the idea of teaming them in 1996. She knew them both, and realized how much they had in common. Neither has ever married, both are Catholic (Paterson often jokes that they should call the show "Two Fat Cats"), both have affluent backgrounds, neither is a chef, but both are cooks, and, well, neither is thin. The result of this collaboration is what the BBC says is their most watched cooking show ever.

"I thought we would have a traditional food audience," producer Llewellyn said in the *Washington Post*, "and maybe a bit of a gay cult following, but I had no idea that middle England would take to them."

Llewellyn thinks the appeal has to do with nostalgia for an earlier time. And, of course, the honesty of the hosts. The BBC tried scripting the ladies, but they wouldn't hear of it. They tried putting makeup on them, but they wiped it off (Clarissa prefers to wear none, but Jennifer likes her red lips and nail polish). So Llewellyn told the ladies to be themselves, supplying no script, and no studio kitchen. They travel all over the United Kingdom, stopping off to cook for cricketers, or, perhaps, at a boarding school for a girls lacrosse team.

In the latter episode, which was titled, simply, "Meat," Jennifer quipped (referring to the girls), "They look very healthy. Shouldn't think they're vegetarians." On another installment, involving buttering a cake pan, Clarissa jokes "Did you see *Last Tango in Paris*? Something like that." On another shoot, this time at a Boy Scout camp-out, upon being asked by Jennifer how one starts a campfire, Clarissa quipped "Rub two Boy Scouts together." And on their September 24, 1997, *Tonight Show* TV appearance, Jennifer told host Jay Leno the story of how, thinking they were sweetbreads, she once cooked sheep's testicles.

At first, many of the male reviewers of *Two Fat Ladies* seemed fixated on the stars' sizes, not the "cookery," as the British call it. The *London Evening Standard* referred to their "uncompromising physical ugliness" and "equally ugly personalities." In looks-obsessed America, people are almost nervously giddy about them. The *Washington Post* reported their weights. (Okay, if you must know, Jennifer is twelve stone six, or about 175 pounds, and Clarissa is sixteen stone four, or about 230 pounds.) Still, no one's reporting Emeril Lagasse's weight.

For some, it's downright shocking to observe overweight women who are comfortable with who they are and the way they look. These two performers knead raw meat with their bare hands, use terms like "slosh it" and "muck it around," wrap everything in bacon and clotted cream, and call a spade a shovel. They mince onions, *not* words. "Political correctness is so patronizing," Clarissa Dickson Wright is fond of saying, "a return to Victorian euphemisms. I am a fat ex-drunk, not a horizontally challenged and chemically disadvantaged person!" She also likes to point out that although she's admittedly overweight, and eats meat and butter regularly, she has the cholesterol level of a two-year-old, and the blood pressure of a five-year-old.

"Fat is extremely good for you," Jennifer Paterson has said. "People aren't eating enough of it. It's not the animal fats that do the harm; it's the lack of vegetables and fresh fruit."

Dickson Wright believes *Two Fat Ladies* is popular in the United States because the hosts are unconventional and eat what they like. She said in the *Washington Post,* "I suspect most Americans actually do like cooking with butter, and things like that, aside from a small nucleus of mutants in Los Angeles." Paterson added, "And I imagine it's rather a relief to people to look at us instead of all those blond bimbos . . . those stick insects."

This attitude is as refreshing to the show's home viewership as the unapologetic title of the show, which is actually English bingo slang— whenever the number eighty-eight comes up, the caller yells out "two fat ladies." Indeed, Clarissa and Jennifer refer to themselves as the "fat ladies." And the real appeal of the program is *not* the food, which some find unappetizing; it's the rapport between the two women. They have not known each other very long and they're getting to know each other as we get to know them. Who wouldn't want to hang out with people who make each other laugh and enjoy each other's company? You could probably learn a lot from spending time with these unique ladies for an afternoon, and not just about clotted cream.

Striking a blow against what they call "food Fascism," the Two Fat Ladies believe their series is about freedom. As Clarissa Dickson Wright says, "It's a cookery show with anarchy and a motorbike."

TV Series

Two Fat Ladies (BBC, 1996–) (Food Network, 1997–) (PBS, 1998–)

TV Specials

Two Fat Ladies Christmas Specials (Food Network, Christmas Week 1997, Christmas Week 1998)

Books

Two Fat Ladies Ride Again by Jennifer Paterson, Clarissa Dickson Wright (Clarkson Potter, 1998)

The Haggis: A Little History by Clarissa Dickson Wright, Clare Hewitt (illustrator) (Pelican Publishing Co., 1998)

Cooking with the Two Fat Ladies by Jennifer Paterson, Clarissa Dickson

Wright (Random House, 1998)

Web Sites

www.cooks-book-shop.co.uk
www.foodtv.com

Caprial Pence: The Caprial World

Born: July 4, 1963.

Hometown: Portland, Oregon.

Parents: Father, Patrick, sculptor; mother, Artheen.

Siblings: Sister, Angela.

School: Culinary Institute of America (Hyde Park, New York).

Favorite Junk Food: "Corn dogs. I get teased about it."

Always in the Pantry: "Olive oil, balsamic vinegar, curry paste, and chili sauce."

Always in the Fridge: "Barbecue sauces, cayenne sauces, olives, wine, butter, mineral water, and milk for the kids."

Favorite Food Smell: "Bacon, onions, and garlic."

Favorite Food Sound: "When you make an Asian dumpling, you put the water in and it hits the oil and makes a great sound and it all explodes and you throw the lid on it really quick. It sounds like an explosion in a pan."

Fantasy Last Meal: "Rack of lamb, foie gras, and for dessert, something with raspberries and chocolate."

Her name is pronounced cah-PREEL, and it was invented by her mother, long before Caprial Pence's (*Cooking with Caprial*, PBS-TV) birth. "My mom and her best friend made it up in high school. They were goofing around and talking about the future." So it's probably safe to say that she is the only Caprial in the world.

Growing up in Portland, Oregon, "Cappy" Horsley wasn't allowed to watch much television. When she did, the only TV show she enjoyed was Julia Child's. "Her humor struck me. She was entertaining, and my parents entertained a lot so I was interested in food. I didn't grow up with macaroni and cheese. The ideas [Child] was presenting I found interesting, and at that point I was given the choice between Julia Child and a Japanese subtitled movie."

Pence grew up in an artistic family. Her father, Patrick Horsley, is an internationally renowned ceramic artist; some of his handmade art can been seen on the set of her TV show (items like teapots, plates, and trays). Her parents are both insatiable when it comes to learning about other cultures and like to research places before they travel there. "I think I got a lot of that hunger and interest from them both. My dad's a really good cook, and my grandfather on mom's side was a really good cook and gardener, and even though he died when I was young, he was a genetic influence. I cooked as soon as I could read."

By the time she was ten, Pence was cooking for her family. She created a complete French dinner for her peers in her high school French class at St. Mary's Academy in Portland. Still, she never considered a career in food. In fact, she was set on becoming a doctor, an idea of which her mother was fond, so she took a job as a hospital volunteer. She soon realized she wasn't cut out for medicine. "I couldn't deal with people being hurt. It literally made me sick. I'd have to step in the hall and double over in pain." She then told her mom she wanted to do something more creative, like being a chef, "like Julia Child."

"My parents always joked about sending me to cooking school, and finally when it dawned on me that I wasn't going to be a doctor, I got a job in a restaurant and I knew the first day that it felt right." She started working at Otto's, a deli in Portland, where she made fresh pastas and salads. She spent a year there, and then it was off to the Culinary Institute of America (CIA) in Hyde Park, New York, in 1982. She was only one of five women in the class at a school where only three of the 100 faculty members were women.

Like many women in the culinary school, Pence experienced sexism. "If I got an A on my test the guys would say, 'Oh, it's because you're a girl.' No, it's because I'm not smoking pot and drinking all night then coming in to try to take the test! Girls who wore makeup didn't survive, or were tortured. Part of why I didn't have so much trouble with [sexism] was that I didn't wear makeup, I kept my head down, and I worked as hard as I possibly could. If someone tried to make me cry, I didn't cry, and once you don't cry they leave you alone."

This sounds more like advice for dealing with grade school bullies. However, Pence isn't complaining. "The hard quality of the education and how it's sort of like going to military school, I don't think that's necessarily bad. I think it really woke people up as to how hard this profession is. If culinary school were gentle, they'd have a really rude awakening [in the real world]. A lot of people drop out in the first six weeks, and it's a good thing. It's like my hospital thing." This experience educated Pence on how to work with difficult people in the restaurant business. "It taught me how to deal with [the situation] when I had a French chef who was sexist who I worked for. I quit. I found somebody who let me do what I wanted to do, instead of staying there and complaining."

By the time Caprial graduated from the two-year program at CIA, twelfth in her class, in 1984, she was nineteen, and had already met her future husband, John Pence. They ran around in the same group at cooking school, and fittingly, their first date was a vegetable-carving demonstration at the institution. After graduation she took an internship at Shoalwater's, a restaurant in Long Beach, Washington. John soon joined her in Seattle, and they found kitchen line jobs at Fullers, a nationally renowned Sheraton Hotel restaurant, and the place for chefs to be in the Northwest. Caprial stood out in a big talented staff. She was promoted to lead line cook, then sous-chef, then chef in 1987.

At the time, Pence was twenty-four and pregnant, with a staff of fifteen, and within three months, she totally changed the menu at Fullers. An advocate of local farmers, she started buying directly from them rather than produce suppliers. She created "Pacific Rim cuisine," which she defines as "local ingredients with strong Asian influences, whether it's Chinese, Japanese, Thai, or Vietnamese."

Why was Caprial drawn to Asian food? "I had really strong people that I worked with when I first got out of cooking school that were very influential and taught me a lot, and one happened to be Vietnamese and one happened to be Malaysian. That's when I became really interested in [Asian] food and how different it was from classical cuisine, which is what I had been doing for the last three years."

Tossed Salad and Scrambled Eggs

If fine restaurants gave out frequent flyer miles, Frasier Crane (Kelsey Grammer) and his brother Niles Crane (David Hyde Pierce) could go to Bali fifty times for free. These Northwestern foodies and wine experts of *Frasier* (1993–) are the spiritual descendants of *The Odd Couple*'s (1970–75) Felix Unger. Frasier's even been known to whip up (or at least order in) gourmet nibbles such as foie gras.

As denizens of the Seattle coffee culture, the Crane brothers wile away the hours at Cafe Nervosa. The dream of their foodie lives occurs in the 1995 episode, "The Innkeepers," in which one of Frasier and Niles' favorite restaurants is going out of business, and, impulsively, they buy it. Re-opening the establishment as "Les Freres Heureux," things go amiss when they accidentally injure several of their staff, and generally wreck the place.

Pence is a firm believer in the melting pot, literally and figuratively. "There are so many ethnic influences that have touched my life. I still consider that American cooking. All that does is expose people to ideas about ethnic people. How can you hate somebody if you enjoy their food and love their culture?"

Pence's impact was felt nationally, and then internationally. In 1988, she and two of her Fullers kitchen staff were flown to the then–Soviet Union to demonstrate Pacific Rim cuisine. They were the first Americans to take part in an exchange of chefs with that country and were invited by the Soviet Georgian provincial government to attend the Goodwill Games.

"Talk about sexist! That was the most sexist country I'd ever been in. I happened to be seven-and-a-half months pregnant with my son Alex at the time, so that freaked them out at first; not only were they not used to seeing women in the kitchen, but a pregnant woman at that!" Caprial describes the experience in the Soviet Union as very intense, and would like to go back in five or ten years and see how different it is. "When I was there you could just see change shimmering on the edge."

The word of mouth from that trip led to an invitation to Washington, D.C., late in the same year to prepare a gala meal at the Soviet Embassy. In 1989, Pence was off to Kuala Lumpur, the capital of Malaysia, flying in with Pacific Northwest ingredients to prepare a birthday dinner for seventy-five people for the Sultan. Pence was named "Best Chef in the Northwest" by the James Beard Foundation in 1991 (James Beard was a fellow Oregonian, by the way). That was the same year her first cookbook came out, *Caprial's Seasonal Kitchen* (1991). It was also in 1991 that she asked her husband to be co-chef with her at Fullers, and they operated the restaurant together for ten months.

During the eighteen months prior to joining Caprial at Fullers, John put his career on hold to be a house-husband and take care of Alex. Though both were chefs, Caprial was becoming much better known. "It had zero effect on us when we were both at different restaurants, but when the [TV] show came along and I was at the restaurant with John and it was our restaurant, [my fame] was harder to deal with. We worked through it and got to the point where we just said, 'It doesn't matter, it's us.' No matter if it's my name and our restaurant, it's our career, it's our success. We couldn't do either one of them without the other."

When the Sheraton hired a new executive chef, the Pences feared they would lose control of the restaurant. They learned from Caprial's mother Artheen that the Westmoreland Bistro was for sale, and they bought it in 1992. The move was supposed to be a slowing down of sorts, an aim at having a life; a thirty-seat restaurant in Portland instead of something big and swanky away from her family. However, Caprial's reputation made the restaurant so popular that business thrived.

Luckily her family was close by, so they could help out. By this time, their second child, Savannah, was born. "Savannah loves to cook, and she's interested in seeing how the restaurant works. She wants to be a part of it. We cook all the time at home together." The Pences also enjoy gardening, camping, and entertaining with friends. "Sometimes our friends who aren't in the industry are intimidated to cook for us. But we're not going to friends' houses to critique what they're making!"

In 1997, the restaurant was rechristened Caprial's Bistro and Wine to make it easier for her fans to find her. She and her husband teach regular Tuesday night cooking classes for the community. But if you can't make it to Portland, there's always television.

Pence's TV career began in 1994 with the premiere of *Caprial's Cafe* on the Learning Channel. In the first year, it was nominated for

Best Television Cooking Series by the James Beard Foundation (fellow nominees were Pierre Franey and Jacques Pépin). The pilot came about after the producer saw a videotape done for the international olive oil commission several years earlier using seven chefs, including Pence. One of the other chefs had sent the producer the tape hoping something would happen. It did—for Pence, who stood out among the others. "I had done a lot of local TV in Seattle and felt very comfortable in front of the camera. It was something that felt very natural and right for me." A show was born, and so was her second book, *Caprial's Cafe Favorites* (1994). *Cafe* aired for two and a half years, and is currently running internationally.

She moved over to PBS with *Cooking with Caprial* in 1996, and released the companion cookbook, *Cooking with Caprial*. She also has a Web site where she answers e-mail from around the world. Her fans like her easy-going style. She is accessible, yet professional, using common language and simple recipes combined with expert techniques.

Pence takes her role as a teacher seriously: "The people that have more backbone and teaching ability with entertainment mixed in there, will last longer than just entertainment. Someone who's just entertainment-based can only write so many cookbooks and come up with so many dishes before it starts to look not real." But all types of cooking shows seem to be popular these days. "Maybe people really miss being in the kitchen. More people go out to dinner than ever before. Fewer people cook and fewer people have mothers who cook. Maybe it's some sort of craving for that. I think it's funny how many people watch the show[s] who don't cook."

Caprial is trying to reach those people too. "I want people to learn something from me. I want to elevate their expectations of food and what they can cook in the kitchen, and I want people to feel comfortable in the kitchen. That's why I design dishes that are really do-able at home but still teach them techniques." And she sees evidence of a food revolution: "Years ago people couldn't or didn't have roast peppers or garlic. When people tell me that now they have roasted peppers in their refrigerator, that gives me a lot of satisfaction. Everyday middle America is not buying canned mushrooms anymore."

There is one type of impact that she couldn't have expected. "Because of the show, I've gotten letters from people who have named their daughters 'Caprial.'"

TV Series

Caprial's Cafe (The Learning Channel, 1994–97)
Cooking with Caprial (PBS, 1996–)

Books

Caprial's Seasonal Kitchen: An Innovative Chef's Mouth-Watering Menus and Recipes for Easy Home Cooking by Caprial Pence (Alaska Northwest Books, 1991)
Caprial's Cafe Favorites by Caprial Pence (Ten Speed Press, 1994)
Cooking with Caprial: American Bistro Fare by Caprial Pence (Ten Speed Press, 1996)
Caprial's Bistro Style Cuisine by Caprial Pence (Ten Speed Press, 1998)
Caprial's Soups and Sandwiches by Caprial Pence, Mark Dowers (contributor) (Ten Speed Press, 1998)

Web Site

www.pacificharbor.com

Jacques Pépin: Jacques Treatment

Born: December 18, 1935.

Hometown: Bourg-en-Bresse, France.

Parents: Father, John, restauranteur; mother, Jeanne, chef.

Siblings: Older brother, Roland; younger brother, Richard.

School: Columbia University (New York City—master's).

Favorite Junk Food: "In our house we don't really go for junk food. I love chocolate. If chocolate is around, I'll eat it."

Always in the Pantry: "Dried mushroom, flour, sugar, dried fruit, and bouillon."

Always in the Fridge: "Eggs, onion, garlic, lettuce, bread, coffee, lemon, lime, and vegetables."

Fantasy Last Meal: "It [would] change, depending on the season; to me it's seasonal. It's the way people feel. Soft shell crab, if it was in season. Maybe roast chicken, boiled potato, salad, and potato and leek soup."

If you ask any TV chef or home cook whose technique they admire the most, everyone names the man who once said of his profession, "We are soup merchants. We're not geniuses." Jacques Georges Germain Pépin was born near Lyon, France. His first exposure to cooking was as a child at Le Pelican, the restaurant that belonged to his parents, where his mother was the chef. In fact, most of the chefs in Pépin's family have been women. He's the first man in the family to go that route.

When Pépin was thirteen, he began his first formal apprenticeship after finishing school exams at the distinguished Grand Hôtel de L'Europe in his hometown. Next it was on to Paris to work at the Meurice and then at the Plaza-Athénée, where he apprenticed under Lucien Diat. From 1956 to 1958, still in his early twenties, Pépin was the personal chef to three French heads of state: Felix Gaillard, Pierre Pfimlin, and Charles DeGaulle. He eventually worked in more than fifty restaurants in Paris.

In 1959, at the age of twenty-three, Pépin moved to the United States. He had no definite plan, and didn't know if he was going to stay or not, but he knew he wanted to learn English. "I am a true American because I am here by choice," he said. He became a naturalized citizen in 1965.

Pépin found the American culinary experience different than other parts of the world, especially France, where almost everyone eats French food. "Cuisine in Italy, France, and Spain was always part of who you are, part of the culture," he told *Nation's Restaurant News* in 1995. "But it wasn't really here. That was, in a sense, the beauty of it. A French chef like me could become 'famous.' There was never a cuisine strong enough to dominate. It was possible to do something with yourself in this country."

After arriving in America, Pépin worked in the kitchens of New York's Le Pavillon, and in the summer of 1960, he turned down an offer from the White House to be the chef for the Kennedys. By today's standards, turning down that job seems hard to understand. But things were different back then.

"You have to remember that chefs were nothing at the time," he explained in the *Hartford Advocate* in 1996. "Cooking for the president of France had been like working in a black hole. It was Jackie Kennedy who first brought chefs out of the kitchen and into the limelight." Instead, he took a job at the Howard Johnson Company, where he served as director of research and development for ten years.

Pépin had also started his Bachelor of Arts degree at Columbia University. He enrolled at Columbia initially to improve his rudimentary English, then after a two-year prep course he entered the School of General Studies, a liberal arts college for students who have to postpone or interrupt their educations. He ultimately earned an M.A. degree in eighteenth-century French literature in 1972. "I did it all for my own gratification," he told the *New York Times* in 1997. "Having an education prevented me from having a complex about not having an education."

His schedule at Howard Johnson's—7 A.M. to 3 P.M.—allowed him to continue his studies. In addition, Howard Johnson's gave him the opportunity to work in an American corporation environment. He wanted to learn things one doesn't experience in a conventional kitchen, such as marketing, mass production, and food chemistry. After working for HoJo's, whose orange roofs are still beacons of hope for many weary drivers, Pépin could say he's really cooked for everyone.

After he left Howard Johnsons in 1970, Pépin was co-owner and developer of La Potagerie, a successful soup restaurant in New York City. In 1975, he was consultant to food operation at the World Trade Center. Then it was time for Pépin to concentrate on writing, and what soon followed were the acclaimed cookbooks *La Technique* (1976) and *La Methode* (1979), two volumes that together present the principles of preparing French cuisine.

Jacques' array of fine books prompted his induction into the Cookbook Hall of Fame at the 1996 James Beard Awards, which is given each year to the author whose contributions to the literature of food have a substantial and enduring impact on the American kitchen. Pépin currently writes a quarterly column for *Food & Wine* magazine. A founder of the American Institute of Wine and Food, he is also on the board of trustees at The James Beard Foundation and a member of the International Association of Culinary Professionals, both of which are based in New York City. Pépin is the recipient of two of the French government's highest honors: he is a Chevalier de L'Ordre des Arts et des Lettres (1997) and a Chevalier de L'Ordre du Mérite Agricole (1992). Pépin contributes 25 percent of his time to fundraising events and festivals and spends thirty to forty weeks out of the year traveling.

Teaching, like cooking, is in Pépin's blood, and he's created many ways to combine the two. He is Dean of Special Programs at the French Culinary Institute in New York and an adjunct faculty member at Boston University. After receiving his master's degree, he proposed a doctoral dissertation on the history of French food, but his advisors said no: food was not for serious historians. Now a professor at Boston University, which offers what is believed to be the nation's first master's degree program in gastronomy, Pépin teaches a course on the development of French food, complete with readings from Montaigne and Rabelais. "For me, the preparation of food is an index of society's values," Pépin told the *New*

York Times in 1998. *Bon Appetit* magazine has said that Pépin is "a born teacher.... Were there a culinary Oscar to bestow, Pépin would capture it by acclamation."

Stop Your Wine-ing

Everyone eats, but not everyone drinks wine, or even likes it. This may explain why shows focusing on wine alone don't really catch on with many home viewers. Television is a visual medium, and all kinds of foods can look yummy on camera. However, looking at a glass of chardonnay on TV isn't likely to make you salivate. Jacques Pépin explains it this way: "After all the smelling, tasting, and gurgling, it would get boring and pedantic."

Wine discussions do seem to work on TV when they are folded into a cooking show in the service of food and wine pairing. This is something that wine expert David Rosengarten does at the end of almost every episode of his show, *Taste*. However, even Rosengarten doesn't think wine can carry a program alone. "American wine culture didn't go as far as the food culture. People get to the end of that road fast. They go, 'Alright, I did the wine thing, I really feel like having a Pepsi.' But that doesn't happen with food. Once you get hooked on this whole philosophy of food, that it's important, that you should pay attention to it, take pleasure from it, let it play a role in your life, it doesn't stop. You don't say, 'I'm not interested anymore. I'm just going to have cereal for dinner.'"

Veteran TV cooking show producer Geoffrey Drummond agrees. "Wine has not made it because it's just so difficult and removed. It gets very cognitive because you're trying to create sensual analogs, basically, and that's going to be really tough to do. [You have to] communicate historical background information about vineyards. But, television is still pretty much an active medium, and you want to see people cook [not just talk and sip]. Something should be happening. If a personality [comes along] that is the 'Julia of wine,' we might be willing to go to vineyards."

There are many who think watching Pépin on television is as good as earning a degree in cooking. He did his first PBS cooking show, *Everyday Cooking with Jacques Pépin*, in the early 1980s, but his real media break didn't come until almost ten years later, when he did a guest appearance on San Francisco's KQED with chef Martin Yan. It went well, and KQED asked if he'd like to have a show of his own. He said sure, and in 1991, *Today's Gourmet with Jacques Pépin* was on the air.

"I don't think that I ever had a distinct philosophy or a goal. I love to cook and teach. Doing television enables me to inform people. I don't try to cook French and don't try not to cook French." Any discomfort being on camera? "I've been in the kitchen almost fifty years," he told the *San Francisco Examiner* in 1998. "Cooking is what I do. As long as I'm cooking I'm fine—I don't even think of the camera."

Today's Gourmet with Jacques Pépin ran for three seasons, 1991 to 1994, and won a Beard Award in 1994. That was followed by the 1995 special, *Julia and Jacques: Cooking in Concert*, with Julia Child, which is popular at pledge time on PBS stations. Next was another Beard Award winner, *Jacques Pépin's Kitchen: Cooking with Claudine* (1996) and *Jacques Pépin's Cooking Techniques* in 1997. He has also cooked on *Late Night with David Letterman*. His latest series is *Jacques Pépin's Kitchen: Encore with Claudine*.

Pépin has been married to his wife, Gloria, since 1966. Their daughter Claudine, who would later share the TV kitchen with her dad, was born in 1968. Today, the Pépins live in Madison, Connecticut, in a former brick factory. The kitchen includes two dishwashers, two sinks, and two stoves. An eight-foot wall in his kitchen holds about 100 pots and pans.

"I rarely watch my show, except the ones my daughter is on, to see her," Pépin says. The aim of having Claudine cook with him on the program was to have Jacques interact with someone who doesn't know as much about food and cooking as he does, and ask the questions that we want to ask, such as "Can I freeze this? What can I do with leftovers?" "She is my '*vox populare*,'" he said of his daughter in the *Hartford Advocate* in 1996. "Claudine is there to ask the questions my audience might ask about the process of creating beautiful and tasty dishes if they were in the kitchen with me."

Pépin shares the stage with Julia Child again, on *Julia Child and Jacques Pépin: Just Cooking*. Veteran cooking show producer Geoffrey Drummond paired them again for a reason. "I feel [Pépin] is the only chef who can play opposite Julia and be strong enough to provide the counterbalance. That's because Jacques is intelligent, highly intelligent. His technical abilities are so much a part of him that you sort of take them for granted but they're very much there. He's articulate and he's extremely generous. Technically he's probably the best teacher, and I think he has a great personality. And he's great looking, which absolutely does not hurt."

Pépin has been called the "Cary Grant of Cooking," a pin-up for the cooking impaired. And the accent doesn't hurt. This gets him quite a few female fans. However, if you're not interested in cooking, you won't last long with his shows. They are fairly serious cooking programs. "He breaks through the lens," says Drummond. "His eye contact, his enthusiasm, he has a warmth, he so much cares about what he does, and you buy into that enthusiasm, and energy, but you have to be willing to put the work in to stay with him. He has probably more of the weekly cooking congregation than most other programs, but he doesn't push himself over the line the way Martin Yan will, where he goes way out of his way to be an entertainer." Pépin's shows are traditional and information-driven, and his fans marvel at the dexterity of his hands (watching him has been compared to observing a skillful ping-pong player) and the clarity of his technique.

"I ask people why they look at my show, and some people will say, 'Oh, I love watching you and your daughter.' Others will say, 'I tried your recipe,' and others look at it and do not cook whatsoever." So, why are they watching? "I don't know!" he laughs. "I don't really see the entertainment value. It's not an hilarious show. . . . I hope it's not!" He laughs again. "It's not a show that would be entertaining unless you use it."

So, it's not surprising that Pépin scoffs at the suggestion people aren't cooking. "When I came to this country, the state of the supermarket [was such that] you couldn't find a leek, or a shallot, and you found two types of lettuce, iceberg and romaine. Now, even at the local Stop and Shop, you have an embarrassment of riches. Professional restaurants are not buying from supermarkets. If no one cooks at home, who's buying it? The truck's coming, someone's got to buy this stuff."

TV Series

Today's Gourmet with Jacques Pépin (PBS, 1991–94)
Jacques Pépin's Kitchen: Cooking with Claudine (PBS, 1996– *)
Jacques Pépin's Cooking Techniques (PBS, 1997– *)
Jacques Pépin's Kitchen: Encore with Claudine (PBS, 1998–)
Julia Child and Jacques Pépin: Just Cooking (PBS, 1998–)

TV Specials

Julia and Jacques: Cooking in Concert (PBS, 1995)
Julia and Jacques: More Cooking in Concert (PBS, 1996)

Books

The Other Half of the Egg by Jacques Pépin (M. Barrows & Co., Inc., 1975)
Jacques Pépin: A French Chef Cooks at Home by Jacques Pépin (Simon and Schuster, 1975)
La Technique by Jacques Pépin (Times Books, 1976)
La Methode by Jacques Pépin (Times Books, 1979)
Everyday Cooking with Jacques Pépin by Jacques Pépin (Harper and Row, 1982)
A Fare for the Heart by Jacques Pépin (Cleveland Clinic Foundation, 1988)
A FareThat Fits by Jacques Pépin (Cleveland Clinic Foundation, 1989)
The Short-Cut Cook by Jacques Pépin (William Morrow and Co., Inc., 1990)
Cuisine Economique by Jacques Pépin (William Morrow and Co., Inc., 1992)
Jacques Pépin's The Art of Cooking Volumes I and II by Jacques Pépin (Alfred A. Knopf, 1988, 1992)
Today's Gourmet: Light and Healthy Cooking for the '90's by Jacques Pépin (Reissue Edition) (KQED, 1994)
Good Life Cooking: Light Classics from Today's Gourmet by Jacques Pépin (Reissue Edition) (KQED, 1994)
Happy Cooking: More Light Classics from Today's Gourmet by Jacques Pépin (KQED, 1994)
Jacques Pépin's Simple and Healthy Cooking by Jacques Pépin (Rodale Press, 1995)
Jacques Pépin's Kitchen: Cooking with Claudine by Jacques Pépin (KQED, 1996)
The Best Bread Ever: Great Homemade Bread Using Your Food Processor by Charles Van Over, Priscilla Martel, Charles Van Over, Jacques Pépin (Broadway Books, 1997)
Maida Heatter's Pies & Tarts by Maida Heatter, Jacques Pépin (Andrews & McMeel, 1997)
Jacques Pépin's Table: The Complete Today's Gourmet by Jacques Pépin (KQED, 1997)

The Strang Cookbook for Cancer Prevention: A Complete Nutrition and Lifestyle Plan to Dramatically Lower Your Cancer Risk by Laura Pensiero, Susan Oliveria, Michael Osborne, Jacques Pépin (E. P. Dutton, 1998)
Jacques Pépin's Kitchen: Cooking with Claudine: Second Helpings by Jacques Pépin (KQED, 1998)

Videotapes

Jacques Pépin Cooking Techniques by Jacques Pépin (VHS Video edition) (Silma Delta Research, 1997)
Guide to Good Cooking Vol. 1: Secrets by Jacques Pépin (VHS Video edition) (Videocraft Classics, 1990)
Guide to Good Cooking Vol. 2: Soup, Fish by Jacques Pépin (VHS Video edition) (Videocraft Classics, 1990)
Guide to Good Cooking Vol. 3: Meats by Jacques Pépin (VHS Video edition) (Videocraft Classics, 1990)

Web Site

www.red-knight.com/napavalley/pepin/index.html

David Rosengarten:
Remembrance of Things Repast

Born: January 25, 1950.

Hometown: Belle Harbor, New York.

Parents: Father, Leonard, garment district worker; mother, Lorraine.

Siblings: Younger brother, Lewis.

Schools: Colgate University (Hamilton, New York); Cornell University (Ithaca, New York—doctorate).

Favorite Junk Food: "I love potato chips, salty peanuts, cheesy tortilla chips. My palate is definitely salt-oriented."

Always in the Pantry: "Brittany sea salt, an array of hot sauces and chili powders, a sauce called West Indies Creole pepper sauce, and chili powders that are specific chilis."

Always in the Fridge: "Rich, French style butter, red wine vinegar— I don't put balsamic vinegar in salads; it's just a special thing for sauces—a sharp fruity red wine, and Korean kim chee."

Favorite Food Smell: "Garlic in olive oil. Growing up in the fifties, that real Southern Italian smell, that was the most exciting thing. I'd smell it at Angelos on Flatbush Avenue in Brooklyn, and I'd smell it in my father's kitchen. It's like turning on a switch."

Fantasy Last Meal: "A huge tray of plateau of French raw oysters (so this would have to be in winter, of course), a simple but slightly aged crisp Chablis with that. Then, choucroute garnie, the Alsacian platter of sauerkraut with all sorts of sausages and cured pork things on top of it, and a simple but slightly aged Alsacian Riesling [wine] with that. Then I would have a fabulous array of French cheeses, and probably drink a great red Burgundy [wine] with that. Dessert would be tarte Tatin."

David Rosengarten (*Taste*, Food Network) likes to say he comes from a food-crazed family, and it goes back several generations. His father's father, also named David, who died before David the younger was born, was an executive for MGM who traveled a lot in the 1920s and 1930s. The elder David developed a passion for variety in food and would come back to New York and bring his son things to taste. "One family story is that he'd wake my father up at two in the morning to go to some speakeasy in the 1920s because they just got a fresh shipment of oysters." This passion for foods and tastes was passed on to David's young namesake.

"My earliest memory is my dad taking me to places to taste different foods, while my friends were all eating chicken soup and chopped liver. Other kids were helping Dad fix the car; I was helping Dad fix Lobster Cantonese." On the weekends, David and his father would bond in the kitchen while cooking up dishes like Lobster Fra Diavolo and Cantonese Pepper Steak. The main culinary adventures were the things that were around the most in the suburbs of New York in the 1950s: Chinese-American and Italian-American food. Every weekend was about food at the Rosengarten house. Saturday mornings they'd make the shopping list and shop, and then either cook that night or eat out that night and cook the next night. During the week, the meals were mostly the domain of his mother, who "believes in meat," and cooked less exotically, though she made "awfully good baked fish and beef stew."

Today, Rosengarten's eighty-year-old father, who worked in New York's garment district, travels with his son quite often. "My dad likes to say, 'When I was a kid, David Rosengarten used to take me around to eat all over New York, and now I'm old and David Rosengarten takes me around to eat all over the world.'"

Even with all this home-schooling in the culinary arts, Rosengarten never considered it a possible career. He went to Colgate University in Hamilton, New York, caught the theater bug, and started directing. "I did acting as well, but I could tell...I would direct a play and people would say, 'That was great!' and I'd cook a dinner and people would say, 'That was incredible!' Then I'd act and people would say, 'That was...[pausing for effect] good.'"

But he couldn't escape the taste his father had awakened in him. "Hamilton, New York, was the middle of nowhere, where the main gastronomic treat was the tuna fish special at the Bluebird. The Student Union had horrible food, and for the first time in my life I was away from restaurants and my father's cooking. So, I started duplicating what I had always done with my dad." Soon Rosengarten's dinner parties gained a reputation and everyone wanted to go to his house for dinner. "But still, I never thought this would be a career for me."

Back in New York City after graduation, Rosengarten started to direct off-off Broadway, and formed a theater company with a college classmate. During the day, David took food and wine jobs to make ends meet. He worked at a wine shop on Madison Avenue, where he obtained much of his wine education. "They wanted the people who worked there to really understand about wine, so they made us keep notebooks and take notes and they kept checking our notebooks. It was like school; it was cool."

Rosengarten soon answered an ad in the *New York Times* for a private chef for a psychiatrist who was head of a New York State mental hospital and who was contractually promised a state-provided chef in his home. "It helped if the chef was insane," Rosengarten explains, laughing. Even though he never had a professional job cooking before, he bluffed his way through the interview and got the position because they "loved the way I talked about food." He stayed there for about four years and had a great time.

He was still thinking theater career but he saw how difficult it was to succeed as a director. "I did like to eat and wanted to have a steady flow of income so I could go to restaurants at some point, so I thought, 'Maybe I should stay in the theater but just get a normal job: I'll become a theater professor.'"

So Rosengarten got his doctorate from Cornell University, and during those years, his food fanaticism grew. "It was like, 'This weekend I'm going to conquer the food of...Afghanistan!' I systematically made my culinary knowledge grow, and in my spare time I was cooking all the time, but I never had career thoughts."

Finally, that changed. While teaching theater at Skidmore College in Saratoga Springs, New York, in 1980, Rosengarten walked into a local housewares and fancy gourmet ingredients store called Mabou. He asked about a sign in the window advertising cooking classes. "I said to the woman very diffidently, 'I'm a teacher at Skidmore and I really know a lot about food and cooking. I could probably teach a good cooking class.'" Because he wasn't professionally trained, the owner said he could teach a free one-hour demo in the store to see how it went. He whipped up Szechuan shrimp with chili sauce, and a crowd gathered. David Rosengarten, the cooking teacher, was finally born, and soon was teaching weekly classes at the store.

This new job changed everything. "I felt so confident and comfortable [giving cooking classes]. I was teaching theater every day, but it was a difficult era for the liberal arts. It was the early eighties, Ronald Reagan had just been elected, and the country was going on its decade-long financial binge." Freshmen would come into his campus office and ask for advice on what courses they should take. "I'd say, 'You should start with History of Western Philosophy, History of Art.' They'd say, 'My dad's not going to let me take that, I have to take Macroeconomics, I'm going to B-school!' I was so disgusted by all that, and then I'd go in and start teaching these cooking classes at Mabou and everybody who's there is passionate and wants to be there. So, maybe it was the time, I don't know, but I ended up feeling, 'This is great.'"

After a few years at Skidmore, Rosengarten's wife-to-be wanted to move to New York to pursue her acting career. So, he figured he'd go to New York for a year and try to get something going as a cooking teacher/food writer/wine writer. That's exactly what happened, and it occurred very quickly. He wrote an article about balsamic vinegar and sent it to *Gourmet* magazine just to see what would happen. To his surprise, they bought it. Next he wrote a column on matching food and wine for *Food and Wine Spectator*, probably the world's most important wine publication. He went on to write for *Bon Appetit*, *Wine Spectator*, and other magazines, as well as the *New York Times*. He was the weekly wine columnist for *New York Newsday* from 1988 to 1993.

Recently appointed New York Restaurant Critic for *Gourmet* magazine, Rosengarten is also the Contributing Food Editor and writes a regular restaurant column called "Food for Thought" for *Departures*, American

Express' magazine for platinum card holders. He also still writes a monthly wine column for *Food & Wine* magazine. His other articles about food, wine, and travel have appeared in *Harper's Bazaar, House Beautiful, Business Week, Metropolitan Home,* the *New York Daily News,* the *New York Observer,* the *San Jose Mercury News, Diversion, 7 Days, Gastronome, Video Review,* and *Market Watch.*

David Rosengarten Reveals Olive Oil's Dirty Little Secret

Bet your pantry has a bottle of olive oil in it right now. Well, David Rosengarten, a self-proclaimed "fanatic about olive oil" has news for you.

"A lot of people don't know this about olive oil, but it degrades fairly quickly. The dirty little secret of olive oil is that it's never better than on the day it was made. Usually one year later it's significantly worse and two years later it's usually dead. I'm always trying to keep current with olive oil. I've got several different kinds. I've got some that I might use for cooking, but I always try to have on hand a bottle of fresh, killer olive oil."

Here's one of his favorite quick meals featuring olive oil.

"I take white beans, soak them for a day, throw them in some boiling water, and boil them. Then I take a fresh bottle of killer Tuscan olive oil, drizzle it on, and have tomatoes on the side. That oil drizzle can make an instant meal."

David is a member of the New York Wine Press and the Wine Media Guild, and he serves on the Book Awards Committee of the International Association of Cooking Professionals. He is also a sought-after jurist for wine, food, chef, and sommelier competitions. He recently served in Paris as the only American judge on an international panel that selected the world's greatest sommelier, and was President of the Jury at the recent selection of America's best sommelier in New York City. He was honored in 1989 by *Cook's* magazine, when he was one of five nominees for "Best Food Journalism of 1989." In 1991, he was one of ten finalists for the James Beard Who's Who in American Food and Beverage Hall of Fame, and in 1993 and 1995 he was one of three nominees for the James Beard Journalism Award, Feature Stories. He is also the Wine

Advisor to Gracie Mansion, in New York City, where he is coordinating a New York State wine program for Mayor Rudy Giuliani.

In 1986, Rosengarten collaborated with the British wine authority Hugh Johnson in the production of *Hugh Johnson's Wine Cellar*, a food-and-wine computer program. His essay on matching wine and food appears in the program's user manual. He also served as associate editor for *A Dictionary of American Wines* (1986). He is the co-author of *Red Wine with Fish: The New Art of Matching Wine with Food* 1989, a cooking-and-wine book. He co-published for four years the highly acclaimed newsletter, *The Wine & Food Companion*. In 1996, Random House released *The Dean & DeLuca Cookbook*, authored by Rosengarten, which is a 500-recipe book devoted to the food and food ideas of America's most famous grocery. David is currently at work on a cookbook based on *Taste*, his cooking show on the Food Network.

Rosengarten's success in food journalism was satisfying, but did nothing to satiate the urge that once made him go into that housewares store in Saratoga Springs. So, he started pursuing the television angle in the late 1980s. He joined with two friends and made a connection with WGBH-TV in Boston. "They were interested in our idea for a wacky, off-the-wall cooking show. They wanted to call it *Three Men and a Kitchen*. I wanted to call it *Mouth Party*, but they didn't go for that." David and his pals went through three program pilots, the last one costing hundreds of thousands of dollars, and then, there was an executive change at the last minute and the new person in charge nixed the entire idea. "Two years of work on this and it was over. I was phenomenally depressed."

David finally found his way to the incipient Food Network in 1993, auditioning for *Food News and Views* (now called *In Food Today*). He was offered the position, but was initially reluctant because they wanted him to be an anchor and read food news. "I wanted to do food on TV; I didn't know if I wanted to talk about other people's food." However, he decided to get in on the ground floor of this fledgling network, and three months later he successfully pitched *Taste*.

Taste doesn't look like a lot of other TV cooking shows. It's more stark, with a seamless white background and a few metal shelving units housing *objet d'art*. Part of that is because, as one of the first shows produced by the novice Food Network, there wasn't a lot of money to put into it. So they went with a minimalist concept, and it stuck. Also, because David is not technically a chef, he doesn't wear the traditional chef's jacket. However, his shirts and ties are chosen to blend with the food he's cooking, or, more specifically, the "third act table setting." His ties sometimes come from Hugo Boss, Armani, and Polo, as well as flea markets and vintage clothing stores.

That mixture of the high and the low can be a metaphor for David's show itself. Tune into *Taste* one day and view an episode devoted to caviar; tune in the next day and the subject might be tuna salad sandwiches. That's how Rosengarten likes it: "By always juxtaposing the high and low, by doing foie gras one day and hamburgers the next, I want people to get the subliminal message that all food is worthy of your contemplation and all food gives pleasure."

Despite his egalitarian tastes, Rosengarten feels he is often misunderstood. "I often hear, 'Hey Dave, I love your show, but I didn't feel that way at first. At first I figured you were this food snob, this show-off with information, and then I watched it again, and I realized you're not a snob, you're nuts, you love this food and you want us to love it, too.' Many people go through that process." This is what's behind the commercials for *Taste*, in which he makes fun of his own reputation by acting like a wine snob, and in the next scene appearing in a biker jacket, or on a skateboard saying, "What up?"

Still, you're not likely to find a more erudite cooking show on television today. Rosengarten will focus on one dish, or perhaps one ingredient, discussing his likes and dislikes, and expounding on its history. This is part of his mission. "I hate food snobbery, and I hate when people focus on only high end ingredients. I mean, I really like potato chips. I really like a hamburger. I really like a tuna salad sandwich, and the bigger picture is that in America we just don't take as much time and pleasure with our eating as they do in some other countries."

David feels he's an educator in the aftermath of a food revolution. "I discovered twenty years ago that there was a whole bunch of dishes that people didn't know about. Now we're a more sophisticated food country. Twenty years ago, no one knew what risotto was, and now you can find it at a diner in Cincinnati. However, even though we can find risotto everywhere we haven't really developed national standards for what is good risotto. So I think the next stage in the education of the American palate is finding out what's good and bad about these dishes. One of the things I wanted to do with *Taste* is look at these dishes from all around the world and look at these new ingredients that we're now seeing in our markets and find standards for them. Or, to take things that we haven't thought about in years, like good old fashioned Fifties Chinese-American and Italian-American food and remind people and talk about those standards."

The food of Rosengarten's father and his youth returns, and he continues the cycle on television—literally. His children, Andrea and Sarah, have been on *Taste* several times. One episode, about the little French cookies called madeleines, was especially fitting. There's a passage in Marcel Proust's *Remembrance of Things Past* about tasting a madeleine and how it took him right back to childhood. A rush of his memories of childhood was triggered by the taste of that cookie, and a whole poetic philosophical discourse on how tasting something can trigger memory follows.

"Foodies all love this passage, and I discussed the whole thing [on the show] while making the madeleines. I said, 'I'm not doing this because madeleines trigger any memory in me. Wanna see my madeleine? Here's my madeleine.' I picked up a napkin, and there's a bagel with a shmear." Then he made up his own Proustian memories. "'I see you all now, Uncle Hymie under the elm, Aunt Esther selling your schmatas....' I did the Jewish Proust. In the third part of the show, I had a little French tea party set up, and I said, 'I wanted to make sure my daughters have a taste of madeleines in youth so they could always remember it after,' and the camera pulled back and there were my two daughters, sitting so pretty at the table, and having the videotape record their first taste of madeleines, with the consciousness of, 'Well, they'll never forget this, in fact they can always refer back to it on videotape,' so it was all folding in on itself. As we're pulling away, the girls were eating their madeleines and I was reading from Proust about the power of memory. It was a very moving show. People who've seen it and paid attention have said, 'I didn't know a cooking show could go there.'"

This coming from a man who thought his lifelong relationship with food had no career possibilities. "The amazing thing is something like this comes along and enables me to blend theater, teaching, and all the different things I know about food. This was the end of that road, but I didn't know it at the time."

What is the appeal of watching a cooking show? "A cooking show has a very interesting rhythm. You start out saying what you're going to do, you spend the middle part of the show doing it, and the third part of the show, you've done it. I always think of my show as a play. People like that play because they know what's coming. There's comfort about it, in a world that's becoming increasingly chaotic and uncertain. I'm going to tune into a cooking show and I'm going to have the satisfaction of seeing something proposed and something executed. It's a nice rhythm for people. The 'thereness' of the Food Network is something that really hasn't been attempted before and I think it's working for a lot of people. People have a romantic view of an older time that not many of us lived through when families were together around the hearth. We all like that image, and nobody has it today in their lives. The Food Network has become an electronic hearth for people [who are] gathering around the cathode tube. We're there, we're your family. Since food is always connected with hearth and family, the connection is easy to make."

TV Series

In Food Today [originally *Food News and Views*] (Food Network, 1993–)
Taste (Food Network, 1994–)

TV Specials

Taste of the Orient—Bangkok (Food Network, October 1997)
Taste of the Orient—Singapore (Food Network, November 1997)
Taste of the Orient—Malaysia (Food Network, December 1997)

Books

Dean & DeLuca Cookbook by David Rosengarten, Joel Dean, Georgio DeLuca, Lori Longbotham (Random House, 1996)
Home Bistro Simple, Sensuous Fare in the Comfort of Your Own Kitchen by Betty Harper Fussell, David Rosengarten, Joshua Wesson (Ecco Press, 1997)
Taste: One Palate's Journey Through the World's Greatest Dishes by David Rosengarten (Random House, 1998)

Web Site

www.foodtv.com

22

Nick Stellino: From the Stock Market to Stock Pots

Born: May 1, 1958.

Hometown: Palermo, Sicily, Italy.

Parents: Father, Vincent, retired art dealer; mother, Massimiliana, housewife.

Siblings: Younger brother, Mario.

School: Arizona State University (Tempe, Arizona).

Always in the Pantry: "Garlic, Italian parsley, olive oil, balsamic vinegar, and red pepper flakes."

Always in the Fridge: "Wine, water, eggs, green beans, asparagus, and mushrooms."

Favorite Cooking Smell: "Sautéing garlic. Not burned. Very few people understand the difference between the gentle sautéing of garlic, which has a celestial aroma, versus the whiff of burnt garlic, which is basically the soul of the garlic leaving the corpse behind. One is a celebration of life, the other one an affirmation of death. It takes the same amount of time, same amount of energy, but an extra amount of sensitivity."

Favorite Cooking Sound: "The blades of a knife hitting the bottom of the wooden board as I go along slicing mushrooms; it makes me feel like I'm unbeatable. The key is to start out with the same number of fingers I'm ending up with."

Fantasy Last Meal: "I would like [my wife and I] to leave [this world] together while we sleep, after having one of the finest meals; spaghetti and tomato sauce, balsamic vinegar and strawberries, and scaloppini á limon. Let me tell you that tomato sauce is not going to come out of a can, that veal scaloppini perfectly sautéed with a wine deglaze and a little bit of lemon is going to be out of this world, and those berries, I'll go and pick them out myself and find the perfect ones and I'll scrub them one by one."

Everybody in Nick Stellino's (*Cucina Amore*, PBS) family—everybody in his neighborhood—cooked and told stories. The kitchen was the gathering place where traditions were passed down. "Cooking was first and foremost a social event as well as providing the fuel for the day. What I liked about cooking was the sense of love that was involved, and tradition. I think of the dinner table then, and still today, as the last family or tribal meeting ground. Even though we think we're so sophisticated because we go around with our laptops, we still have primitive rituals. I do believe that my love for food is my attempt to try and preserve those wonderful family moments. I believe that every time I reproduce this food I can feel them around me. That's what inspires me and gives me the great love for what I do."

Stellino fondly remembers being a child in Sicily shelling peas, chopping onions, and then standing on a stool so he could reach the pot to stir them. He also recalls the reverence with which America was described. If you ask him what he wanted to do when he grew up, he'll say "To go to America."

"As a child growing up, everything that I saw on TV was American. John Wayne, *Leave It to Beaver*, all, of course, spoken in Italian. America was this incredible country where every wish and hope materializes, and people were bigger than life, as portrayed in films and TV shows. Plus, my father always spoke of America as a wonderful place full of open space where great dreams can be realized by common people."

In the summers, Stellino and his father would go into a village in interior Sicily to buy fresh tomatoes to make *conserva*. It was a whole day affair, and on the way home, they'd enjoy the sunset together. "My father would say, 'Nicolino, on the other side of the ocean where you cannot see anymore, there is a whole new land, called America, where the ocean is always full of fish and all your dreams will come true.' If you put this in the back of your mind as a child, even though you grow up and read the news and watch TV, the sensation of this being the country of opportunity and dreams stayed with me. These are things we all have inside of us. Some express it through music and some are able to write poems, and some aren't able to express it at all, but have it in their hearts. I express it through my food."

Stellino came to America in 1974, when he was sixteen, and cooking helped him miss his family less. "I love to cook because that's how I bring all these people back. When I went to America alone, I remember longing for my family like you wouldn't believe. I'd call on Sunday just to hear their voices and hear who was at the dinner table. And I would prepare myself these dinners, copying my mom and dad's recipes. My love of food is a symbolic rite to get in touch with what I left behind."

Stellino became a naturalized U.S. citizen and earned his B.S. in Marketing from Arizona State University. He still didn't know cooking was in his future. But why marketing? "I thought, you get a degree and you get a job. I come from a family of traders. My grandfather traded olive oil and grain. My great grandfather before him did the same thing. My father was basically an entrepreneur who's ability to survive was based on building personal relationships and selling products. So genetically speaking, inbred in me there is a basic understanding of the value of the human relationship and the ability to sell product." Settling in southern California, his marketing skills landed him a job as a stock broker in 1984, where he worked for seven years.

A family tie would change the direction of Nick's life and career. His favorite uncle, Giovanni, was dying of cancer in the early 1990s, and all the cousins flew back to see him in his last days of life, to pay their respects. "This was the crazy uncle that everyone has in their family, who you just love. The guy who always gave you candies, who would always make you smile when you were sad, who always thought and acted like a child because basically he was a child and understood us better than our own parents did. He was coming in and out of sleep, and as we were leaving the room he grabbed my hand and said, 'Nicolino, I have to speak to you . . . you should never die without following your dream.' I am looking at him and I do not know if he knows who I am, or what he's saying."

"That stood in the back of my mind for so long, that mysterious phrase kept popping back. Every day that I went back to work, the phrase came, first a murmur, then a resounding voice, and then a scream. I remember coming unexpectedly one day [in 1991] looking out the window of my office, saying to myself, 'I quit.' It was not planned, I didn't discuss it with my wife [Nanci, whom he wed in 1983, and who is currently his business partner], and trust me, I discuss everything with my wife. I went to my boss and quit. I was thirty-three."

Realizing his dream was the restaurant business, he started looking in Los Angeles for a job cooking, which had always been a hobby. "You must understand that at this point I was a very dangerous man. I had a collection of 500 cookbooks that I memorized from page to page. I was comparable to a man who had read a book on thoracic surgery and assumed that because he read the book, he could operate on a live patient."

Stellino interviewed for a position at a small restaurant run by a French man, who almost hired him until he asked Stellino where he worked before. When Stellino answered Merrill Lynch, he was thrown out. Then he remembered something his father told him about a time when he was having trouble finding a job in Italy after World War II. His dad paid a shipping department supervisor to let him work there. "I heard this story a thousand times, and at the age of thirty-three somebody opened that door and it came right back at me. I turned [to the man] and said, 'You also need a dishwasher. I'll give you five dollars a day if you let me wash dishes in your restaurant.' That is how I got my first job in the restaurant business."

Stellino worked his way up from washing dishes to gutting chickens to cleaning calamari, and finally, to making lunches. He moved on to several other Los Angeles eating establishments, including Drago, Farfalla, and La Terraza. In 1993, he worked one year as the spokesperson for Ragu, the Italian food products company.

One night, sharing with his wife the last bottle of wine from his days as a broker, Nick envisioned his own TV cooking show. More than two thousand phone calls later, it all came together. Making pitch phone calls was something in which he had experience. "As a trader, I was selling securities for investments which were based on the performances of others. Today, what I sell is me. I'm a hell of a lot better product because I know what I can deliver and in which form I can deliver it."

In 1995, *Cucina Amore* was born. The TV show takes place in the titular fictitious restaurant, where Stellino greets his customers and then takes the viewers into the kitchen to watch him prepare the specials for that night. There is a reason behind this trickery. "People are intimidated by restaurant food. [This is] empowering. [Viewers will think], 'It's so easy, I can make it.' It worked well, but what I never counted on is the fact that people would take it to the next level."

Mama Mia!

From March 7 to July 21, 1984, the CBS network gave us the only TV sitcom (to date) revolving around a cooking show. And nobody came to dinner.

Mama Malone was written by playwright Terrence McNally (*Love! Valour! Compassion!*) and starred Shakespearean-trained actress Lila Kaye as Mama Renata Malone, the Italian widow of an Irish cop, whose cooking series, *Cooking with Mama Malone*, aired live from her fourth-floor Brooklyn walk-up and was carried by a local TV station. During the taping of the show-within-a-show, neighbors and family members wandered in and out, airing their dirty laundry. Of course, Mama would solve all problems, the whole time talking to the camera and ostensibly cooking the dish of the day.

The characters were a cavalcade of walking, talking ethnic stereotypes that seemed prevalent on TV in the 1980s: Mama herself, stirring the pasta sauce and dispensing "Old Country" wisdom; her "hot-to-trot" daughter Connie Karamakopoulos (Randee Heller), divorced from a Greek guy; grandson Frankie Karamakopoulos (Evan Richards); younger brother Dino Forresti (Don Amendolia), a lounge singer who wanted to be Frank Sinatra and whose car horn played the theme from *The Godfather*; Padre Guardino (Ralph Manza), the ancient parish priest; and Father Jose Silva (Richard Yniguez), his handsome young Hispanic assistant who walked around in cut-off shorts, whom Connie lusted for until she found out what he did for a living.

Everyone, including the priests, got schooled by Mama on homespun morality. And, with the help of Austin (Raymond Singer), the nervous director of *Cooking with Mama Malone*, she did tie the problems of the day into the dish of the day, with lessons such as, "People who try to get away with stuff in cooking do the same in life."

Indeed, fans of *Cucina Amore* have tried to make reservations, only to find out that the restaurant does not exist. Aren't they miffed? "They feel cheated, so I take great personal care in handling those requests whenever I have the opportunity, so that they understand why that was done. Maybe that was a sign from God that I should look into opening a chain of restaurants." The fiction worked into the show has led some people to speculate that maybe Nick isn't for real, either. And granted, he's not for everyone, with his tales of family and his overt emotion. However, his loyal fans feel Stellino, who has been on TV's *Today, Good Morning America, CBS Saturday Morning, CNBC Business Center,* and a PBS documentary on Italian-Americans that also featured Alan Alda and Danny Aiello, is a family member.

Italian food is the food cooked most requently on television. What is it about Italian food and Chinese food that made them the first ethnic foods to really catch on in America? "Italian food perpetuated itself through the ceremony and celebration of the family dinner. The non-Italians had the opportunity to taste this food, and they found it fascinating. It's flavorful, it's easy to prepare, with ingredients you can grow yourself or find easily in the supermarket and basic preparation techniques. If you look at the Chinese way of doing things, very strong respect for the family, family and food very closely connected together, the cultures are very similar. Italian-American [cooking is a] different interpretation of the sauces and cooking of the meat. Americans need to have the meat, the starch, and the vegetables. That's not the way things are done in the old country. [There] people can make a meal out of a vegetable, like braised artichokes. Try to give to a paying American customer a plate of braised artichokes as an entree."

What is the secret of good home cooking? "Cooking is 20 percent technique and the other 80 percent is pure passion and love. If you are the greatest technician, but have no passion and no love, your food will always look great, but never taste great. It takes as much time to cook something badly as it takes to cook something perfectly."

TV Series

Cucina Amore (PBS, 1995–)

Books

Cucina Amore by Nick Stellino (Doubleday, 1995)

Nick Stellino's Glorious Italian Cooking: Romantic Meals, Menus and Music from Cucina Amore by Nick Stellino (Putnam Publishing Group, 1996)

Nick Stellino's Mediterranean Flavors by Nick Stellino, E. J. Armstrong (photographer), Patty Wittmann (illustrator) (Putnam Publishing Group, 1997)

Three Dog Bakery: It's a Dog's Kitchen

Mark Beckloff

Born: June 22, 1964.

Hometown: Kansas City, Missouri.

Parents: Father, Gerald L., an M.D., formed a pharmaceutical research and development company; mother, LuAnn, teacher, then bookkeeper for her husband's company.

Siblings: Older brothers, Mike and Mitch.

School: Baker University (Baldwin, Kansas).

Dan Dye

Born: June 28, 1959.

Hometown: Kansas City, Missouri.

Parents: Father, Virgil, import business owner; mother, Annetta, homemaker.

Siblings: Older brothers, Mike, Gerard, and Tim; younger sister, Theresa.

School: Rockhurst College (Kansas City, Missouri).

Always in the Dog Biscuit Pantry: Whole wheat flour, cornmeal, wheat germ, eggs, and vegetable oil. Then the flavorings: apples, honey, cinnamon, and molasses.

Dogs' Favorite Cooking Smells: Garlic and cinnamon.

Some would argue there's been a food revolution over the last thirty years; we're not just eating instant mashed potatoes, canned mushrooms, and iceberg lettuce anymore. Tell that to your dog. He's still eating biscuits filled with so many preservatives that they'll stick around longer than he does.

Not anymore, since dog lover Mark Beckloff got a Christmas present from his mom—a dog bone-shaped cookie cutter. She thought he should bake treats for his dogs. Beckloff and his partner Dan Dye started baking the biscuits in their home near Kansas City, Missouri, in 1990 to satisfy the in-between-meal cravings of their dogs Sarah, Dottie, and Gracie. They experimented with recipes in the basement, test marketed on neighbors' and coworkers' canines and consulted with area veterinarians. Then they started selling their KC-K9 biscuits on a wholesale basis only. The biscuits are made of all-natural products, ingredients like whole wheat and oat bran flour, cornmeal, eggs, spinach, carrots, and wheat germ (which helps promote a shiny coat), with no added sodium, sugars, or preservatives. "[The biscuits are] almost too healthy for human consumption," Beckloff jokes.

Mark Beckloff and Dan Dye have known each other since the mid-1980s when they worked together part-time on a customer service phone line in Kansas City. Later, when Dye was a copywriter for an advertising firm and Beckloff was an accounting clerk for a pharmaceutical company, they decided to start some kind of business together. "We were watching people get promoted just on longevity and not so much merit, and didn't really like that game. We wanted to start our own business, but we didn't know what we wanted to do. But we truly loved animals and knew we wanted to do something with animals, and something just clicked. We love dogs so much, we were doing this from the heart, not from the wallet side of it. We laugh because we didn't have any baking experience, business experience, or money, we just had a true love for dogs. Our arms are all scarred with burns from trial and error, and the dogs aren't picky... well, some are."

Pet stores and vet clinics began featuring their creations. Shortly, the company outgrew its basement facilities and transferred to a small, very inexpensive storefront in a bad area of Kansas City. There the partners spent twelve hours a day baking for their wholesale accounts. Then they thought, "Why don't we just open the doors and see if people will buy these fresh biscuits?" Beckloff was the first to quit his regular job and as soon as the Three Dog Bakery was ready, Dye joined him.

The enterprise soon outgrew that store as well. Dan and Mark found a new location in the entertainment district of Kansas City, known as Westport. Once opened, their shop began getting attention, in particular from print and broadcast media. The partners developed a Dogalog (like a catalog, see?) to complement their mail-order business, and their customer base continued to expand. Today the Dogalog is sent to more than 60,000 dog owners all over the world and offers treats such as Boxer Brownies, Puptarts, Pupcakes, and Big Scary Kitties.

In 1993, a reporter from the *Wall Street Journal* who just happened to be in Kansas City spotted the bakery and was inspired to do a story on the unique operation. The story appeared on the front page of the "Market Place" section. The guys had no idea what being featured prominently in the *Wall Street Journal* would mean. That showcase literally changed their lives. Five years later Beckloff, Dye, and the dogs were featured on the cover of the June 15, 1998, issue of *Forbes* magazine, which discussed entrepreneurs. They've also been profiled in *People* magazine, the *New York Times*, the *Los Angeles Times*, the *Boston Globe*, to name just a few, and have appeared on *The Today Show*, *The Dick Cavett Show*, the BBC, CNN, National Public Radio, and PBS.

When they appeared on the *Oprah Winfrey Show*, Oprah tasted a dog treat on camera. "My dogs've got your biscuits. They love them," she said. "And I was thinking of sampling these, because they do smell sort of like cookies—regular cookies." After tasting it, and hearing that they're low in fat, the talk show maven waved the biscuit to the audience and declared, "My new snack." (Interested? Call 1-800-4TREATS.) The men opened sixty bakeries in 1998 alone, including one in London.

Beckloff and Dye wrote the cookbook/memoir *Short Tails and Treats from Three Dog Bakery* (1996), which is the story of the business, with a few recipes included. To promote the book, they went on a ten-city tour, and hired a public relations firm that got them a five-minute segment on Food Network's *In Food Today*. The cable channel was interested in doing a cooking show for dogs, so Beckloff and Dye were invited to do

Chef du Jour four months later. Their appearance earned a great response, and they were invited back to do a full-fledged TV series. "They offered us a series called *Three Dog Bakery*," says Beckloff, "which was really great because they could have called it something like 'K9 Kitchen,' but this was our company name." Actually, the program was almost called "Three Dog Bakery Unleashed."

"One of things we tried to do on the show," Beckloff explains, "is keep everything very basic, because people are watching treats being made for the first time, probably. When you think of a dog treat you're thinking of chicken lips and feet and beaks. And now you see things like cornmeal, things that you may have eaten yourself. We wanted it not to be a chore for them to cook for their dogs, and there's nothing in the bakery that you wouldn't be able to eat. We aren't trying to be gourmet chefs. Kids love the show and baking the treats, and we kept it simple so kids could participate in that."

Fans of their TV offering don't seem to be limited to dog owners. "People tell us, 'We watch your show all the time and we don't even have a dog.'" Nevertheless, dogs and their owners are the target market. "People are realizing the entertainment value. There's a lot of violence and weird shows on TV, and cooking shows [in general] are very clean. It's fun to watch people create; there's an artistic value to it. It's also health consciousness, people taking more responsibility for what they're eating." And responsibility for what their dogs are consuming. "I don't like the word 'pamper,' but the dog's an important member of the family, and we want to try to make sure that dogs all across the country are being taken care of as best they can. It gives people something fun to do with their dogs, too."

Beckloff and Dye appear monthly on the Fox News Channel's *Pet News*, as well as Health Network's, *Ask the Vet*, shown locally on NBC Channel 41's *Kansas City Today*. They also participate monthly on a new interactive Internet Web site called Critter Connection. Their new show, *Unleashed*, can be seen on the Animal Planet channel starting in the fall of 1999.

Sara, Dottie, and Gracie (who is deaf) are very tied to the business, and they're all getting up there in years. They also get lots of mail, not to mention the collars, bowls, beds, and leashes. "At Christmas time you can't even imagine how many gifts they got from viewers," says Beckloff. "Gracie even got a wedding proposal from a Great Dane in Atlanta, who wrote, 'I usually don't write to girls who I haven't sniffed before but it was love at first sight when I saw you on TV.' They get more mail than we do."

Fans know that these dogs are pretty relaxed, and just sort of lounge around until it's time to eat the finished products. "People like to watch them get their treats. We filmed thirteen shows in five days, and they were so mellow, acting like [filming a TV show] is the most common thing." Mellowness is important, because Beckloff and Dye always drive with the dogs instead of flying.

So, did these guys ever really cook before? Beckloff's grandmother taught cooking at a university, and baking was her specialty. He used to spend time with her in the kitchen and watch her bake. When he was in second or third grade, he had an Easy-Bake Oven. "I always ended up eating more of the dough than what was actually baked, so I'd always feel sick by the time I finished." Fittingly, he grew up to bake dog treats, so he's not as inclined to eat the dough. Both guys did have food service jobs when they were teenagers. "In high school we both worked at Baskin Robbins," Beckloff said. "I ate ice cream all day and I gained, like, forty pounds when I worked there. So I'm just thankful [we're making] a dog treat, and it's very low in fat so even if you do eat it, it's healthy."

Although the idea of making home-baked treats for your dog may seem frivolous, it's not without sincerity for Mark Beckloff and Dan Dye. "Dogs are such great companions," says Beckloff, " and they offer so much unconditional love. We get so many people in the bakery who say, 'I've got nothing for my kids but I'm in here buying something for my dog.' We know people for whom the only reason to get out of bed is because of their dogs."

TV Series

Three Dog Bakery (Food Network, 1997–98)
Unleashed (Animal Planet, 1999–)

Books

Short Tails and Treats from Three Dog Bakery by Dan Dye and Mark Beckloff (Andrews & McMeel, 1996)
Three Dog Bakery Cookbook: Over 50 Recipes for All-Natural Treats for Your Dog by Dan Dye and Mark Beckloff (Andrews & McMeel, 1998)

Web Site

www.threedog.com

Jacques Torres:
The French Confection

Born: June 14, 1959.

Hometown: Bandol, France.

Parents: Father, Jean, carpenter; mother, Terese, housewife.

Siblings: Older brothers, Jean-Claude and Gaby.

School: Centre de Formation Professional (Carros, France, near Nice).

Favorite Junk Food: "We all snack. Chefs don't always eat well at the restaurant; we eat leaning on the corner of the table. I like everything American. I will snack on anything I have."

The Pastry Pantry: "Flour, sugar, eggs, butter, a little bit of salt, milk, perhaps vanilla, and some fruit. Then you are already way ahead. You can do lot of things with just those ingredients. Chocolate would help."

Favorite Food Smell: "Hot chocolate, a baking tart in the oven, or croissant, pan au chocolate. Go to a pastry shop when they make croissants in the morning. It smells so good."

Fantasy Last Meal: "Mom's food. I do believe we relate to what we grew up with and Mom's food is like home. Potato gratin with cream and cheese, a beautiful fricassee of rabbit with polenta and olives. And for dessert, fresh out of the oven with a nice puff pastry crust, a good apple tart with vanilla ice cream with extra cream in the vanilla ice cream."

Jacques Torres (*Dessert Circus*, PBS) grew up in a small village in the region of Provence, in southern France, on the Riviera. When he was a boy, he thought he wanted to be a diver, something a lot of people do in that region. However, that didn't last long. "I was afraid to hit my head coming up on the boat." Later, he considered becoming a carpenter, like his father. "Then I saw my dad cutting himself with carpentry equipment, so I thought, 'That's not for me.'" Number three on his list was chef, and his third choice was the charm. Wasn't he worried he'd cut himself with a knife? "Yeah, but I could eat as much as I want."

Not just any food, but pastry. Why? "I love to work with my hands, I love craftsmanship. And I love to eat. The combination of the two made me think about pastry. There's a lot of craftsmanship in pastries. It's a little bit like mathematics, it's very scientific. You have to learn why things interfere together the way they do, how things work together, and then you can come up with your own recipe. That actually makes the profession very interesting."

Pastry is scientific. After all, one of the most important pieces of pastry equipment is a scale. But it's also artistic. After school, Torres went to a drawing school located on Bendor, an island offshore from Bandol. "Imagine, you come out of school and you have to take a small boat to an island to go to art school. That was so cool. That made me very interested in drawing."

When he was fifteen, Torres decided to try the world of baking. During his next vacation, he began an apprenticeship at La Frangipan, a small pastry shop in his home town of Bandol. After two years, he completed his training requirements and graduated first in his class. He continued his practice of pastry-making in the town of La Cadiere d'Azur while waiting to fulfill his obligatory year of military time.

Then, one day in 1980, he was walking by the Hotel Negresco in Nice with a friend. "It's a very impressive hotel. You have the doorman with the hat and the feather on top of the hat, with his uniform, and it's a big white building with big windows, very, very luxurious, gold all over. It's like you go in here, and you picture when you're a kid these guys kicking you out! I was twenty years old, coming out of my military time, so I was looking for a job, and I said to my friend, 'Hey, what about here?' and she said, 'I bet you don't go there.'" However, Torres was feeling lucky. He went in and asked the Michelin two-star chef Jacques Maximin for a position. Maximin gave him sixty minutes to return to work with a chef's coat, thus starting a relationship that lasted eight years and took Jacques around the globe.

"I was so surprised, because usually, for that kind of place, you need to know someone, or there's a waiting list, and here I walk in, and an hour later I was in the kitchen working, and I was like, 'What the heck is going on?' It was so strange. I've always been very lucky, always been at the right place at the right time. That's luck. That's pure luck."

Torres settled in as a pastry worker at the Negresco, rising to the pastry chef's post the very next year. From 1980 to 1983, Torres went back to school (to the Centre de Formation Professional in Carros, near Nice on the Riviera) on his days off to earn the degree of Master Pastry Chef. He taught pastry at a local culinary school in Cannes from 1983 to 1986. During this time, he was also honing his skills in preparation for the daunting Meilleur Ouvrier de France competition. In 1986, at the age of twenty-six, Torres was awarded the prestigious medal, the youngest chef to earn the distinction.

The list of Torres' many culinary awards and achievements during this period includes consulting and product development for Cointreau and Valrhona; participation in the rededication ceremonies for the Statue of Liberty honoring French President Francois Mitterand and U.S. President Ronald Reagan; Le Figaro's Culinary Cruise through the countries of the Mediterranean; receipt of the gold medal of the Japanese Pastry Chef Association; winner of the 1986 French Championship of Desserts; culinary weeks in Tokyo, Sydney, Melbourne, and Spain; as well as participation in numerous competitions and culinary events in France.

In 1988, the Ritz-Carlton hotel chain invited Jacques to America as corporate pastry chef, shunting him through the pastry departments (with an emphasis on training personnel) in Laguna Niguel in California, Naples in Florida, and Atlanta. It was in that Georgia city in 1989 that Torres got the call from legendary restaurateur Sirio Maccioni of Le Cirque in New York, luring him to work in a $100,000 custom-built pastry kitchen. Torres quickly relocated to Manhattan, where he still lives today. Soon his creations at Le Cirque were praised as some of the most innovative desserts around.

Torres has opened his pastry kitchen at Le Cirque to aspiring students and shares his passion for the art of pastry. He serves as Dean of Pastry Arts at the French Culinary Institute in New York, where he designed the pastry school and its classrooms, created and wrote the curriculum, and continues to give lectures and demonstrations. He's been the James Beard Pastry Chef of the Year; Chefs of America Pastry Chef of the Year; one of *Chocolatier* magazine's ten Best Pastry Chefs; one of the "Masters" of The Masters of Food & Wine (a culinary Olympics in which top chefs and wine makers from around the world gather for what has been termed an "international culinary summit"); Chartreuse Pastry Chef Award winner; and a member of Academie Culinaire de France. Some of Jacques' TV appearances during the last decade include participation in *Merci Julia—the World's Top Culinary Professionals Salute Julia Child*; and Julia Child's *Master Chefs* television series. Torres has donated time to many national charity organizations such as the American Red Cross, Meals on Wheels, Gods Love We Deliver, New York's Hard of Hearing Association, Sloan Kettering Cancer Research Center, the Association to Benefit Children, and many others.

When Torres decided it was time to write a book on his art, he wanted it to reach a wide audience, not just professionals. So he turned to television. "I love what I do. My profession gave me what I have and what I am. I wanted to tell other people and give back to that profession what I get from it, so I wanted to teach people, to share where I am today and what I know today." This decision led him to talk with his colleagues, Jacques Pépin and the late Pierre Franey, and to contact Franey's producer, veteran cooking show producer Charles Pinsky, who was ready to do a pastry program. Once Pinsky and Torres found sponsors, *Dessert Circus* was born, and the companion book, *Dessert Circus: Extraordinary Desserts You Can Make at Home*, was published in 1997.

Dessert Circus was one of the first TV cooking shows filmed in front of a live audience. This was Torres' idea. "I give a lot of classes with 100 people in front of me. I told Charlie [Pinsky], 'If you give me an audience and let me interact with them, I will forget about the camera.' I talk to the people, and I tell them what I'm doing and I ask them questions and they ask me questions. And if I don't like them I throw food at them!" The audience also gets to taste his creations at the end of the show, which has to be worth the price of admission. "Most of the time I ask kids [to taste], because kids will tell you if they don't like something, and that's funny."

Children are also a big part of the *Dessert Circus* home audience. A lot has to do with the circus-like animation that pops up throughout the TV program. "We put those animations in the first show just to keep the circus spirit up, and when we got email that kids look at the show and love to see the show because of the animation, we started to put more of them. We have some complaints from some adults who say, 'Why do you put those animations in? They have nothing to do with a cooking show.' But I interact a lot with kids during the show. They are fun; I love kids. So that's why the animation and that's why I want that audience. More and more I receive email from parents thanking me, and saying, 'Now I can watch something with my kids besides cartoons.' Kids look at the animations, they look at the cooking show, they get interested in food, and the parents learn something. We didn't plan it at the beginning, but that was a good direction."

Apparently dogs are interested, too. "Every time I cook [my dog Mindy] sits in the kitchen, and nothing can bother her. She just looks at me and what I'm doing, so I always say, 'She wants to learn how to cook.'" Mindy is a thirteen-year-old lab and golden retriever mix with arthritis who "still has that puppy face." She travels everywhere with Torres and his girlfriend, Kris Kruid, a contributor to his cookbook. Torres enjoys going back to his hometown and visiting his parents in the south of France. "You get up early, get some fresh bread, make coffee and have breakfast outside, think about what you're going to do for lunch, nap in the afternoon, go to the beach, and think about dinner. The vacation goes very fast."

Most of us probably imagine we'd expand to blimp size if we were surrounded by pastry all day. Torres is in great physical shape, but he admits to being a sugar addict. "I need my 'fix,' I think you call it, of sugar each day. Sugar is a drug, it keeps you up. When I go home after hours of not eating sugar all day, I need sugar, so if I have a box of M&Ms, I'll eat them. I don't get sick of it, I just miss it if I don't have it."

Nonetheless, having a sweet tooth is not enough to propel someone into the career of pastry chef. Few people outside the food world know that the pastry kitchen is a completely different arena than the cook's kitchen, and meant for entirely different people. In fact, at the French Culinary Institute, students are given a test to assess which kitchen they'd be happier in. Torres borrows an analogy from a friend to explain the difference. "[If chefs were doctors,] the guy in the emergency room would be the cook—somebody's sick and you have to take care of him right away and anything can happen, and things are going very fast and you have to fix people. Now, the pastry chef would be the surgeon. He can plan, he can think about it, he can look at all the x-rays, then he's going to do the surgery, then he can do another patient. It's a lot more planning, and not as crazy as the emergency room." In fact, like surgeons, pastry chefs often suffer from carpal tunnel syndrome.

"In the kitchen it's the same; if you come during the [dinner] service you can see the cooks running all over, and doing things last minute. In pastry you cannot do anything last minute. Everything has to be ready; it's a completely different job. Somebody who doesn't like to plan in advance, who doesn't like mathematics, who doesn't like to be organized, cannot be a pastry chef."

Still, the message Jacques wants to get across is that, despite its reputation, pastry is not that complicated. "If you understand why things work the way they work, why you are going to use bread flour or cake flour, and actually, what is bread flour and what is cake flour, what's in the flour, to me that's the most important thing. People are scared of pastry because they don't know beforehand, before the end of the recipe, what's going to happen. If you know the step by step, if you know what's happening during the time you do it, you can fix mistakes before they happen, before that cake comes out of the oven."

"I always tell people you have to know your ingredients, you have to know your techniques. Then making desserts becomes really easy. They become idiot-proof because you know what you're looking for. When you start the recipe: read the recipe a couple of times and understand what the chef wants; have all the ingredients ready; have all the right equipment. Then you have to take the time to do it. If it doesn't work the first time, that's okay, you can do it again another time. Try it a few times. People think a recipe is going to work perfectly the first time. Yes, sometimes, but it's like driving. Somebody gives you directions and you go a little on the left and it's not there, and you go a little bit on the right and it's not there, and then you find where you want to go, so the second time, you're going to go a lot faster. Following a recipe is a little bit like that."

The freedom with a cooking show about pastry comes from the fact that no one is thinking about diet and health; you can't complain about calories if you tune into a dessert show. It's pure fantasy with no apologies. Why are people tuning into cooking shows in general? "You have to cook everyday. You have to fix dinner, you have to fix lunch. It's something you cannot avoid; most everybody must do that at home. So automatically you develop an interest [in cooking shows]. We all have a little repertoire of what we like to cook at home. I do. I'm part of those people who have those ten things I like to cook at home, and I like to look at cooking shows because sometimes you find something easier or something faster."

TV Series

Dessert Circus (PBS, 1998–)

Books

Dessert Circus: Extraordinary Desserts You Can Make at Home by Jacques Torres, Christina Wright, Kris Kruid, John Uher (photographer) (William Morrow & Co., 1998)

The French Culinary Institute's Salute to Healthy Cooking: From America's Foremost French Chefs by Alain Sailhac, Jacques Torres, French Culinary Institute (Rodale Press, 1998)

Web Site

www.jacquestorres.com/jtmain.htm

Ming Tsai:
Food Tsai-ence

Born: March 29, 1964.

Hometown: Dayton, Ohio.

Parents: Father, Stephen, mechanical engineer and author; mother, Iris, ex-restaurant owner.

Siblings: Older brother, Ming-Hsi, engineer (Chef Ming's full name is really Ming-Hao).

Schools: Yale University (New Haven, Connecticut); Cornell University (Ithaca, New York) (Master's).

Favorite Junk Food: "We go through barrels and barrels of pretzels at home, but that's not really junk food because there's no fat. I actually don't do junk food, but I do love fried foods."

Favorite Cooking Smell: "Caramelized garlic and onions, or garlic and ginger. Second to that, the yeast-y smell of fresh baked bread."

Favorite Cooking Sound: "The super-hot wok or sauté pan; you add your ingredients, and you have that huge sizzle."

Always in the Pantry: "Pretzels, soy sauce, sesame oil, garlic, ginger, all types of oils, and fleur de sal."

Always in the Fridge: "Fifteen to twenty different hot sauces, all Asian types, also Southwest and Caribbean hot sauces, beer, miso paste, and assorted cheeses."

Fantasy Last Meal: "I'd have toro, the lower belly of the tuna; it's the filet mignon of a tuna, and o-toro is the premium of toro. You eat it on a little bit of rice and it's the most succulent fish you'll ever put in your mouth. It just melts in your mouth. I'd probably throw in some truffles and foie gras."

Ming Tsai (*East Meets West with Ming Tsai*, Food Network) grew up in Ohio, and at thirteen, started cooking in his mother's Chinese restaurant, Mandarin Kitchen. He did everything there, from being prep cook to manager. "It became my instant summer job. That was really my first taste of cooking professionally. I always loved eating, and even as a kid would be in the kitchen to see my grandpa cooking. [In] the Chinese heritage, food is more than just a means of eating. And we always based our decisions of travel around food—a typical conversation while eating is, 'Where are we eating next?'"

After graduating from Phillips Academy (in Andover, Massachusetts) in 1982, the analytically minded Tsai was off to Yale University to earn a degree in mechanical engineering to follow in the footsteps of his father and brother. "It seemed like a natural for me to do that, so when I got to college I was very gung-ho about it and took more courses than normal, but then, by the end of sophomore year, I decided this was for the birds. I just couldn't see myself being an engineer for the rest of my life."

Deciding that it would be easier to finish the program than start all over with something else, Tsai completed his engineering degree in 1986. The summer between junior and senior year, he continued his cooking education in France at the Cordon Bleu. "I thought 'Wow, the French know how to cook too!' Especially in desserts. The Asians don't have anything worth talking about with desserts."

After finishing up at Yale, he went back to Paris to work as a pastry cook at Fauchon and a sous-chef at Natacha. It was at the latter place that Tsai first experimented with East-West cuisine, combining his knowledge of Asian ingredients with the French technique, sometimes called fusion cuisine. "This was really pivotal. It was a platform to try [the food out] on real people, not just at home."

Back in the United States, Ming furthered his education in the food business by attending Cornell University's Hotel School in Ithaca, New

York, where he earned his master's degree in 1989. Next, he spent two years in the business, rising from Assistant Food and Beverage Director to Food and Beverage Director at the Hotel Inter-continental in Chicago. "I decided this was, again, for the birds. Being in the hotel business is thankless. It's low-paying, extremely long hours, ninety-hour weeks, and it's more about kissing [the General Manager's] ass than your ability. I also just really missed cooking; I felt I'd rather be chopping garlic than doing [some] budget. I started just 'jonesing'—I needed to get back to the kitchen."

In 1992, Tsai accepted a job as executive sous-chef at Silks in San Francisco. The East-West cuisine proved to be a perfect fit, and it was there that he met one of his mentors, Ken Hom. "That really got me back into the kitchen and since then I have not turned back." When he took that assignment, he had prearranged to spend the summer in Japan, studying that cuisine firsthand as a sushi chef. "That was an incredible experience because the Japanese certainly have their own way of cooking; incredible discipline and organization of the kitchen, and very specialized. I'm a huge believer that you need to learn how to do something traditionally first; in other words, you need to learn how to make sushi rice the correct way before you start to do it differently in fusing it and combining it with other elements. The problem is young chefs out there who read about five-spice powder, throw a handful in, and say, 'Fusion cuisine!' but they have no understanding. It doesn't mean you have to go to Japan; you can work in the restaurants here. But there is a right and a wrong way. Learn the right way, then, with respect to the ingredient, bring it into your cuisine."

Ming also added to his culinary education in 1994 when he became the executive chef at the Ginger Club Restaurant in Palo Alto, California, which specialized in tropical Southeast Asian cuisine. The next year found him in a new position as executive chef at Santa Cafe in Santa Fe, New Mexico. The Cafe served up "East meets Southwest" cuisine. In a short time, he was honored as best chef in Santa Fe. Tsai then set up shop in the Boston area in 1998 with Blue Ginger, a 130-seat East-West bistro in Wellesley, Massachusetts. Here, a Feng Shui Master was consulted on the design of the restaurant.

Tsai's wife, Polly Talbott-Tsai, is a trained nurse whom he married in 1995, and she is very involved in the restaurant operation. "When I decided to do Blue Ginger, I gave her free option: 'If you want to work with me, great, if you don't, power to you because the marriage is more important than the job.' At the beginning she continued being a hospice nurse, but once we started doing the 'build out,' she realized she was actually part owner and, having put the house up and having both our money involved, she said, 'So, if this thing goes down, we're out!'" So Talbott-Tsai got involved, even with very little restaurant experience. Not only does she helps with the hostessing duties, she taught herself accounting and does all the books. "It's great," says Tsai, "because I don't have to worry about the trust issue."

Chinatown, My Chinatown

Why is Chinese cuisine the most popular Asian food in America? Chef Ming Tsai explains: "When the Chinese were brought here to do [build] the railroads, a lot of Chinese restaurants started opening up because their kids need some kind of métier to support themselves. Cooking just seemed a natural because that was something that you could have full control of and you can be your own business. It was a means of survival. Chinese food and Asian food in general have never been considered upscale food. When French cuisine came over, it was brought over with Rene Verdon [the Kennedys' chef], so everyone looked at French food as haute cuisine; that was its introduction to this country. Chinese food, or any Asian food, was really brought over by the lower middle class, and those restaurants that flourished from that were really the working class people who needed a means of survival. Plus, there are lots of Chinatowns; in the major cities there are two Chinatowns. As with any immigration, [Chinese immigrants] went to the lowest rent district first because they couldn't afford anything else. So, funnily enough, almost every Chinatown is next to every red-light district in the world. I guess it's convenient if you're a pervert and Chinese!"

Ming and his wife, who have a "four-legged daughter" named Jasmin (an Australian shepherd/collie mix), could have encountered one another as kids, but they didn't. "She's Caucasian, and was actually born in Dayton, Ohio. We never met in Dayton even though I lived there eighteen years. Her brother was my squash coach at Yale; he introduced us when

I was a sophomore at college. Polly was at Colorado University in Boulder, majoring in Chinese. Because she was studying Chinese, David the coach said, 'Hey, you should meet this guy.' She speaks great Chinese, according to my parents she has a better accent than I do, which really pisses me off! We speak Chinese together, especially at the restaurant when we want to talk about someone."

Tsai channels his competitive nature by continuing to play squash. "I love squash. I still compete when I can, and play tournaments. In the winter, I love to ski and snowboard. My new-found love is scuba diving, something that my wife and I love doing together—she's much better than me, so she loves doing that!"

Tsai's TV career began when Food Network's *Dining Around,* a show that often scouted out new chefs for use on the network's other shows, came to film in his restaurant kitchen. Tsai was called back for *Ready...Set...Cook!* and *Chef du Jour* in 1997. It seemed ludicrous to him that the Food Network had no Asian-influenced show, and he told them so. "I was persistent. I did a lot of *Cooking Live* [filling in] for Sara Moulton. I was her pinch-hitter over the last year and a half. I was a guest on *In Food Today.* Whenever they asked me to do anything, I would go to New York. I was chugging away." Finally, the premise for his own show was agreed upon, and it became *East Meets West.*

"The mission of the show is: don't be scared of a cuisine that you may not be familiar with, i.e., Asian cuisine. Nowadays you can almost get any ingredient anywhere in the world because of transportation. Something like ginger—if you don't know how to use it, it's just like an onion, which is used in every other cuisine. Asian cuisines are just as easy as any other ones; people are just unfamiliar with them, having not grown up with them. [I want to] get people to feel comfortable using these ingredients and to really demystify Asian cuisine."

Are there misconceptions about Asian cuisine? "People think it's extremely prep intensive, that they have to chop all day to get it together. That might be true, you might do a little more prep, but the cooking time is much faster. A lot of the stir fries, you cook them in five minutes and you're done, as opposed to a lot of other cooking techniques that take a lot longer. So at the end of the day, it takes no longer to make a meal. People are comfortable making a meatloaf and roasting a turkey and did not grow up cutting lemon grass and using soy sauce, but they certainly used Worcestershire sauce. If you can use Worcestershire you can use soy sauce."

And why is cooking on television so popular these days? "It's not junk TV. People don't think they're wasting time as much as if they just watch eight hours of TV because they are learning something."

TV Series

East Meets West with Ming Tsai (Food Network, 1998–)

Web Site

www.foodtv.com

Martin Yan: Yan the Man

Born: December 22, 1950.

Hometown: Guangzhou, China.

Parents: Father, Tak-Ming, restaurant manager; mother, Xi Mei, store manager (in China).

Siblings: Younger brother, Michael.

Schools: Overseas Institute of Cookery (Hong Kong, China); University of California at Davis (Davis, California).

Favorite Junk Food: "You can call me a chip-a-holic. Put a bowl of tortilla chips and fresh guacamole or tomato salsa in front of me and I will lose all forms of self-control. My favorite Mexican restaurant nicknames me 'Mr. Chip.'"

Always in the Pantry: "My pantry will never be without soy sauce, sesame oil, five-spice powder, hoisin, and oyster flavored sauce."

Always in the Fridge: "I love tofu so I will always have that in my fridge. Also, soy milk, ginger, some lemon grass, and yes, my mother's favorite, Chinese sausages."

Favorite Food Smell: "Lemon zest, and fresh cut ginger.... I wish they would make a perfume with that combination."

Favorite Food Sound: "The sound of chopping is always in my mind. I guess it is like the case of a musician hearing imaginary drumbeats.

I tap my chopsticks or pencils on the desk sometimes just to remind myself of it. Tap, tap, tap, chop, chop, chop, just like a cleaver hitting a chopping board."

Fantasy Last Meal: "I always like my meals simple, so my last meal should be like all my other meals: light, simple, healthy, and tasty. My personal favorite is tofu, with lots of vegetables. It is my link to nature."

Martin Yan (*Yan Can Cook*, PBS) can debone an entire chicken in under twenty seconds, and his cleaver has clocked so many miles traveling the world with him that it qualifies as a frequent flyer on its own.

Yan was born in the eastern part of China, about 200 miles north of Shanghai, where his father ran a restaurant named Tac Kee and his mother operated a grocery store. His father died when Martin was three. His mother sold the restaurant but kept the store to support the family. As a result, the Yans didn't have much. "When I was about four or five in the mid-1950s," Yan told the *Boston Globe*, "China was probably like the Depression in this country, and everything was rationed. One time I went home and it smelled so good I ran into the kitchen. Then I noticed it was not food; My mother was stir-frying marbles. We were just kind of pretending psychologically. We'd eat our rice and suck on a marble and get the sauce."

The Cultural Revolution of the 1960s took its toll. "All our property was nationalized, taken away. All my relatives told me I better leave, so I left when I was thirteen." Yan was sent to Hong Kong for high school. For five years, he lived, apprenticed, and slept (he laid a plank across a booth for his bed) in a distant uncle's Kowloon restaurant. Because of the scarcity of housing in Hong Kong, this was not uncommon. Poor families often sent their children to live and work in restaurants because there's always food for them. Nonetheless, Yan took to it. "When other children were outside playing sports and games, I was busy playing chef. I guess I knew early on that my place is in the kitchen."

Martin soon earned his diploma from the Overseas Institute of Cookery in Hong Kong, where he shopped for food for classes in exchange for tuition. It was there that he met his mentor, chef Dick Chu, from whom Yan learned his now famous cutting techniques and his obsession with cleanliness. Yan then traveled to Canada for further schooling, but, preferring a warmer climate, transferred to California. "I came to California because there are too many chefs in China and not enough TVs," he once told the *San Jose Mercury News*.

Yan earned his bachelor's and master's degrees in Food Science from the University of California at Davis in 1975. He had originally thought about becoming a pharmacist or chemical engineer, and was interested in the science of why things happen to food. Yan literally cooked his way through school. After seeing Julia Child perform her culinary magic on television, he proposed teaching a cooking class at the University of California, Davis Extension (UC-Davis), in Davis, California, eighteen miles west of Sacramento and about fifty miles north of San Francisco. His course, which taught students how to make Chinese homestyle meals, was called "The Art and Science of Chinese Cuisine," and was held in a local coffee shop.

Having learned English at age sixteen, Martin found it difficult to shake his accent, and had difficulty engaging the students. In fact, they would sometimes fall asleep. During one class, a student was snoring so loud he was distracting his classmates. Yan grabbed his wok and spatula, stood right over the guy, hit the wok with the spatula like it was a gong, and said, "You paid a fortune to go to sleep? Go home!"

Everybody laughed, even Snoring Guy, who was now wide awake. Yan got the message: humor is a good teaching method. If people are having fun, they'll learn more and faster, and it was more fun for the teacher, too. A persona was born.

After finishing up at UC-Davis, Yan returned to Hong Kong for two years to work as a food technologist. Despite the cold he then moved to Calgary in the western province of Alberta, Canada. As the Cultural Revolution was ebbing, the Red Guard dragged his mother into the streets and publicly humiliated her for being a capitalist. Yan knew he had to get her and his brother out of China, and Canada offered new immigrants the opportunity to petition immediately to bring over their relatives. Yan credits his mother with his success. "Without sounding overly sentimental, I must say that I owe much of my professional career to my mother. She will always be the best cook in my mind. I remember growing up and seeing her happily buzzing around our tiny kitchen. She looked so happy. I couldn't wait until I was old enough to pick up the wok."

Martin's big TV break occurred in 1978 after he began teaching Saturday cooking classes at his newly opened restaurant in Calgary. One of his students was a local TV producer, and invited him to do a twelve-minute spot on a talk show to fill in for the scheduled chef, who was ill. Yan turned that one appearance into a daily cooking program, *Yan Can*. (He added the "Cook" when people were calling up to ask "Yan Can what?") In 1982, public television station KQED began producing *Yan Can Cook* in San Francisco, and the rest is media history. And even though the guy can debone an entire chicken in less than twenty seconds, he usually ends his show with "If Yan can cook, so can you!"

No Soup for You

Though not quite foodies, TV's *Seinfeld* (1990–98) clan was almost always discussing food, and spent quite a bit of time at Monk's Diner (which is really Tom's Diner on Broadway in Manhattan's Upper West Side). There was the copious supply of cereal boxes in Jerry's kitchen (the very first cereal box to be shown on *Seinfeld* was on the pilot, called the *Seinfeld Chronicles*—it was a package of "Oaties"). The Seinfeld universe includes foods, the mention of which can instantly bring to mind, for a true *Seinfeld* fan, the episode in which they were featured. Some of the items from that world: chocolate babka, marble rye, black and white cookies, Bosco, Chunkys, Jujyfruit, Junior Mints, Kenny Rogers Roasters, Macinaw peaches, muffin tops, paella, Pez, Tic Tacs, Twix, and Yoo-hoo.

But *Seinfeld*'s greatest impact was felt by the soup world. After the "Soup Nazi" was featured in the November 2, 1995, episode of *Seinfeld*, soup restaurants sprang up everywhere. Ali "Al" Yeganeh, the real-life inspiration for TV's "Soup Nazi," was *not* very pleased about this whole *Seinfeld* thing, and when Jerry Seinfeld came by to apologize for calling him "Soup Nazi," Yeganeh told him to apologize nationally, which never happened.

Keen observers of the human condition, the gang also noticed food behavior, such as George double-dipping a chip, Elaine's boss eating his Snickers candy bar with a knife and fork, and George's girlfriend moaning louder for risotto than she did for him.

Germophobe Jerry said it all in the episode where restaurateur Poppie didn't wash his hands after using the bathroom, and proceeded to knead the dough for Jerry's special pizza meal: "A chef who doesn't wash is like a cop who steals—it's a cry for help."

Martin has been a guest chef/instructor at many professional chef programs, including the California Culinary Academy and Johnson & Wales University (he also serves on both schools' advisory committees), the University of San Francisco, and Chinese chef-training programs across North America. He founded the Yan Can International Cooking School in Foster City, California, in 1985. *Yan Can Cook* was recognized twice by the James Beard Foundation with the James Beard Award for Best TV Cooking Show in 1994 and Best TV Food Journalism in 1996. In 1998, the television series received a Daytime Emmy for best cinematography.

Yan has also been honored with the prestigious Antonin Careme Award by the Chef's Association of the Pacific Coast and the Courvoisier Leadership Award by Courvoisier. He was named Culinary Diplomat for the American Culinary Federation, and received an Honorary Doctorate Degree in Culinary Arts from Johnson & Wales University. He has appeared on *The Phil Donahue Show, The Home Show, Live! with Regis and Kathie Lee,* and *The Tonight Show with Jay Leno.*

Fans of *Yan Can Cook* know that the vegetables may be fresh, but the puns are not. Especially in the early years, you could expect to hear G-rated groaners like "The Chinese eat anything that flies except a kite!" or "No one used to eat beef in China because cattle were needed to help cultivate the land. After all, why would anyone be so foolish as to stir-fry their tractors?" And if it's time to cook salmon, you can expect to hear "Something fishy here!" Some viewers have genially compared him to an old-fashioned snake oil salesman, or called him the Soupy Sales of cooking, or the Chinese Jackie Mason, which is interesting, considering that Yan himself has said that the Chinese culture does not really have stand-up comedy.

On any given day, *Yan Can Cook* airs in one of seventy-five countries, including China, India, Italy, Northern Ireland, South Africa, New Zealand, and Spain. This means the potential audience is more than one billion people each week. This is a man who has shot more than 1,500 shows. He attributes his success, in part, to timing. Martin came onto the scene in the early 1980s, just as the wave of food shows hit America. He feels he's demystifying Chinese cuisine, introducing one culture to another, just like an ambassador. In fact, changing people's perception of Chinese food, getting across the message that it's not chop suey, is Yan's mission.

"Americans are becoming more aware of their health and how a light healthy diet can contribute to their well-being. Chinese food is well-balanced, rich in grain and vegetables, and we always emphasize fresh ingredients. The Chinese have been advocating healthy eating for thousands of years. I am glad that it is finally being brought to the attention of the average American family." Yan's own family includes Susan, his wife of ten years and office manager, and their twin sons, Devin and Colin, born in 1994.

What makes a cuisine is the way it's prepared, not the ingredients, which Yan does play with. However, no matter what he prepares, he's cooking it the Chinese way. For example, in Chinese cooking, you wouldn't roast a whole piece of meat, as in Western cuisine. The Chinese always cut up the meat. Meat is also often used as a seasoning, not a main course. Besides, you can't use chopsticks to eat a whole piece of meat. It's really the difference between a culture where meat was readily available and cheap, and one where it wasn't.

The popularity of Chinese food caught on in America in the 1950s, like Italian food, and before other Asian foods. Yan believes that's because Chinese cuisine is not too hot or spicy, uses common, easy-to-find ingredients, and does not demand an acquired taste like other Asian cuisines, such as Thai food. In that way, Chinese dishes are probably the most "mainstream American" of the Asian cuisines. As Asia's standard of living keeps rising in the 1990s, and people all over the world explore Thai, Vietnamese, Malaysian, and Korean foods, Yan's latest TV shows are on hand to help viewers through this adventurous journey. In Yan's explorations of Asian cuisines other than Chinese, he is more of a travel partner, and more introspective than in his early live-audience shows, when he was more about entertainment.

Martin is quick to acknowledge his colleagues. "I have always been a big fan of cooking shows. I must have watched every single episode of Julia Child and Graham Kerr and I am the number one fan of my great friend, Master Chef Jacques Pépin. These shows are entertaining and you know, you can really learn a thing or two if you pay attention."

Is cooking on TV more popular now than it was when he first started? Yan thinks so. "Life in the nineties is all about getting back to basics, but in a quality way. Ask any homebuilder and he will tell you that the new homebuyers are getting more and more demanding on what types of appliances go into their new kitchens. The kitchen is quickly becoming the most popular room in the house as people are entertaining more and more at home. When people are emphasizing food more, there is a greater need for the knowledge of food and cooking. Maybe this explains the recent rise in the popularity of cooking shows. [Still], many people still believe that cooking delicious meals is something for the professional chefs. Not true at all. Anyone with enthusiasm and will-power can do it. Of course, a nice sharp cleaver won't hurt either. . . . "

TV Series

Yan Can Cook (PBS, 1983–) (also Food Network, 1996–97)
Martin Yan's Sizzling Wok (Chinese-language cooking show, 1995–)
Yan Can Cook in China (China's first cooking show, 1996–)

TV Specials

Edible Roots: Singapore (Food Network, 1996, 1997)
Edible Roots: Philippines (Food Network, 1996, 1997)
Edible Roots: Hong Kong (Food Network, 1996, 1997)

Books

Yan Can Cookbook by Martin Yan (Doubleday & Co., 1982)
The Joy of Wokking by Martin Yan (Doubleday & Co., 1982)
Martin Yan, the Chinese Chef by Martin Yan (Doubleday & Co., 1985)
A Wok for All Seasons by Martin Yan (Doubleday & Co., 1988)
Everybody's Wokking by Martin Yan (Harlow & Ratner, 1991)
The Well-Seasoned Wok by Martin Yan (Harlow & Ratner, 1992)
Simply Delicious by Martin Yan (Culinary Connection, 1993),
Too Easy Gourmet: The World's First Non-Fiction Cookbook by Ben Levitan, Martin Yan (Too Easy Gourmet Press, 1994)
A Simple Guide to Chinese Ingredients and Other Asian Specialties by Martin Yan (Yan Can Cook, 1994)
Martin Yan's Culinary Journey Through China by Martin Yan (KQED, 1997)
Martin Yan's Asia: Favorite Recipes from Hong Kong, Singapore, Malaysia, the Philippines, and Japan by Martin Yan, Geoffrey Nilsen (photographer) (KQED, 1997)
Well-Seasoned Wok by Martin Yan (Fine Communications, 1998)

Web Site

www.yancancook.com

PART

3

Appendices

Vast Tasteland:
An A-to-Z List of
Fictional TV Food Folks

Adam (*Northern Exposure*, 1991–95): condescending chef hiding out in remote Cicely, Alaska, who was initially mistaken for Bigfoot. Often heard to cry, "Bacon is not pancetta!" Played by Adam Arkin.

Alice (*The Brady Bunch*, 1969–74): purveyor of traditional, suburban, stick-to-your-ribs grub for a man named Brady and his family. She loved meat so much she waited around for a butcher to propose to her. Played by Ann B. Davis.

Anal Retentive Gourmet (*Saturday Night Live*, 1986–94, occasional) Spoof of a cooking show starring a gourmet who liked to line up his vegetables in order of size. Played by the late, great Phil Hartman.

Arnold/Al (*Happy Days*, 1975–83): Arnold's was the hangout for the *Happy Days* gang, and Arnold (né Matsuo Takahashi), the cook/proprietor, was played by Pat Morita (1975–76, 1982–83), a character actor who often played food service guys on TV. He played Yamata, Felix and Oscar's partner in a Japanese restaurant on *The Odd Couple*, and reprised his role as Arnold (from *Happy Days*) on the short-lived *Blansky's Beauties* (1977). Morita's Arnold (on *Happy Days*) was replaced for five years by Al, played by Al Molinaro, also an *Odd Couple* alumnus (Murray the cop).

Gareth Blackstock (*Chef!* 1993–) (British): the high-strung chef de cuisine at England's upscale restaurant, Le Chateau Anglais. Played by Lenny Henry.

Sheila Bradey (*Tattingers/Nick and Hillary*, 1988–89): no-nonsense chef at New York restaurant, Tattingers, a show that was first an hour "dramedy," then a half-hour comedy, then canceled. Played by Mary Beth Hurt.

Fritz Brenner (*Nero Wolfe*, 1981): gourmet cook for rotund gentleman detective Nero Wolfe (portrayed by portly actor William Conrad). Played by George Voskovec.

Don Brockett (*Mister Rogers' Neighborhood*, 1968–95): gruff-voiced chef in Fred Rogers' neighborhood bakery. Played himself.

Nat Busiccio (*Beverly Hills, 90210*, 1990–): father figure and free food supplier for a bunch of spoiled rich kids whose weekly allowances add up to more than his yearly take from the "Peach Pit" diner. Played by Joe E. Tata.

Sara Campbell (*The Simple Life*, 1998): Martha Stewart clone who relocates her TV show from Manhattan to upstate New York to practice what she preaches. Played by Judith Light.

Chuy Castillos (*Golden Palace*, 1992–93): cook at the Golden Palace hotel, the business bought by sans–Bea Arthur *Golden Girls*. Played by Cheech Marin.

Chef of the Past/Future (*The Honeymooners*, 1955): characters played by Ralph Kramden and Ed Norton to sell the Handy Housewife Helper on television. Played by Jackie Gleason and Art Carney.

Frasier and Niles Crane (*Frasier*, 1993–) Seattle psychiatrist brothers who enjoy finer foods and wine so much they are likely to have major arguments over them. Played by the Emmy-winning Kelsey Grammer and the Emmy-winning David Hyde Pierce.

Nat E. Dred (*Fridays*, 1980–82, occasionally): I-ree! The one-joke wonder from *Fridays*, ABC's attempt at a *Saturday Night Live*-type show, Dred was known as the Rasta Chef, whose favorite ingredient was his beloved herb. His motto was "Where there's smoke there should be ganja." Played by Darrow Igus.

Earl (*Amanda's*, 1983): excitable chef at Amanda's By the Sea on this American rip-off of Britcom *Fawlty Towers* starring Beatrice Arthur as Amanda. Played by Rick Hurst.

Vernon Gaines (*A Different World*, 1988–93): gruff fry cook who dispensed advice to the students at Hillman College, after Lisa Bonet left. Played by Lou Myers.

Edna Garrett (*The Facts of Life*, 1979–86): meddling matronly housemother, cook, and nutritionist for the Eastland School for Girls. She pulled Tootie (Kim Fields) out of a jam or two. Played by Charlotte Rae, in a role she originated on *Diff'rent Strokes*.

Monica Geller (*Friends*, 1994–): extremely thin chef who supposedly used to be fat. She lives in a huge apartment in New York City with her friends and never seems to really work. Played by Courteney Cox.

Igor (*M*A*S*H**, 1976–83): Chipped beef on toast, anyone? At the M*A*S*H* 4077 you can get it with a smirk from mess hall guy Igor, played by Jeff Maxwell, who recently cashed in on the series role with a cookbook.

Laura Kelly (*Duet*, 1987–89): California caterer and Mary Tyler Moore clone who met her writer boyfriend Ben in a supermarket. Played by Mary Page Keller.

Lunch Lady Doris (*The Simpsons*, 1990–): a woman in a hairnet who loved her work. When Lisa Simpson was looking for something meatless to eat at the school cafeteria, Doris suggested, "Try the meatloaf." Voiced originally by Doris Grau.

Renata Malone (*Mama Malone*, 1984): stereotypical Italian mama who hosted her own fictional cooking show from her Brooklyn apartment, and taught everyone everything. Played by Lila Kaye.

Sarah Marshall and David Stuart (*Working It Out*, 1990): two divorced single parents who meet in a night-school cooking class and make beautiful ravioli together. Starring two veterans of food-based shows, Stephen Collins, late of *Tattingers*, and Jane Curtin, who played a divorcee-turned caterer on *Kate & Allie*. Mary Beth Hurt, also of *Tattingers*, was also on this show. Six degrees of (food) preparation!

Kate McArdle and Allie Lowell (*Kate & Allie*, 1984–89): Can two divorced women live together, with their kids, without driving each other crazy? Susan Saint James and Jane Curtin did in Manhattan, and in the last few years of the series, they even worked together, running a catering business.

Jerome "Chef" McElroy (*South Park*, 1997–): employee of South Park Elementary, and a friend and advisor to Stan, Kyle, Eric, and the ill-fated Kenny. "Chef" often breaks into song about "laying down" whatever woman happens to be around. Perfectly voiced by Isaac Hayes, the first African-American composer to win an Oscar. In the 1970s, he won a Grammy and a Golden Globe for his score to the movie *Shaft*.

Howard Miller (*It's a Living*, 1985–89): acerbic chef at Over the Top, a posh Los Angeles restaurant. Played by Richard Stahl. He was the longest-running chef on this sitcom, replacing Earl Boen (1981–82) as Dennis, who replaced Bert Remsen (1980–81) as Mario.

Sue Ann Nivens a.k.a. "The Happy Homemaker" (*Mary Tyler Moore Show*, 1973–77): man-hungry host of a Minneapolis TV cooking show who would smile at you while sleeping with your husband. Emmy-winning role played by Betty White.

Dana Palladino (*Love & War*, 1993–95): temperamental chef at The Blue Shamrock, a New York restaurant/bar, who had quit her job at a fancy French restaurant when she was passed over for the post of executive chef. Annie Potts earned an Emmy nomination for this role that hardly anyone remembers. She costarred with Jay Thomas, who was no stranger to food-based comedy—he played Remo the pizza guy in *Mork & Mindy*.

Mel Sharples (*Alice*, 1976–85): gruff fry cook and owner of Mel's Diner in Phoenix, Arizona, who liked to yell "Dingy!" and get taught stuff by his waitresses, especially the titular one. Played by Vic Tayback.

Chelsea Stevens (*Style and Substance*, 1998): short-lived Martha Stewart clone who oversaw her own domestic arts empire. Played by Jean Smart.

Ted Stoody (*George and Leo*, 1997–98): Martha's Vineyard restaurateur and son of prissy bookstore owner George (Bob Newhart). Played by Jason Bateman.

Swedish Chef (*The Muppet Show*, 1976–81, occasional): incomprehensible chef who once made a sandwich so big it flew away, so he shot it. Dig the Asian subtitles.

Terry (*Fawlty Towers*, 1975–76, 1979–80) (British): chef at Fawlty Towers, the hotel and restaurant in Torquay, England, owned by Basil Fawlty and his wife, Sibyl. One of Terry's specialties is ratatouille. Played by Brian Hall.

Jack Tripper (*Three's Company*, 1977–84; *Three's a Crowd*, 1984–85): king of the cooking school graduates, Jack's kitchen skills were one reason Janet and Chrissy let him move into their apartment in swinging 1970s southern California. Jack, played by pratfall king John Ritter, did eventually open his own restaurant, the cleverly titled "Jack's Bistro," near the end of the *Three's Company* run.

Felix Unger (*The Odd Couple*, 1970–75): king of fictional foodies. The TV role of Neil Simon's classic neatnik, played by Tony Randall, must have been the inspiration for Phil Hartman's "Anal Retentive Gourmet." And yes, for you sticklers, the role was played by Jack Lemmon in the 1968 movie and by Ron Glass in the 1982–83 ill-fated *The New Odd Couple* (but we don't need to get into that).

Hollyfood:
A Filmography of Food Movies

Sure, food doesn't always take direction, but it doesn't demand a huge trailer and a three-picture deal, either. Here are twenty-one movies starring food:

Babette's Feast (1987, 102 minutes, Danish) Written and directed by Gabriel Axel; starring Stéphane Audran and Bibi Anderson. Based on Isak Dinesen's short story. Two beautiful minister's daughters in a nineteenth-century Danish seaside town grow older and more religious together. They hire a Parisian cook/maid, who turns out to be a world-class chef, and introduces them to the sensual enjoyment of fine dining. Recipient of a Best Foreign Film Oscar.

Big Night (1996, 107 minutes) Written by Stanley Tucci and Joseph Tropiano; directed by Stanley Tucci and Campbell Scott; starring Stanley Tucci and Tony Shalhoub. Italian immigrant brothers are restaurateurs on the New Jersey shore during the 1950s, with the exacting Primo (Tony Shalhoub) in the kitchen, and Secundo (Stanley Tucci) running the business. "Big Night" refers to the evening that Louis Prima (the vintage musician and band leader) is invited to the restaurant.

A Chef in Love (1996, 100 minutes, French/Georgian) Written by Irakli Kvirikadze; directed by Nana Djordjadze; starring Pierre Richard and Nino Kirtadze. Oscar-nominated, sentimental movie about the star-crossed relationship, seen through flashbacks to the 1920s, between an old chef

(Richard) and a proud, young Georgian princess (Kirtadze) forced apart by the Russian Revolution. Richard's character sums the film up with this line: "Bolshevism will disappear; fine cuisine won't."

Combination Platter (1993, 84 minutes) Written by Tony Chan and Edwin Baker; directed by Tony Chan; starring Jeff Lau and Colleen O'Brien. A newly arrived immigrant from Hong Kong gets a job as a waiter at the Szechwan Inn in Queens, New York, and learns about American culture.

The Dead (1987, 83 minutes) Written by Tony Huston; directed by John Huston (his last film); starring Angelica Huston and Donal McCann. Based on the James Joyce short story of the same name about a festive holiday Irish feast in 1904, followed by a loveless married couple confronting each other.

Diner (1982, 110 minutes.) Written and directed by Barry Levinson; starring Mickey Rourke, Daniel Stern, Kevin Bacon, Paul Reiser, Ellen Barkin, and Steve Guttenberg. Several friends doing regular late-night hanging out in a Baltimore diner in 1959 try to grow up and understand the opposite sex. Remember when Mickey Rourke and Steve Guttenberg were watchable onscreen?

Eat Drink Man Woman (1994, 124 minutes, Taiwanese) Written by Ang Lee, James Schamus, and Hui-Ling Wang; directed by Ang Lee; starring Sihung Lung and Kuei-Mei Yang. This follow-up to Lee's *Wedding Banquet* concerns a moody Taipei master chef named Chu who has grown apart from his three daughters, is being pursued by the neighborhood widow, and probably worst of all, has lost his taste buds. Over a hundred recipes!

Eating (1990, 110 minutes.) Written and directed by Henry Jaglom; starring Frances Bergen (Candice's mom), Mary Crosby, and Toni Basil. Low budget and talky, in other words, Jaglom-esque. A group of women talk about food, obsessions, desires, sex, and life.

Hamburger... The Motion Picture (1986, 90 minutes) Written by Donald Ross; directed by Mike Marvin; starring Leigh McCloskey and Dick Butkus. Students at Busterburger University, the only college devoted to hamburger franchise management, learn about life and love.

La Grande Bouffe (1973, 125 minutes, French-Italian) Written by Marco Ferreri and Raphael Azcona; directed by Marco Ferreri; starring Marcello

Mastroianni, Ugo Tognazzi, Michel Piccoli, Philippe Noiret. Graphic tale of four bored middle-aged men who decide to commit suicide by eating themselves to death.

The Last Supper (1996, 94 minutes) Written by Dan Rosen; directed by Stacy Title; starring Cameron Diaz and Ron Eldard. Five grad students invite the right wing extremists and other jerks who don't agree with their views to dinner, kill them, and bury them in the vegetable garden. .

Life Is Sweet (1990, 103 minutes, British) Written by Mike Leigh; directed by Mike Leigh; starring Stephen Rea and Jane Horrocks. A chaotic working-class English family and the role of food in their lives. Mom's always cooking, Dad's a chef who buys a snack truck, the kids (one's bulimic) eat meals in front of the TV.

Like Water for Chocolate (1992, 113 minutes, Mexican) Written by Laura Esquivel (based on her novel); directed by Alfonso Arau (Esquivel's husband); starring Lumi Cavazos and Marco Leonardi. In the early twentieth century, a young woman is dominated by her strict mother but thanks to her housekeeper's cooking lessons, has a mystical way with food (especially quail in rose petal sauce, into which her very essence is cooked). It provides a sensual outlet and helps her gain control over her life as well as others. The highest grossing foreign food film of all time.

Love Is All There Is (1996, 98 minutes) Written and directed by Renee Taylor and Joseph Bologna; starring Angelina Jolie, Paul Sorvino, Renee Taylor, and Joseph Bologna. A comedic *Romeo and Juliet* featuring two Bronx restaurant rival families.

The Meal (1975, 90 minutes) Written and directed by R. John Hugh; starring Dina Merrill and Carl Betz. A brutal, symbolic movie about a wealthy woman who invites several rich and powerful people to a banquet, and lets them "devour" each other as they feast on their meals.

My Dinner with Andre (1981, 110 minutes) Written by Wallace Shawn and Andre Gregory; directed by Louis Malle; starring Wallace Shawn and Andre Gregory. Actor-writer Shawn has dinner with his friend, theater director Gregory, at an elegant New York restaurant. They chat about Gregory's experiences, and philosophize about life in general.

Soul Food (1997, 114 minutes) Written and directed by George Tillman Jr.; starring Vanessa L. Williams, and Vivica A. Fox. Matriarch Mama Joe has held her family together for forty years around a Sunday dinner of soul food. When diabetes hospitalizes her, the dinners stop and tensions among her three daughters rise. Grandson Ahmad cooks up a plan to bring the family back to the table.

The Story of Boys and Girls (1991, 92 minutes, Italian) Written and directed by Pupi Avati; starring Lucrezia Lante della Rovere and Massimo Bonetti. A wedding banquet featuring a twenty-course meal brings together two very different families in 1930s Italy.

Tampopo (1986, 114 minutes, Japanese) Written and directed by Juzo Itami; starring Tsutomu Yamazaki, Nobuko Miyamoto, Koji Yakusho, and Ken Watanabe. An original comedy about a truck driver who helps a widowed noodle shop owner make the perfect noodle.

The Wedding Banquet (1993, 111 minutes, American-Taiwanese) Written by Ang Lee, Neil Peng, and James Schamus; directed by Ang Lee; starring Winston Chao and May Chin. A gay Taiwanese-American tries to fool his parents with a fake wedding, resulting in lots of comedic complications.

Who Is Killing the Great Chefs of Europe? (1978, 112 minutes) Written by Peter Stone; directed by Ted Kotcheff; starring George Segal, Jacqueline Bisset, and Robert Morely. A whodunit with a real 1970s feel, set amid lavish European scenery and cuisine, and featuring Morley as the world's foremost gourmand.

It's People!

There are many ways in which cannibalism has been brought to celluloid: zombies (*Night of the Living Dead*), stranded travelers (*Alive!*), Oscar-winning movies about psychopaths (*The Silence of the Lambs*), and just plain old campy horror (*Three on a Meathook*). Here are ten movies that feature people eating food that happens to be made of people—elegantly or grotesquely, deliberately or unwittingly. What this says about our relationship with food is the subject for another book.

Consuming Passions (1988, 95 minutes, British) Written by Michael Palin and Andrew Davies; directed by Giles Foster; starring Vanessa Redgrave and Jonathan Pryce. Black comedy about a man who kills his way up the corporate ladder in a chocolate company that uses a secret ingredient.

The Cook, The Thief, His Wife & Her Lover (1989, 120 minutes, French-Dutch) Written and directed by Peter Greenaway; starring Richard Bohringer, Michael Gambon, Helen Mirren, and Alan Howard. Pretentious parable about love, revenge, and greed at a fancy restaurant.

Delicatessen (1992, 99 minutes, French) Written by Gilles Adrien; directed by Marc Caro and Jean-Pierre Jeunet; starring Marie-Laure Dougnac and Dominique Pinon. A comedy-horror-romance about a futuristic world with food shortages, and an ex-clown seeking work at a tenement, only to find that the landlord, a butcher, feeds his tenants on other fattened-up renters.

Eat the Rich (1987, 88 minutes, British) Written and directed by Peter Richardson; starring Nosher Powell and Lanah Pellay. A transvestite is fired from his restaurant job, goes back to leading a band of revolutionaries, and starts turning the diners into menu offerings. But who cares? We've got a score by Motorhead, and cameos by Paul and Linda McCartney, Bill Wyman, Miranda Richardson, and Koo Stark.

Eating Raoul (1982, 83 minutes) Written by Paul Bartel and Richard Blackburn; directed by Paul Bartel and Mary Woronov; starring Paul Bartel, Mary Woronov, Robert Beltran (now on *Star Trek: Voyager*), Ed Begley Jr., and Buck Henry. Black comedy about the Blands, an extremely square couple who, aiming to finance a restaurant and get rid of swingers and other "perverts," lure them to their apartment, kill them for their money, and "recycle" the bodies.

Ice Cream Man (1995, 84 minutes) Written by Sven Davison and David Dobkin; directed by Norman Apstein; starring Clint Howard (yes, that's Ron's brother), Sandahl Bergman, and Jan-Michael Vincent. Disgusting horror flick. After being released from the Wishing Well Sanitarium, a not-quite-cured Gregory reopens the old ice cream factory, where all the kids are reprocessed into ice cream.

Lucky Stiff (1988, 82 minutes) Written by Pat Proft; directed by Anthony Perkins; starring Joe Alasky and Donna Dixon. A rotund nerd is seduced by a beautiful blond, only to find he's been chosen as the main course for Christmas dinner for her inbred cannibalistic family.

Motel Hell (1980, 92 minutes) Written by Steve-Charles Jaffe; directed by Kevin Connor; starring Rory Calhoun, Nancy Parsons, and Wolfman Jack. Out in the boondocks, a farmer kidnaps tourists to obtain the key ingredient in his smoked sausage.

Parents (1989, 82 minutes) Written by Christopher Hawthorne; directed by Bob Balaban; starring Randy Quaid, Mary Beth Hurt, and Sandy Dennis. Black comedy set in the suburban 1950s about a kid who wonders where his square, conformist parents get all the meat they eat.

Soylent Green (1973, 95 minutes) Written by Stanley R. Greenberg; directed by Richard Fleischer; starring Charlton Heston, Chuck Conners, and Edward G. Robinson. A detective investigating a murder in the twenty-first century discovers what constitutes the people's primary food source. Dark movie, lightened unwittingly by Heston's overwrought performance.

Celebrity Dish: Celebrity Cookbooks

In an odd cocktail of pop culture and cooking, here's a smorgasbord of cookbooks cashing in on TV shows:

Alice's Brady Bunch Cookbook by Ann B. Davis (Rutledge Hill Press, 1994)

Are You Hungry Tonight? Elvis' Favorite Recipes by Brenda Arlene Butler (Grammercy, 1992)

Aunt Bee's Mayberry Cookbook by Ken Beck, Jim Clark (Rutledge Hill Press, 1991)

Bewitched Cookbook: Magic in the Kitchen by Kasey Rogers, Mark Wood (Kensington Publishing Corp. 1996)

Cooking with Days of Our Lives by Paulette Cohn, Dotty Griffith, Greg Meng, Maureen Russell (Rutledge Hill Press, 1997)

Cooking with Friends by Amy Lyles Wilson (Rutledge Hill Press, 1995)

Cooking with Regis & Kathie Lee: Quick & Easy Recipes from America's Favorite TV Personalities by Regis Philbin, Kathie Lee Gifford, and Barbara Albright (Hyperion, 1993)

Disney's Cooking with Mickey & Friends by Patricia Baird, Cindy Sass (Disney Press 1998)

Eat This . . . It'll Make You Feel Better: Mama's Italian Home Cooking and Other Favorites of Family and Friends by Dom DeLuise (Pocket Books, 1994)

Elvis in Hollywood: Recipes Fit for a King by Elizabeth McKeon (Rutledge Hill Press, 1994)

Florence Henderson's Shortcut Cooking by Florence Henderson (William Morrow & Co., 1998)

I Love Lucy Cookbook (Hollywood Hotplates) by Sarah Key, Vicki Wells (Abbeville Press, 1994)

In the Kitchen with Miss Piggy: Fabulous Recipes from My Famous Celebrity Friends by Moi (Time-Life, 1996)

Mary Ann's Gilligan's Island Cookbook by Dawn Wells, Ken Beck, Jim Clark (Rutledge Hill Press, 1993)

Murder, She Wrote Cookbook by Tom Culver (editor), Nancy Goodman Iland (editor) (Chicago Review Press, 1997)

Northern Exposure Cookbook: A Community Cookbook from the Heart of the Alaskan Riviera by Ellis Weiner (NTC/Contemporary Books, 1993)

*Secrets of the M*A*S*H Mess: The Lost Recipes of Private Igor* by Jeff Maxwell (Cumberland House, 1997)

Star Trek Cookbook: Food from the 23rd Century and Beyond by Theresa Robberson (Citadel Press, 1998)

Tossing the Virtual Salad: Web Sites and Usenet Groups

The cooking show is the ultimate in educational television; throw in the Internet and the learning is instantaneous. We no longer have to jot down measurements while we watch our favorite chefs cook, or even wait until we buy the cookbook. We can download the recipe and serve it up that very night.

A Sampling of Foodie Web Sites

Electronic Gourmet Guide: www.2way.com/food/egg
Epicurious magazine: www.epicurious.com
Famous Chefs: www.planettexas.com/8004/gourmet-food/Chefs
Food Network: www.foodtv.com
Gemini and Leo's Meal-Master Software and Recipes:
    www.synapse.net/~gemini/mealmast.htm
Microsoft Julia Online: microsoft.com/masterchef/
StarChefs: www.starchefs.com
Vicki's Vast List: Food and Drink: www.gulf.net/~vbraun/food.html

Food and Cooking Usenet Groups

alt.college.food	alt.creative-cooking
alt.cookies.yum.yum.yum	alt.creative_cooking
alt.cooking-chat	alt.food
alt.creative-cook	alt.food.asian

alt.food.barbecue
alt.food.chocolate
alt.food.cocacola
alt.food.coffee
alt.food.dennys
alt.food.diabetic
alt.food.fast-food
alt.food.fat-free
alt.food.grits
alt.food.hamburger
alt.food.ice-cream
alt.food.low-fat
alt.food.mcdonalds
alt.food.mexican-cooking
alt.food.olestra
alt.food.pancakes
alt.food.peeps
alt.food.pez
alt.food.professionals
alt.food.red-lobster
alt.food.safety
alt.food.squeezepop
alt.food.sushi
alt.food.taco-bell
alt.food.vegan
alt.food.waffle-house
alt.food.wine
alt.restaurants
alt.restaurants.professionals
alt.tv.networks.tvfood
rec.food.baking
rec.food.chocolate
rec.food.cooking
rec.food.cuisine.jewish
rec.food.drink
rec.food.drink.beer
rec.food.drink.coffee
rec.food.drink.tea
rec.food.equipment

rec.food.historic
rec.food.marketplace
rec.food.preserving
rec.food.recipes
rec.food.restaurants
rec.food.sourdough
rec.food.veg
rec.food.veg.cooking

Glossary of Cooking Terms and Ingredients

Don't know dicing from mincing? Or arugula from tapanade? Here's a list of terms and ingredients to help you get the most out of TV cooking shows and this book:

al dente (al-DEN-tay) Italian for "to the tooth." Pasta is al dente if it's cooked until it's firm to the touch and still slightly chewy without being tough, and not so cooked that it's soft or overdone.

arugula (a-RU-gah-la) A salad green with a bitter, mustard flavor.

au gratin (aw-GRAH-tin, aw-grah-TAN) Vegetables, meats, or fish are broiled or baked with a layer of bread crumbs and/or grated cheese on top until a thin brown crust forms.

balsamic vinegar Aged Italian vinegar made from white grape juice.

basmati rice Long-grained fragrant rice found in Indian and Middle Eastern dishes.

baste To spoon or brush food before and/or as it cooks with melted butter or other fat. Basting adds color and flavor, and it keeps food from drying out. A bulb baster helps drizzle the liquid over the food.

beurre manie (burr mah-NAY) see **roux** French for kneaded butter, beurre manie is a paste made of equal amounts of softened butter and flour creamed together. It is then beaten into a soup, stock, or stew to be thickened and simmered.

blanch [see **parboil**] To briefly cook by plunging a food (usually vegetables or fruit) in and out of boiling water, and then into cold water, to loosen its skin (as in tomatoes) or prepare for freezing. Blanching removes strong flavors from foods, and enhances the color of fresh vegetables.

blend To combine all ingredients until they are uniform and smooth.

bouquet garni (boo-KAY gar-NEE) One of the three classic combinations of herbs used in cooking. Parsley, thyme, and bay leaf are tied together or bagged so they can be removed before the dish is served.

braise (brayz) To cook meat or vegetables, tightly covered, in a small quantity of liquid at a low temperature for a long time. Braising develops flavor and tenderizes by breaking down fibers.

branston pickles British pickles.

broccoli rabe A vegetable related to the turnip and cabbage families, with a pungent flavor.

brown To cook something quickly with a little fat over high heat, until the outside of the food turns brown while the inside stays moist.

bruise To partially crush an ingredient, especially herbs and spices, to release the flavor.

calamari Squid.

caramelize To melt sugar over low heat until it liquefies and becomes a clear syrup ranging in color from golden to dark brown. It refers to plain sugar or to the natural sugar in other foods, such as onions. Caramelized sugar is also called burnt sugar.

chantrelle mushrooms Orange-yellow wild mushrooms shaped like trumpets.

chop To cut into bite-size pieces using quick, heavy blows of a knife or cleaver. The results of chopping should be coarser than that of mincing.

choucroute garnie (shoo-KROOT gahr-NEE) Sauerkraut garnished with assorted meats such as sausages and pork, and potatoes (choucroute is the French word for "sauerkraut").

clarify To make a cloudy liquid clear by removing the sediment, or by separating solids from a liquid. The term most often refers to butter when the golden oil is poured off from the whey that settled to the bottom when the butter was melted. The most common procedure is to add egg whites and/or eggshells to a liquid, like stock, and simmer for 10–15 minutes. The egg whites attract any particles floating around in the liquid like a magnet. After it cools for an hour, it is poured through a sieve.

compote Fresh or dried fruit that's been cooked slowly in a sweet syrup.

confit of duck Duck preserved by salting it and slowly cooking it in its own fat.

conserva The result of cooking down peeled fresh tomatoes; the starter for an Italian tomato sauce.

cream To beat with a wooden spoon or a large fork against the sides of a bowl, just enough to make the mixture smooth, light, and fluffy. The result should contain no particles. Butter is the most commonly "creamed" food, usually with sugar or herbs.

crème de cacao Chocolate flavored liqueur.

crush To reduce a food to its finest form (crumbs, paste, or powder). Press with garlic press, side of knife, or mallet to release the juice of an ingredient.

cube To cut into cubes of a half inch or larger. The result of cubing is larger than that of dicing.

curdle To coagulate, or separate into curds and whey; to bring about the undesirable effect of overcooking (usually a dairy product–based sauce or custard).

cut in To mix in a solid fat (butter) with dry ingredients (flour) by chopping with two knives or fingers or using a pastry blender, until the combination is in particles.

deglaze To add liquid to a degreased cooking pan after the food (usually meat) has been sautéed or roasted. While the liquid simmers, the browned bits of food and cooking juices on the bottom of the pan are loosened. The resulting deglazed liquid adds flavor, color, and substance to stock or sauce.

dice To cut into chunks of a half inch or less. The result of dicing is smaller than that of cubing.

dredge To lightly coat with flour, bread crumbs, or sugar. Dredging helps food to brown easily by forming a dry coating on the outside before cooking.

dust To sprinkle lightly, or give a light coating.

Edamame (edah-MA-meh) Fresh soy beans (edamame is the Japanese word for soy beans).

emulsify To make a mixture thick and satiny in texture.

en croute (en CROOT) French for "crust." En croute refers to food that is baked in either a pastry or a bread crust.

fillet To cut the bones from a piece of meat or fish, thereby creating a meat or fish fillet.

fines herbes (FEEN erb) One of the three classic combinations of herbs used in cooking. Chervil, chives, parsley, and tarragon, which, unlike bouquet garni, are not removed before serving the dish.

Fleur de Sal French salt.

flute To decoratively finish off the edges of a pie crust by pinching it against the edge of the pan. Also, to cut out a repeating pattern on mushroom caps or other vegetables or fruits.

foie gras Goose liver marinated in wine and baked (sometimes duck liver is used).

fold To blend light, whipped foods such as egg whites or whipped cream into a heavier substance. Folding is done gently with a rubber spatula by pushing the lighter food down into the heavier mixture, then raking along the bottom and up the sides again and again, gradually rotating the bowl to reach all the corners. The key to folding is to not reduce the volume of the mixture or make it heavy.

glaze To coat food with a thick liquid or sauce that adds flavor, smoothness, or shine. Breads can be glazed with egg yolks for a glossy crust; roasted birds can be glazed with melted marmalade or jelly.

grate To cut into tiny pieces using the small holes of a grater.

herbes de provence (ERB du pro-VANCE) One of the three classic combinations of herbs used in cooking: basil, fennel seed, lavender, marjoram, rosemary, sage, savory, and thyme.

hoisin sauce Sweet and spicy reddish-brown Chinese cooking sauce made of soybeans, garlic, chili peppers, and spices.

julienne (joo-lee-EN, zhoo-lee-EN) To cut into long, very thin strips. This is most commonly done to vegetables that are then sautéed or used as a garnish.

marinate To immerse certain foods (generally meats) in a seasoned liquid (called a **marinade**) for several hours or longer, in order to enhance and often tenderize. Acids such as lemon juice, vinegar, and wine do the tenderizing. Marinating should never be done in aluminum, but glass, ceramic, and stainless steel are fine. By the way, when this process is done to fruit, it's called **macerating**.

mascarpone A rich, buttery Italian cream cheese.

meringue sponge An airy gelatin-based dessert made with whipped egg whites, sometimes flavored with fruit puree.

mince To cut into very small pieces; the results are smaller than chopping, but not as small as crushing.

miso Japanese fermented soybean paste.

pan broil To fry foods using a preheated skillet instead of broiling under heat.

pancetta Italian bacon that is not smoked, but cured, with spices and salt.

parboil [see **blanch**] To cook in water for a few minutes to tenderize slightly. Parboiling can be done to onions, green peppers, or cabbage for stuffing.

peel To strip off the outer covering, skin, or rind.

pinch An immeasurable small amount, like a dash; the tiny amount of seasoning that can be held between your thumb and forefinger.

piri piri sauce (PI-ree PI-ree) A hot sauce made from olive oil, chili peppers, and bay leaf.

poach To cook in liquid just below the boiling point when the liquid's surface is beginning to quiver.

polenta Northern Italian cornmeal mush which can be eaten hot with butter or cool after being cut into pieces and fried.

proof To dissolve yeast in warm liquid and set aside in a warm place for 5–10 minutes until it swells and gets bubbly. This "proves" it's alive and capable of leavening.

puree Any food that has been turned into a smooth, thick consistency with a sieve, food mill, blender, or food processor. As a verb, it means to grind or mash food until smooth.

ragout A French thick stew of meat, fish, or poultry, with or without vegetables.

reduce To boil a liquid rapidly, usually stock, wine, or a sauce mixture, until the volume is reduced by evaporation. This thickens the consistency and intensifies the flavor. The resulting mixture is sometimes called a reduction.

risotto An Italian rice made by sautéing rice and chopped onions in butter, then stirring in stock.

roux [see **beurre manie**] A mixture of any hot fat and flour that is first cooked together then used as a thickener in stocks, sauces, or stews. There are three classics: white, blond, and brown. The color and flavor are determined by how long the roux is cooked.

saffron A bright, yellow spice that is the most expensive in the world. This pungent accent is used in paella and bouillabaisse (among others).

sauté To cook quickly in small amount of fat over direct heat.

scald To bring a liquid, usually milk, to just below the boiling point.

score To cut shallow slits in meat or vegetables at regular intervals to tenderize, keep flat during cooking, and/or aid in flavor absorption.

sear To cook at a high temperature over direct heat until the meat's surface is brown, sealing in the juices.

234

shitake mushrooms A Japanese and Korean mushroom with a steak-like flavor.

shred To cut into thin, narrow strips using the large holes of a grater or by hand.

simmer To cook gently in liquid just below the boiling point, low enough so tiny bubbles just begin to break surface.

sliver To cut into long thin pieces.

snip To cut into very small pieces without any chopping action, using scissors.

sommeleir (so-mahl-YAY) The French term for a waiter or steward in charge of, and possessing an extensive knowledge of, wine.

sous-chef A cook who supervises food production and reports to the executive chef in the kitchen. The French word "sous" literally means "under," so it's the person who is under the chef, that is, the second in command in the kitchen.

steam To cook on a rack or in a double boiler just over boiling water. Steaming retains flavor texture and vitamins more effectively than boiling or poaching.

steep To infuse tea and other dried foods such as mushrooms by placing them in water that was first brought to a boil. Steeping hydrates the food and brings out its flavor.

stew To simmer slowly in a liquid just deep enough to cover food, tightly covered, for a long time. Stewing tenderizes and allows flavors to blend.

stir-fry To quickly fry thinly sliced food in a large skillet or wok, over very high heat, stirring constantly.

sweat To cook ingredients, usually vegetables, in their own juices and a small amount of fat over low heat, to soften them without browning them. The vegetables are covered directly with a piece of foil or parchment paper, then the pot is tightly covered.

tapanade (ta-pen-AHD) A French thick paste made of olive, capers, anchovies, olive oil, lemon juice, and seasonings.

tarte Tatin A French upside-down apple tart.

toss To tumble and turn ingredients over and over, using a light lifting motion, thereby mixing. Usually done to a salad.

truffle oil Oil made from truffles, which are an extremely expensive fungi, found mostly in France.

truss To secure a bird with string so it holds a compact shape. Trussing keeps the wings and legs of a bird from overcooking or burning during cooking by tying them close to the body. On large birds such as turkeys, the wings and legs should be released for the last segment of cooking so the meat under them can fully cook.

uni A sea urchin, considered a Japanese delicacy.

vinaigrette An oil-and-vinegar combination, usually also containing salt, pepper, and various spices.

whip To beat ingredients rapidly, like egg whites, till light and fluffy, to add air and increase volume.

Bibliography

All quotes are from interviews conducted by the author, unless otherwise noted in the text.

Interviews

Curtis Aikens: June 24, 1998.
Mario Batali: September 22, 1998.
Mark Beckloff: June 9, 1998.
Sissy Biggers: July 7, 1998.
Bob Blumer: June 9, 1998.
Kimberlee Carlson: June 10, 1998.
Julia Child: July 22, 1998.
Amy Coleman: September 21, 1998.
Geoffrey Drummond: July 28, 1998.
Susan Feniger: June 3, 1998.
Bobby Flay: August 14, 1998.
Paul Gilmartin: July 23, 1998.
Annabelle Gurwitch: August 19, 1998.
Mollie Katzen: May 20, 1998.
Graham Kerr: September 11, 1998.
Jim Lautz: August 4, 1998.
Michael Lomonaco: August 5, 1998.
Claud Mann: June 9, 1998.
Mary Sue Milliken: June 3, 1998.
Sara Moulton: May 21, 1998.
Molly O'Neill: September 23, 1998.
Jennifer Paterson: via mail.
Caprial Pence: June 24, 1998.
Jacques Pépin: June 9, 1998.
Charles Pinsky: July 21, 1998.
Marjorie Poore: September 11, 1998.
David Rosengarten: June 17, 1998.

Nick Stellino: August 11, 1998.
Jacques Torres: July 24, 1998.
Ming Tsai: September 13, 1998.
Clarissa Dickson Wright: via mail.
Martin Yan: September 10, 1998.

Periodicals

Allen, Robin Lee. "Jacques Pépin: Enjoying 'Un-presidented' Success." *Nation's Restaurant News* (September 4, 1995).

Asimov, Eric. "Bits and Bytes." *New York Times* (September 24, 1997).

Avashti, Su. "A 'Sein-Feast' A to Z." *New York Post* (May 11, 1998).

Bates, Caroline. "Specialites de la Maison." *Gourmet* (April 1986).

Bates, Tom. "The Real Caprial." *The Sunday Oregonian* (April 19, 1998).

Beale, Lewis. "What's in Store for Two Fat Ladies." *New York Daily News* (February 25, 1998).

Berman, Karen. "To Cook Is to Delve into a Culture." *New York Times* (January 18, 1998).

Booe, Martin. "Cooking with Lagasse." *The Web Magazine* (January, 1998).

Brass, Dick. "Kerr Finds New Recipe." *New York Post* (1976).

Carlin, Peter Ames, and Tirella, Joseph V. "Fresh Pince." *People* (November 2, 1998).

Castro, Peter. "Fare maidens: 'Two Fat Ladies,' cable's new hit cooking show, makes macro waves." *People* (October 20, 1997).

"Chronicle" *New York Times* (April 10, 1997).

Cibellis, Matthew. "Cooking Good." *Lesbian News* (January, 1996).

Citara, Bill. "Cue the 'Chokes! Zoom in on the Salmon!" *San Francisco Examiner* (May 6, 1998).

Cohen, Lisa. "Tamale the World." *Out* (June 1997).

Crewe, Candida. "The Lady Who Lunches." *The London Times Magazine* (April 27, 1996).

Dam, Julie. "Telly-Tubbies." *Entertainment Weekly* (July 17, 1998).

Fletcher, Janet. "The Enchanted Mollie Katzen." *San Francisco Chronicle* (September 17, 1997).

Gardella, Kay. "TV Gourmet's Aim: To 'Turn On' Women." *New York Daily News* (February 23, 1969).

Gliatto, Tom. "Having Seen the Lite, Graham Kerr Now Preaches a Low-Cal Gospel." *People* (October 22, 1990).

Green, Michelle. "Season's Eatings." *People* (December, 1997).

Grimes, William. "If You Can't Stand the Heat, Change the Channel." *New York Times* (August 24, 1998).

Grossman, John. "Recipe for Success." *Cigar Aficionado* (February 1998).

Hesser, Amanda. "'Here's Emeril!' Where's the Chef?" *New York Times* (November 4, 1998).

Hicklin, Aaron. "Consuming Obsession." *Spectrum* (April 20, 1997).

"Hot List." *Rolling Stone* (August 20, 1998).

Isele, Elizabeth. "Recipe for Success." *Hartford Advocate* (December 19, 1996).

Jones, Madeline. "Know Your Neighbors." *CT Life* (February 1996).

"Katzen, Mollie." *Current Biography* (October 1996).

Koch, John. "The Interview: Martin Yan." *Boston Globe Magazine* (1998).

Lee-Potter, Lynda. "The Telly Tubbies." *Weekend Magazine* (August 30, 1997).

Lehrman, Karen. "What Julia Started: Julia Child Made America Mad for Food and Changed Notions of Class and Gender." *U.S. News & World Report* (September 22, 1997).

"Martha Stewart (The 50 Most Beautiful People in the World 1996)" *People* (May, 1996).

Miller, Samantha, and Greissinger, Lisa Kay. "Hot Hands Chef Bobby Flay Sizzles His Way to Culinary Stardom with Spicy Southwestern Fare." *People* (July, 1998).

Neill, Michael and Wescott, Gail Cameron. "Southern Comfort." *People* (September 28, 1998).

Okamoto, David. "Chef!: Sugar, Spice and Nothing Nice." *Dallas Morning News* (January 19, 1997).

Paglia, Camille. "Sugar and Spice." *The Advocate* (April 30, 1996).

Parseghian, Pamela. "Sara Moulton: Keeping Her Plate Full with 3 Jobs, Family, Humor." *Nation's Restaurant News* (April 20, 1998).

Richards, David. "Big and Getting Bigger." *Washington Post* (1998).

Ridenhour, Ron. "Spotlight On . . . Emeril Lagasse." *People* (May 27, 1996).

Romig-Price, Mary Beth. "Chef of the year: Emeril Lagasse, makin' music in the kitchen." *New Orleans Magazine* (September, 1993).

Stone, Judith. "Trust Us." *Mirabella Magazine* (January, 1998).

Sutel, Seth. "Japanese Indulge a Taste for Fine Food." *Los Angeles Times* (January 6, 1998).

Terada, Jason, and Steepleton, Scott. "Porn Video Is Recipe for Trouble on Cooking Show." *Los Angeles Times* (January 31, 1997).

Walkup, Carolyn. "Emeril Lagasse: The Essence of the Big Easy's TV-Star Chef Is That Food Is His Life, His Love, and His Passion." *Nation's Restaurant News* (January 1997).

White, Erin. "TV's Diva of Domesticity for the Clueless." *Wall Street Journal* (August 20, 1998).

Wohl, Alexander. "Martha Stewart."*Biography* (May 1998).

Books

Bickerton, Anthea. *American-English/English-American*. London: Abson Books, 1994.

Brooks, Tim and Marsh, Earle. *The Complete Directory to Prime Time Network and Cable TV Shows 1946–Present*. New York: Ballantine Books, 1995.

Connors, Martin, and Craddock, Jim, Editors. *Videohound's Golden Movie Retriever 1999*. Detroit, MI: Visible Ink, 1998.

Fitch, Noel Riley. *Appetite for Life: The Biography of Julia Child*. New York: Doubleday & Co., 1997.

Herbst, Sharon Tyler. *The New Food Lover's Companion*. New York: Barron's, 1995.

Katzen, Mollie. *The Moosewood Cookbook*. Berkeley, CA: Ten Speed Press, 1977, revised 1992.

McNeil, Alex. *Total Television*. New York: Penguin, 1996.

Web Articles

starchefs.com/ELagasse_interview.html

starchefs.com/MBatali/bio.html

TBSsuperstation.com/d_and_m/

www.abcnews.aol.com/onair/gma/html_files/moultons.html

www.channela.com/food/bio/myan.html

www.channela.com/food/feature/970205/guestchef.html

www.foodtv.com/bio/rosengar.htm

www.foodtv.com/scenes/drosen.htm

www.grahamkerr.com

www.greatchefs.com/chefs/j_mcdavid.html

www.greatchefs.com/chefs/j_torres.html

www.hotel-online.com/Neo/News/PressReleases1988/
    NYCChefBackgrounds_Feb1998.html
www.justinwilson.com
www.mrmedia.com/mrmedia/97/02.10.97.html
www.neworleans.com/no_magazine/31.06.64-THEEMERIL.html
www.osia.org/pub/chefs.html
www.pacificharbor.com
www.pbn.com/W072296/Johnson.htm
www.petlifeweb.com/on96/f1on96-1.htm
www.restaurant.org/RUSA/1996/9611p27.htm
www.restaurantreport.com/Departments/w_juliachild.html
www.restaurantreport.com/Departments/w_lagasse.html
www.starchefs.com/BFlay/interview.html
www.starchefs.com/FoodWine/sissy.html
www.starchefs.com/MLomonaco/bio.html
www.starchefs.com/MONeill_QA.html
www.surrealgourmet.com
www.threedog.com
www.Torrestorres.com/jt_bio.htm
www.washingtonpost.com/wp-srv/digest/daily/july/12/dogbakery.htm
www.whirlpoolcorp.com/cookin/chefs/my.html
www.wine.brats.org/Surreal/SurrealGourmet.html

Index

242

About the Author

Favorite Junk Food: Chips and dip.

Always in the Pantry: Peanut butter.

Always in the Fridge: Ruby Red grapefruit juice.

Favorite Food Smell: Garlic.

Favorite Food Sound: The doorbell (delivery's here!).

Fantasy Last Meal: Barbecued ribs, well-done french fries, and pecan pie with cream.

Karen Lurie is a professional researcher and pop culture writer who has written extensively about television and whose credits include *The St. James Encyclopedia of Pop Culture* (Gale Research). She is a weekly contributor to the Web magazine *Hole City* (www.holecity.com). She was educated by the state of New York, and lives in the city of New York. This is her fifth book.

Also available from Renaissance Books

ELEGANTLY EASY CRÈME BRÛLÉE
by Debbie Puente
ISBN: 1-58063-008-1 • $14.95

THE ASIAN GROCERY STORE DEMYSTIFIED
by Linda Bladholm
ISBN: 1-58063-045-6 • $14.95

BOOKS

TO ORDER PLEASE CALL
1-800-452-5589